CLUT!

The Top Home Runs in Baseball History

DAN VALENTI

The Stephen Greene Press
Pelham Books

THE STEPHEN GREENE PRESS/PELHAM BOOKS

Published by the Penguin Group
Viking Penguin Inc., 40 West 23rd Street, New York, New York 10010, U.S.A.
Penguin Books Ltd, 27 Wrights Lane, London W8 5TZ, England
Penguin Books Australia Ltd, Ringwood, Victoria, Australia
Penguin Books Canada Ltd, 2801 John Street, Markham, Ontario, Canada L3R 1B4
Penguin Books (N.Z.) Ltd, 182–190 Wairau Road, Auckland 10, New Zealand

Penguin Books Ltd, Registered Offices: Harmondsworth, Middlesex, England

First published in 1989 by The Stephen Greene Press
Published simultaneously in Canada
Distributed by Viking Penguin Inc.

10 9 8 7 6 5 4 3 2 1

Photo Credits
Pages 30, 90, 126, 146: National Baseball Library, Cooperstown, New York
Pages 10, 20, 40, 48, 60, 80, 98, 108, 136: Wide World Photos
Page 70: Courtesy of the Atlanta Braves
Page 156: Courtesy of the Los Angeles Dodgers, photo by John Soohoo
Page 118: Courtesy of the Oakland A's

Library of Congress Cataloging-in-Publication Data
Valenti, Dan.
    Clout : the top home runs in baseball history / by Dan Valenti.
        p. cm.
    ISBN 0-8289-0706-4
    1. Home runs (Baseball)—United States—History. 2. Baseball—United States—
Records. I. Title.
GV868.4.V35   1989
796.357'27'0973—dc19   88-37641 CIP

Printed in the United States of America
Designed by Joyce Weston
Set in Palacio, Korinna Bold and Frontiera by CopyRight, Bedford, MA
Produced by Unicorn Production Services, Inc.

This book is dedicated to

132323222729

212149514555

122011116013

to Edgar Allan Poe

and to Chris Resnik

Also by Dan Valenti

Red Sox: A Reckoning
From Florida to Fenway
Cities Journey
December Sunlight

By Dan Valenti and Ken Coleman

Diary of a Sportscaster
The Impossible Dream Remembered
Grapefruit League Roadtrip

Dan Valenti is a writer who lives in the civilized wilds of the Berkshire Hills in western Massachusetts. *Clout* is his eighth book.

CONTENTS

ACKNOWLEDGMENTS

First, thanks to those who talked to me, often at length and on little or no notice. These include Bobby Thomson, Bill Mazeroski, Bobby Richardson, Tony Kubek, Bill Virdon, Hal Smith, Ted Williams, Cliff Keane, Bobby Doerr, Pat Olsen, Tracy Stallard, Bernie Carbo, Walt Hriniak, Robin Roberts, Dick Sisler, Eddie Gold, Bill Jenkinson, Dusty Rhodes, Bob Watson, Bucky Dent, Dale Long, George Brett, Kirk Gibson, Jack Buck, Ken Coleman, and Lou Gorman. Many other baseball people and members of the press shared insights and opinions at various times. They're too numerous to mention, but thanks to all.

Next, the following PR people provided assistance: Duffy Jennings of the San Francisco Giants; Greg Johnson of the Pittsburgh Pirates; Jim Schultz and Melanie Jesse of the Atlanta Braves; Dick Bresciani and Mary Jane Ryan of the Boston Red Sox; Dean Vogelaar of the Kansas City Royals; Ned Coletti of the Chicago Cubs; Jay Alves of the Oakland A's; Larry Shenk of the Philadelphia Phillies; Harvey Green of the New York Yankees; Mike Williams of the Los Angeles Dodgers; Helene Bleiberg of CBS Radio; Doug Baldwin of Baldwin Associates; and Lloyd Johnson of the Society for American Baseball Research.

Helpful organizations include The National Baseball Hall of Fame, especially photo manager Pat Kelly and Scott St. John of the research staff; the Berkshire County Historical Association; Arrowhead; The Port Authority of New York; The Media Services Group; Literations; the Williams College Library; and the Berkshire Athenaeum. Book people include Tom Begner, Gordon Hardy, Martha Amidon, Priscilla Miller, Rickie Harvey, and Thomas S. Hart Literary Enterprises.

Others contributed in ways they don't know (nor do I, fully). These include Miss Candle; Molly Fuller; Nitchsky; The Big Five, Syracuse, N.Y.; Bruce Weber; Innocence (in a sense); and Hollis Hodges.

Finally, personal thanks go to Paula, Chubby, Princess, Dolores and Fred, my mother and father, Pete McGuire, and especially Mike.

— Dan Valenti

PREFACE

Let's not make too much of it. It's only baseball. But...

...if only we could see. I mean, learn how to observe totally, with all our senses, all our energy, unconditionally. If only we could live our lives with complete attention. If we could do this, we would have no need for the past. We could forget it and not be condemned to repeat it.

Because if we could see in this way, we could live in the present, moving moment to moment in wisdom. Instantly. Such living obliterates time. It allows enlightened experience without the need for memory in the development of knowledge. It allows spontaneous, creative knowing. When you see in this way, you live in the *now*, all the time. This isn't some "new age" bull. This is fact. The rest is fiction.

But the truth is, we don't know how to see in this way because we aren't serious about looking (yes, I include myself). We chain ourselves to our problems, allowing fear and insecurity to scare us off of reality. And so we turn to the past.

The past. No one can add to it. No one can take it away. It can be a gold mine or a cesspool. It can help set us free, or it can trap us. It all depends on the quality of our looking. When we look seriously, with intent, we find in history things we didn't realize were there the first time around.

So it is with famous home runs. There's much to be found.

My approach has been to allow history to speak for itself—through me. Sometimes, the truth goes beyond the mere facts. Sometimes, the truth is actually more myth than memory. Sometimes it speaks closer to poetry than prose. This approach stems from my belief that baseball, no more and no less than all experience, can tell us something about ourselves. To me, sports is not the toy department. And my idea about myself is this: I'm not a baseball writer but a writer whose topic often is baseball.

Of course, as a game, baseball should first retain its surface pleasure, its simple joys. Always—before anything else—we should be able to sit carefree in the stands and have fun.

But when we go back *after* the fact, as I do in this book, we must make full use of the past by squeezing from it as much as we can. We must snorkel the surface but also dive deep. My assumption is that readers want not only to be entertained, but also to be treated with respect. If you are that reader, then we will click.

I hope you enjoy this work.

Dan Valenti
Pittsfield, Massachusetts

WALLOPS

It is The Moment.

It is the moment of confrontation. Team sport's ultimate one-on-one. The challenge is offered from the mound, the pitcher's office, where he scowls in, his eye contact received by the hitter like a formal invitation to the dueling green. The challenge looms in the air like a scent as the batter prepares to step in, senses animal-alert. The space defined by the pitching rubber and home plate hums like a steady tone, the inviolate beam of an electric eye that will go off when a ball breaks its plane. Sixty feet six inches of drama, 726 inches that yield a result for the batter—humiliation back to the dugout or some tour of the bases...a baby's first step, a Fred Astaire dance, a death march, and every type of journey in between.

The back foot digs in. The batter will make his stand in the box, a four-foot by six-foot rectangle that proves out a classic notion of relativity, namely, that an event has no meaning unless it is known *where* it occurs. It is the batter's box that makes the action come alive, because a swing anywhere else on the field is mere practice. Once the game begins, and the batter enters the box, it becomes real, a gut check, literally an uphill struggle as he attempts to hit from sea level the pitcher's throws as they angle down from The Hill, Mound Olympus.

Does this sound too dramatic? Not if you've ever stepped in and tried to hit the ball—9 inches in circumference, $4\frac{5}{8}$ ounces in weight, 216 stitches—as it comes in on you from different deliveries to different locations at speeds up to 100 mph. You have a fraction of a second to make your decision to swing or not.

The ball bites in on the hands, making them feel as if ten thousand fire ants are stinging inside. Or it slides outside, a sibilant blur that makes a reptilian *s-o-o-o-ssshh* as it hits the corner. It is true. One of the most important but least discussed elements of successful hitting is overcoming fear. Quite simply, the ball can maim. It can blind. It can destroy a career. It can kill. You can look up Carl Mays and Ray Chapman.

This entire action is summed up by an icy statistic, one that derives from all the hundreds of thousands of major league games ever played, the millions of innings, the tens of millions of at bats, the hundreds of millions of pitches. One stat, one cold fact: even the best hitter will fail seven out of ten times. And more than ninety-five times out of a hundred, a home run hitter will fail to hit one out.

Against all this, the batter gets in the box. Much depends on the circumstances. When it's September in the eighth inning of a 12–2 game, bases empty, two outs, your team 18 games out, some of the edge is off (not all of it, though; the fearsome possibilities that occur when a ball blazes in the proximity of essentially unprotected flesh remain intact). But when a batter steps in at a big moment, with a record, a game, or even a championship on the line, the encounter becomes larger than life. For this is when faith gets tested, and fate intervenes, if it ever does in human events.

No wonder that the moment burns with blue-flamed intensity. No wonder that when under such circumstances the batter not only gets a hit but hits a home run, the feat takes on a life of its own. It lives, then it lives on. Inasmuch as anything can become immortal in this tenuous earthly life, the *big* home run never dies. It shocks like madness, surprises like magic, endures like myth.

This is a book about such home runs, the most memorable in baseball history. These are home runs that were hit when, logically speaking, one couldn't expect them to be hit. If we can accept a loose definition of the word "prayer," each home run answered one ("...please, just let Thomson hit one out.").

Writing a book about the top home runs, I imagine, is like writing a book about art history. Recognizing that you cannot cover everything, you get selective—an editorial process forced on you by simple lack of space. You become ruthless. You look for the milestones through the triple lens of feel, research, and consensus. You make your choices.

The masters and the movements virtually name themselves: the Van Goghs, the Da Vincis; the Renaissance, Cubism. Because of the limitations, artists and developments otherwise worthy of discussion are left out. The adherents protest.

So it is with home runs.

Ross Barnes of the Chicago White Stockings hit the first home run of all time on May 2, 1876 against Cincinnati's Cherokee Fisher. From the account in the *Chicago Tribune:* "Barnes, coming to bat with two men out, made the finest hit of the game straight down the left field to the carriages, for a clean home run." Since then, there have been more than 150,000 home runs hit. Like people in the Naked City, each one is a story. Each one is an event. Each one was important to somebody, sometime.

But, as with my art analogy, the masters name themselves: Ruth, Williams, Aaron. The rest assume the small type of footnotes at best, or are simply forgotten. The "movements" are also self-evident (i.e., home runs that, because of the circumstances, must be included): Bobby Thomson on October 3, 1951, Bill Mazeroski in Game Seven of the 1960 World Series, and the like.

This being said, I admit that the home runs chosen for a book like this are somewhat arguable. I say "somewhat." I think my inclusions are indisputable. They belong. Period. Beyond that, certainty dissolves, and subjective colorings come into play. Arguments will be made for some home runs *not* featured. The exclusions will draw the debate. I expect that.

Consider a home run such as Babe Ruth's "called shot" in the 1932 World Series against the Cubs. Why leave that out? Why, at the expense of, say, the chapter on Mark McGwire? Two reasons. One is a practical concession to my younger readers, for whom the immediacy of McGwire as a hero eclipses their awe of Ruth as a legend. The other reason is that Ruth's "call" probably never happened. Most accounts agree the "call" was actually a finger pointing to the heckling Cub bench. But since there is no videotape, we won't ever know. Some will argue that that's precisely the point. Because there is no record, the home run is a fable and should be included simply on those grounds. I disagree. With every home run in this book, the circumstances that make it "memorable" are indisputable. Besides, if "myth" were the sole criterion, how could I have left out several of those "600-foot" home runs that were never actually hit?

"Top"—I Know It When I See It

How did I define a "top" home run, a "most memorable" home run? Basically, by my intuitive understanding of the word *impact*—and that's a hard word to define. Like the Supreme Court said of pornography: We can't define it, but we know it when we see it. In selecting my home runs, I paid a great deal of respect to memory. These blasts for the most part live on through the years because they exist in the mind. And the mind preserves experience. Psychic pickling. These home runs, therefore, obliterate time. They will not die, fade away, or vanish.

Ingrained thought, based on memory and fed off of drama, keeps these home runs as fresh as the day they were hit. Oh, the details dim, but the essential truths remain intact. There were 34,320 in the stands when Bobby Thomson said hello to Ralph Branca; about a million claim they were there. Millions more remember or know of it. True and serious baseball fans must know of this home run the same way believers must know the tenets of their particular faith. The knowledge of these homers becomes a "confirmation" in which the believer reaffirms his commitment to the sport. So high drama goes into my selections. Home runs to win crucial games. Home runs to set records.

With one exception, length was not a factor in my choices. That may seem strange. In fact, when friends would ask me about my new writing project, I would say I'm doing a book on baseball's most memorable home runs. They would assume I was going to discuss tape-measure blasts, which have a strange and fascinating pull on the imagination. But accounts of gargantuan home runs are sketchy, especially those 600-foot-plus blasts that Ruth, Foxx, and others are alleged to have hit. My exception to length is Mickey Mantle's moon shot off Chuck Stobbs on April 17, 1953 in Washington. This one home run indelibly altered Mantle's career. It also ushered in the tape-measure era and changed the way baseball thought of itself.

Length, in fact, is an unimportant consideration in what makes a top home run. The more important consideration is really time, not distance. Not "how long," but "when." Look at Dusty Rhodes's home run to win Game One of the 1954 World Series. It was a pop fly not even 260 feet long. Compare this with a ball that Vic Wertz hit in the same game. Wertz's smash went 460 feet before it was caught by Willie Mays. In the box score, Rhodes hit the ball better. Wertz's drive is remembered only as the showcase for what is perhaps Mays's most fantastic catch.

It's interesting the way a box score in particular, and numbers in general, can rob an event of its truth. Perhaps that's at the heart of the controversy surrounding two other home runs of this book: Ruth's sixtieth and Roger Maris's sixty-first. In 1961, Commissioner Ford Frick forever shackled Maris to an asterisk, responding, perhaps, to this quality of numbers, that they often do not embody the true circumstances behind them. Frick found it necessary to add what he felt was a certain truth to Maris's 61 by putting an asterisk next to it. He felt the naked numbers didn't say all there was to say. If they had, Maris would have supplanted Ruth in the record book. Sixty-one is higher than sixty.

I'm not saying Frick was right. In fact, I don't think he was. But I am saying that when the only thing you have in your hand is a number, walk carefully, evaluate slowly, and judge without haste. The nose of a number grows very long indeed for the lies it can tell. Remember that, not only when looking at a box score or a batting average, but also the next time you examine statistics showing the "necessity" of weapons spending, or when the Administration releases its figures on the economy.

After first coming up with my own intuitive list of memorable home runs, I spent time getting a consensus from baseball people—players, old-timers, writers, broadcasters, general managers, fans. Time and again, the same home runs were mentioned.

As I hope you see by now, my selection takes into account many factors: drama, import, memory, consensus, and—in one case—the bizarre. That case is George Brett's "Pine Tar" home run in 1983, a home run too unusual to be left out of this book. In fact, strange home runs could easily have warranted a book of their own. The more I researched, the louder they screamed for attention. These home runs can't be considered "top," but a few are worthy of mention.

My personal favorite is the one hit by Hoyt Wilhelm on April 23, 1952. Rookie Wilhelm came into a game against the Boston Braves in the third inning for middle relief. He batted in the bottom of the fourth at the Polo Grounds. He homered. The fact that Wilhelm, a pitcher, put one out in his first major league at bat shines oddly enough. But no one could imagine how truly unusual this home run would become. Wilhelm went on to pitch in 1070 games over twenty-one years. He ended up hitting a career .088 on 38 hits. He never hit another home run.

Or how about a home run hit by Andy Oyler, a shortstop for the old Minneapolis Millers in the early 1900s? Oyler hit what surely had to be the shortest home run of all time. The Millers were playing rival St. Paul. The game was tied in the last of the ninth. There was a steady rain, and by the ninth, the infield was a deep wallow of mud. Oyler stepped in; the first pitch came whizzing toward his head. He tried to get out of the way, and the ball hit the bat with a loud crack.

Oyler scrambled to his feet and ran madly around the bases as everyone looked for the ball. The catcher was looking up, thinking it had been popped up. The first baseman checked around the bag. The pitcher and third baseman charged; the umpire lifted his feet. But still no sign of the ball. Somebody yelled from the stands, "He's got it in his pocket." As Oyler touched home for the run, the catcher accused Oyler of pulling the hidden-ball trick. But Oyler quickly pointed to a spot in the mud about two feet in front of home plate. The ump reached down. There was the ball, almost buried. Since it was in fair territory, it was a home run—a two-foot home run.

Babe Ruth hit one almost as strange while playing for the Boston Red Sox. He hit a gargantuan pop-up against Lefty Leifield of the St. Louis Browns. The ball was hit so high, that, in Leifield's words, the infielders "were running around like chickens with their heads off, yelling that they couldn't see the ball." When it finally came down, Ruth was rounding third. The ball hit the ground about in front of the plate, between the mound and the first-base line. Ruth and two base runners scored on the 20-foot, three-run homer.

Then there was a home run hit by Billy Purtell in 1910. Purtell was batting for the Red Sox at the team's old Huntington Avenue park. He hit a hard line drive to Browns third baseman Art Griggs. The ball was lined so hard, in fact, that Griggs didn't have time to react. The ball hit him in the forehead, then ricocheted into the left-field seats. Home run.

Other oddities. John Cooney of the Boston Braves played in 1172 major league games and hit only two home runs. They came on successive days, on September 24 and 25, 1939. Joe Kuhel hit an inside-the-park home run for the Washington Senators on September 7, 1945. So what, you say? It was the only home run hit by a Senator at home in Griffith Stadium all year (77 games). Bob Nieman of the St. Louis Browns hit home runs on his first two times up in the big leagues on September 14, 1951, the only man in history to do it. In 1902, Corsicana's Justin "Nig" Clarke hit eight—yes, eight—home runs in one game at Ennis, Texas, where the right-field fence was 210 feet from the plate.

Uniquely American?

I'd now like to turn to a more generic consideration of the home run itself. Not any one home run. All home runs. Home runs are so self-evident that you might feel it's unnecessary to ponder their nature. Let me respond by saying that the opportunity to analyze something we all take for granted—the opportunity to penetrate the obvious—must always be taken, especially if you're a writer. Because only by stripping the facade of the obvious can we ever learn anything. Nothing is obvious. Not even home runs.

The home run. There is nothing in sport so explosive. There is nothing so alert (unless it is a sleeping cat) as a buzzing crowd when a home run hitter steps up to the plate with the game on the line. There is, as someone once said, something "uniquely American" about a home run.

That statement always intrigued me: something "uniquely American." Exactly what? Why isn't the home run "uniquely Japanese" or "uniquely Mexican"? They play baseball, too. Or "uniquely" anything else? What is it about America and hitting one out of the park? What is it that presumes that we, this nation, can claim ownership of the four-bagger? Ugly Americanism? A pigheaded remnant of an imperialistic mind-set? No, for I believe the statement is true. There *is* something uniquely American about it.

I honestly don't know what. Maybe truths like that are best left unexplained. But I will offer a few speculations.

The first point is that we invented this game of baseball. Cartwright and Doubleday and many other people created this game here, for a healing nation just about to end the horror of the Civil War. They made the game pastoral. They made it fun. Since then, all of the major innovations in the game of baseball were brought about in America. So one can see why the home run—the game's most hoped-for play—can be called ours.

The next point is that the home run can be seen as an encapsulation of the American Dream. In the moment of a home run, the batter has taken the game into his own hands. He has taken the ultimate responsibility for his actions by actually driving himself in and scoring his run totally on the merits of his own efforts. This mirrors the concept of rugged individualism that has such a historical grab on the psyche of our country.

Work hard and be rewarded for it. The American Dream. Doesn't that, in a sense, describe a home run? By doing something difficult, the batter is rewarded with his run, with the runs of all those who happen to be on base, and with a special exemption.

Exemption? I refer to the Trot, that luxurious tour around the bases that follows the home run itself. By belting one out, a batter exempts himself from the urgency of hustling out his hit. Instead of a headlong rush toward second base to beat a throw, instead of the need to crawl in the dirt with a slide, he can loaf. Doing that at any other time on the base paths risks a fine and benching. Doing it after a home run brings accolades. It's baseball's equivalent of a luxurious, long, hot bath.

There's nothing quite like the Trot—idleness on the paths. Joy and lolling. You don't have to look back; nothing's gaining on you. The home run does the actual damage to the opponent, but the Trot also can be a weapon. It can rub enough salt into the hide of the pitcher that retaliation may be warranted. The pitcher knocks down the next batter.

As part of the hitter's reward for the home run, the Trot can be a form of self-expression. The "hot dog" can use it as a deliberate taunt, as Darryl Strawberry did off Al Nipper in Game Seven of the 1986 World Series. It can be used as a spike of defiance in the way of Ted Williams and his head-down lope, ignoring not only the fans but also the extended hand of the on-deck batter. It can be the expression of inexpressible elation, as it was for Bill Mazeroski after winning the 1960 World Series. Or it can be a monument of self-aggrandizement; one need only picture Reggie Jackson standing still in the box to admire a home run going over the fence, then taking the first, few, walking steps.

But whatever it is, all batters leave home plate and move around the bases counter-clockwise (symbolically stopping time? Ask anyone who's hit a big home run, and they'll tell you how the moment becomes frozen and unreal). They touch the white, 15-inch-square bags unchallenged. Hopeless defenders can do little more than walk away, stare at the ground, or observe powerlessly. There's nothing they can do to prevent this strolling person from scoring a run right under their very noses.

Part of the research for this book involved looking at photographs of home runs. I found them interesting, especially those that show the batter in various stages of the Trot. I paid particular attention to the body language of the infielders. The first baseman usually expresses some intimation that the ball will be in play. The body is coiled, maybe to get ready for a relay or to backup somewhere. For in the average home run (a contradiction in terms?), the batter doesn't realize it's gone until he's between first and second. Either the second baseman or shortstop is probably on his way to the outfield, in case the ball doesn't make it out, and a relay is necessary. The other half of the keystone combination remains near the second-base bag for a possible play.

It's with the third baseman that the situation sinks in, because by the time a runner gets to third, the home run is definite. Hopes for a miraculous catch are over. The ball is out. The third baseman can be seen, oftentimes, with hands on his hips, shoulders slouched, either staring into the dirt or looking on disgustedly. The man at the hot corner does a slow burn. The catcher and pitcher experience what can only be...well, what is the exact word for a combination of anger and embarrassment?

The run scores. One man slowly tours the bases. Nine men look on, not a damn thing they can do about it. The ultimate personal triumph. It fits so well on men who have, on the whole, a bit more ego than most: the Sluggers. What did Ralph Kiner once say? Home-run hitters drive Cadillacs; singles hitters drive Fords. These Sultans of Swat swagger more than other ball players, experiencing a thrill that is both primitive (the weapon is a war club) and childlike (what kid has not at one time or another imagined hitting one out of the park?). The home-run hitter meets the man-to-man challenge of pitcher versus batter in the most definite way. And when the home run is *big*, everything gets magnified, and the adrenaline shoots through the veins on warp drive. Delirium reigns. The media report the act, and millions stand in awe of this man who did not allow pressure, the insidious crippler of internal response, to invade the will. We have a Hero. And who (George Washington) worships heroes (Abe Lincoln) more than (Davy Crockett) Americans (Bobby Thomson)?

Arisen from the Dead

Where did all this start? The home run was not a part of early baseball. In fact, it came to prominence from the dead—the dead ball, that is. Lon Chaney as the commissioner, Boris Karloff as Home Run Baker. In 1901, Boston (American League) and St. Louis (National League) led the majors in home runs with respective (and for those days, respectable) totals of 36 and 39. The loosely wound balls would not carry out of the parks. Most of the home runs from baseball's beginnings through the 1910s were inside-the-parkers.

But change was in the air. In 1910, the National League hit 214 home runs and the American 144. By 1925, with a tightly wound rabbit ball, those numbers were up respectively to 684 (a 300 percent increase) and 533 (up 350 percent). This change caused no small amount of turmoil. Fundamentally, the issue of increasing home runs went right to the heart of how baseball thought of itself. The fans loved the home run, but league officials were out of touch with the fans (it wouldn't be the last time). With its identity on the line, the game resisted. Baseball's brass called the rise in home runs disturbing. An article in the April 1926 issue of *Baseball* magazine put the "growing problem" succinctly: "(The home run) has introduced a hazard into the average game that has proved a disquieting factor in team play...Yes, the homer is under suspicion...Not a few Major League owners have advocated drastic action to curb home run hitting."

One suggestion was the modification of stadium walls to prevent balls from leaving the park; another was putting certain areas of the bleachers out of play. Fortunately, none of these were enacted. In fact, the attempt to limit home runs was doomed to utter failure. One man saw to that. George Herman Ruth.

To try and sum up Ruth's impact on the game in a few paragraphs would be futile. Whole books have tried and failed. Ruth was gigantic not only as a player but as a social force. When he hit home runs in record numbers, the home run and home run hitters became impossible to ignore. Soon, others imitated his swing. Imitation: the sincerest form of long ball.

Before Ruth, ballplayers were like busy little ants. They lacked identities but moved quickly around their hill, building runs, manufacturing results in bits and pieces, base by base in a chain of walks, bunts, singles, hustle, and scrappiness. Baseball was an endless parade of powerless wonders, gnats in gray flannel, nickel and diming you to death , banjo hitters plucking out twangy little notes, all in search of the Lost Chord—which just happened to be the Babe. Babe was the maestro, the cannon effects to the *1812 Overture,* eschewing baseball's early silence and putting a new noise into the ballparks: the sound of a hundred thousand hands going in an instant from still-ness to clapping, the voices of tens of thousands of throats going from silence one second to screaming the next. Through the home run, a capacity crowd could sud-denly become transformed into unified exaltation, a primordial, almost pagan rejoic-ing. It fit Ruth's style perfectly.

All of baseball since then has been shaped by this man, whose image on those grainy black-and-white newsreels haunts us still—those mincing, measured, pigeon-toed steps around the bases, in whose wake all baseball has since followed. It was undeniable and inevitable. Ruth's popularity at the gate convinced owners to embrace the home run, and soon each team went after its own Bambino. The home run was here to stay.

The late twenties, thirties, and forties saw the rise of such power hitters as Chuck Klein, Rogers Hornsby, Fred Williams, Hank Greenberg, Jimmie Foxx, Lou Gehrig, Ted Williams, Joe DiMaggio, Ralph Kiner, Johnny Mize, Rudy York, Junior Stephens, Hack Wilson, Mel Ott, and Bill Nicholson.

But it was left to the fifties and early sixties to mass-produce the proper power prototype straight from the mold: Gus Zernial, who was Roy Sievers, who was Rocky Colavito, who was Ted Kluszewski, who was Hank Sauer, who was Jim Lemon, who was Gus Triandos, who was Vic Wertz, who was Bob Nieman, who was Ed Mathews, who was Bob Allison. The prototype begat the pinnacle, in 1961, when Roger Maris hit 61 and the Yankees hit 240. It gave continued rise to such batsmen as Ernie Banks, Hank Aaron, Carl Yastrzemski, Dick Stuart, Tony Conigliaro, Norm Cash, Willie Mays, and a string that continues to today, with Eric Davis, Mark McGwire, Jose Canseco, Kirk Gibson, Darryl Strawberry, and the like.

The home run continues to draw controversy. Think back to 1987. Home runs went out of the park at such an alarming rate that fans, writers, officials—just about every-one—felt compelled to investigate, to explain. Some blamed the ball, others the lack of quality pitching, others the increasing power of today's young sluggers. Numerous home run records were shattered. McGwire set the rookie record at 49, the Toronto Blue Jays set the record for most home runs in a game by one team at 10. The American League blasted 2634 for another mark, and for the first time, the league had twenty players with 30 or more home runs, and fifty-one with 20 or more. Beneath it all was a sneaking feeling probably not dissimilar to what the baseball establishment felt in the mid-twenties, that the home run had gotten out of hand.

Yet the game has survived, to no one's surprise, and the number of home runs most likely will continue up. Except for a slight dip in the war years, the number of home runs has been rising since the beginning of the century. Of course, it must stabilize somewhere, sometime. There are outer limits to such things. But even so, big home runs will continue to happen. Be sure of it: the twenty-first century will produce its equivalent of Thomson's shot, or Mazeroski's blast.

Homers of the Holy

When the bases are circled, and the foot descends on home plate, the run scores. The game is over, and this highest of high moments crescendos. A home run will live on, but it will never actually live again. The instant is so brief. One moment Thomson rides off the field on a quilt of shoulders, and Mazeroski dances his way toward the locker room as a city loses its mind in glee. The next moment, they are taking the steps that lead to. . .

. . .silence. And suddenly it's thirty or forty years later. One moment, they are young men. The next, they are talking about these long-ago moments to someone named Dan Valenti. They mention teammates who are no longer alive. They mention places that don't even exist anymore.

The Polo Grounds and Forbes Field and every home run hit in this book are earth-bound spirits. Ghosts. But this isn't a ghost story. Because in the calling up of phantoms, there is cleansing. Why can't a home run hit long ago in a torn-down ballpark help us find, in our awareness, something that comforts, something that can make us look beyond our troubles and find some relief? Why can't a home run do that? Why can't baseball do that?

I believe they can. I believe it's possible, even in the present age, when the glare of light blinds, the screech of noise deafens, when cynicism hardens, and the business of shallow activity prevents a resolute walk through the silent hallways of the mind. This is ground close to holy. That's where the Polo Grounds still stands. That's where Bobby Thomson still swings on that gray day of early October 1951.

If we lose access to these hallways, what good will home runs—or anything else, for that matter—what good will they be? They will exist like majestic trees continually falling in empty forests, making no noise because no one knows how to hear. It would be as if Thomson keeps coming to the plate to hit his home run, only no one is there. The stands are empty. The pitch never comes. He waits at the plate, forever. There is no resolution.

We must never allow that to happen in life. Always, we must be in the stands cheering.

BOBBY THOMSON
October 3, 1951

2

Giants 5, Dodgers 4

"The magic number is down to one," Ralph Branca sang as he combed his hair in the victorious locker room of the Brooklyn Dodgers. He and his teammates had reason to be happy. Clem Labine had just shut out the New York Giants in the Polo Grounds on six hits in a 10–0 rout. The win not only evened the 1951 playoff series at one game apiece; it also gave Brooklyn the momentum.

The Bums had manhandled the Giants this October 2 afternoon, with four of their thirteen hits going for home runs (Jackie Robinson, Gil Hodges, Dixie Walker, and Andy Pafko).

Over in the Giants clubhouse, manager Leo Durocher was talking to the writers.

"Tomorrow will be another day and another game," Leo said. No one could dispute that, but the sight of the normally spirited Durocher reduced to uttering truisms gave hint of a pervasive uncertainty in the Giant air.

Back on the other side, the Dodgers seemed confident. There was horseplay and joking. Branca eased the comb across his head like a rake gingerly pulling over a faultlessly manicured lawn.

The Giants took the first game at Ebbets Field, 3–1, the winning runs scoring on Thomson's two-run homer off Branca in the fourth. The 10–0 laugher evened things up. The Dodgers felt a reprieve. All they had to do was win tomorrow, and they could erase the stigma of blowing a 13½-game lead, a stigma sure to follow if they dropped the rubber match. Instead of being known as the team that choked, they would be remembered for their comeback.

The Brooklyn team of 1951 was a true powerhouse, a team cresting on a wave of— not success, really, more like great expectations. They had won pennants in 1947 and 1949, tied in 1946 (losing the playoffs), and missed out on the final day of 1950, when the Whiz Kid Phillies beat them in extra innings at Ebbets. So here they were again. Tied for the lead, with one game to decide the whole thing.

The Giants, on the other hand, were a team of destiny in 1951. They had a talented pitching staff, led by starters Sal Maglie, Larry Jansen, and Jim Hearn, who accounted for 63 of the team's 98 wins. The keystone combination of Al Dark at short and Eddie

Stanky at second held down the infield, while hitters like league RBI king Monte Irvin and Thomson produced runs in bunches. Add to the mix nineteen-year-old rookie Willie Mays. Willie was called up from Minneapolis on May 24, and Durocher immediately put him in center. Say Hey got off to an 0-for-12 start and begged Leo to send him back down.

"Nothing doing, kid," Durocher snapped. "You're playing." In his thirteenth official at bat, Mays homered off Boston's Warren Spahn.

But despite all the talent, the Giants got off slowly. They won their first three games, then dropped eleven straight. They didn't reach the .500 mark until May was nearly over. The Dodgers rolled, and on August 11, this wonder team, this dynasty in the making, led the Giants by 13½ games. They seemed unstoppable. But the Giants got hot. On August 12, they swept a doubleheader and went on to win sixteen straight. For the remainder of the season, they went 39-8, a stretch drive topped only by Boston's 1914 Miracle Braves.

New York finally caught up, with three games left in the season. The next day, with the two teams tied, their aces turned in blue-chip performances. Maglie beat Boston 3–0 at Braves Field while Don Newcombe whitewashed the Phillies in Phila-delphia, 5–0. On the last day of the season, Jansen beat the Braves 3–2. The Dodgers, meanwhile, were struggling in the City of Brotherly Love. The Phils hammered Preacher Roe and led 6–1 after three, 8–5 after five. By that time, the results of the Giants game were in. The Dodgers knew they had to win or be eliminated. They tied the Phils 8–8 with three in the eighth. The game went into extra innings; then Jackie Robinson took over. He saved it with his glove in the twelfth, when he caught a sizzling low line drive with the bases loaded, two outs. In the fourteenth, he did it with the bat, hitting a home run off Robin Roberts to win it, thus creating the need for a playoff series.

In New York City interest was intense. Daily events took on a baseball flavor, even in the financial district, where the staid and proper Dow Jones wire mixed its daily reports with game updates, such as this example from Game Two:

> Dow Jones 2 P.M. stock averages. 30 industrials 274.20 up 1.64 or 60 pc. Baseball, second inning Giants—no runs, two hits, no errors. Lockman grounded out, Labine to Hodges. Thomson doubled to left. Mays beat out a slow roller to Reese, Thomson taking third. Westrum popped to Cox. Jones grounded out, Reese to Hodges. Score at end of second— Dodgers 2, Giants 0. Continuing with stock averages. . .

On Rikers Island, prisoners were afforded the rare luxury of listening to the games on the radio. At Belmont Park, track goers heard race announcer Fred Capossela update the baseball results. On the streets of Manhattan and the other boroughs, the usual greetings were replaced by a simple, "What's the score?"

For Game Three, Charlie Dressen went with Newcombe; Durocher countered with Maglie. It seemed fitting that a game of this importance would be decided with the two aces going. The afternoon was dark, with overcast skies and a threat of rain keeping the crowd down to 34,320.

Maglie had control trouble in the first, walking Pee Wee Reese and Snider with one out. It cost him, as Robinson singled, driving in Reese to make it 1–0. Sal the Barber (known for his shaves to hitters digging in too close to the plate) then settled down, pitching strongly through the seventh and giving up no more runs. Newcombe held the Giants scoreless through six innings, giving him 21 straight shutout innings. He was lucky to escape in the second, but he did so due in large part to a base-running blunder by Thomson.

Trailing 1–0 and one out, Whitey Lockman singled. Thomson then drove a low liner down the left-field line. Lockman hesitated at second, not sure if Pafko could make a play in the air. Thomson, though, kept running. He was almost to second when he saw Lockman on the base. He retreated, but was caught in the rundown, killing a potential rally.

"I really pulled a rock on that one," Thomson recalled. "But I thought my single was going to hit the wall, and Whitey would reach third. So I kept right on going, running with my head down, so that I didn't see Fitz (first-base coach Freddie Fitzsimmons) trying to flag me down."

Finally, in the bottom of the seventh, the Giants tied the game 1–1 on Irvin's double and Thomson's sacrifice fly. But in the top of the eighth, the Dodgers struck for three runs, stunning the crowd into funereal quiet. Reese singled and went to third on Snider's single. Maglie then lost his concentration, throwing a wild pitch that scored Reese, making it 2–1. Durocher ordered the dangerous Robinson intentionally passed. But Pafko followed with a single off Thomson's glove at third, scoring Snider. Billy Cox ended the scoring by bulleting a double down the left-field line, plating Pafko for a 4–1 bulge. Maglie slowly walked off the mound when the inning ended, tasting failure, bewildered. This man was lost.

As were his teammates and their fans. Hopelessly trailing, they went down without incident in the bottom of the eighth against Newcombe, who towered like a bear, owning the mound, owning the game. He could smell blood. Jansen came on to pitch a 1-2-3 ninth, but few fans had the heart to care. Those fans who really didn't understand baseball streamed for the exits. The rest sat in the seats, bracing for the inevitable, trying to block out the cheers and occasional taunts of the Brooklyn fans.

As the Bums took the field for the bottom of the ninth, there were two announcements. The first was for the fans: "Following the game, nobody will be allowed on the field until all the players have reached the clubhouse." The second was for the press on the subject of World Series credentials: "Please pick up your Dodger credentials at press headquarters in the Biltmore Hotel tomorrow night."

Dodger rooters continued to celebrate. They were convinced they had just witnessed a miracle in the top of the eighth. But maybe, just maybe, that "miracle" was false. There are false miracles, you know. There is also a way to distinguish between true and false miracles. Otherwise, miracles would be useless. But what way? The Giants, who had scored two runs in the previous 22 innings, needed three to tie, four to win. What way?

Dark, first up against Newcombe, hit a sharp grounder to Hodges, but it went off his glove for a single. Don Mueller then singled to right. First and second, no outs, and the cleanup hitter due. Stirrings. The fans in the exits paused. They couldn't see, but could hear something building in the crowd. What? Newcombe reached back and got Monte Irvin to pop up. The crowd groaned, the noise distinct and mournful. But Lockman came through with a a double to left, scoring Dark. Resurrection. Mueller raced into third but slid awkwardly. His left ankle caught the bag, and something broke. Time was called as Mueller writhed in agony. For several minutes, maybe ten, play stopped. Some teammates huddled around Mueller, including the next batter, Thomson. Bobby stood there, talking to Durocher. Mueller was carried off on a stretcher, almost symbolic of his team's slim chances. Durocher sent Clint Hartung in to run.

During the delay, Charlie Dressen was pondering. Newcombe seemed to be running out of gas. He called the bull pen, where Ralph Branca and Clem Labine were heating. They were both ready. "Who do you want, Charlie?"

"Give me Branca."

It was a curious choice, one ripe for second-guessing. Branca was a 21-game winner. But Thomson owned him at the plate all year, hitting five home runs off him, including a home run to win the first playoff game. Labine went nine shutout innings the day before, including fanning Thomson with the bases loaded.

"Labine says he's strong, Charlie."

"Give me Branca."

Dressen went to the mound, took the ball from Newcombe, and called for No. 13. Newcombe steamed in anger. He wanted to finish what he had started. But it was nothing doing, and big Don stalked off the mound with his head down.

Branca warmed up. Thomson was not near the batter's box but still chatting with Durocher by third base. Bobby walked back to the box, mumbling something to himself. Then he stepped in. With runners on second and third, one out, Dressen made another debatable move. Playing it strictly by the book, he decided not to put the winning run on, that Branca would pitch to Thomson. He passed up on an intentional walk to Thomson, even though rookie Mays was on deck, even though Mays was in the midst of a dismal Series: one infield single in ten trips.

Branca came in with a fastball, which Bobby took for a called strike, his 35-ounce bat not moving. Branca went into his motion and delivered. The pitch came in high and tight. Thomson was ready, hips turning into the ball, wrists exploding. *Cra-c-k!*

The ball with the signature of Will Harridge kept rising, rising. Then sinking, sinking. Pafko raced back to the wall, ran out of real estate, and watched hopelessly as the ball landed in the lower left-field seats, a little beyond the 315-foot mark.

It was strange. At first, the crowd at the Polo Grounds didn't react. But as Thomson trampolined around the bases behind Hartung and Lockman, a celestial light switch flipped, and it started to sink in. A deafening roar arose from nowhere. It wasn't a gradually building sound, but a sound sprung fully from silence out of the forehead of some baseball Zeus.

The noise drowned out all reason, all logic, all thinking, all despair. It rang wild, guttural, and unrestrained. Confetti and papers flew. Fans were hugging each other. As Thomson hit third, a hysterical Durocher had to be restrained by Eddie Stanky so he wouldn't tackle his savior. Stanky rode on Leo's back as Bobby sprinted by, his arms pumping, his face marked by a huge smile. The Giants surrounded the plate. Bobby leaped the last 10 feet, and stomped on the plate with both feet. By that time, fans were streaming onto the field. As soon as he scored, the turbulent crowd nearly pummeled Thomson into submission. The stunned Dodgers walked back in shock across center field to the clubhouse. Only Jackie Robinson stayed behind, refusing to give in. He waited and checked to make sure Thomson touched all the bases.

The revelers tried to hoist Bobby to their shoulders, getting him about half-mast before he tore loose. Thomson then began a mad dash from behind home plate all the way to the clubhouse in center, some 500 feet away. It was one of the greatest pieces of open-field running the Polo Grounds had ever seen.

With the players inside the relative safety of the locker room, thousands and thousands of fans gathered outside the clubhouse steps, spilling into center field. They began a chant: "We want Thomson! We want Thomson!" They would not let up. They started to climb the stairs. Worried police went into the locker room, pleading with Bobby to make an appearance at the window. He did, and the cheering began all over again. He was forced to make several trips to the window.

The clubhouse, of course, was chaos. Club officials, the press, league executives, players, friends, family, photographers, and assorted hangers-on mingled in a euphoric daze. Giant President Horace Stoneham was crying. Durocher was speechless. Reporters were trying to talk to him. Leo said nothing. He then hugged his adopted son Chris, age five, who was dressed in a child's Giant uniform.

"He said to me this morning, 'Daddy, let me come out and put my suit on, and we'll win. I'm good luck.'"

Thomson was besieged by the media. He had to stand on a stool and shout to be heard by reporters. "If I was a good hitter, I would have taken that one," he said, referring to Branca's pitch. "Going around the bases, I couldn't believe what was happening to me. I felt I was actually in one of those middle-of-the-night dreams. . . everything was hazy. I heard yells. I saw paper flying. I noticed people jumping in the air, but through it all I kept riding high on that cloud."

A Dodger contingent of President Walter O'Malley, Dressen, Roy Campanella, and Labine came over to offer congratulations. Labine offered his hand to Thomson.

"Who are you?" Thomson asked.

"Labine," the pitcher answered.

"Oh, sure. I remember you from yesterday."

Next door, Branca was sprawled on the floor, sobbing, his uniform (No. 13) still on. He didn't move or say anything for quite some time, a man lost in a nightmare from which there would be no waking; for Branca, there were only clicks of time. Maybe, someday, enough of them would pass so that this, too, would fade away. But not for now. Not for a long while. The muffled shouts from the Giants' clubhouse mocked the Dodger silence. Finally, Branca said softly, "I guess we weren't meant to win it. The ball was high and inside, not a good pitch, and it cleared the wall by that much." He spread his hands to show about two inches.

Newcombe, who had pitched almost twenty-four innings in five days, could not speak. He showered, dressed, and hurriedly left the park. Over in Brooklyn, outside the Dodger offices at Court and Montague streets near Borough Hall, angry fans clustered. An irate man in a blue suit with a briefcase under his arm lectured the crowd, right in front of the team's office windows, "Thomson had hit six home runs off Branca already this season. As soon as Branca walked to the mound, I said, 'Get out the crepe.'"

Telephone traffic was so heavy in New York that many businesses were cut off from the outside world. The phone company blamed fans calling up friends to discuss the game.

"Smoke Screen"

The three-game playoff between the Giants and the Dodgers became historic for Thomson's epic blast, but also for something else. The games were televised nationally, and Chesterfield, the cigarette company, made history when it became the first sponsor of any coast-to-coast network sports event.

Amazingly, the October 1 contest from Brooklyn was broadcast by CBS *unsponsored*. But when the series shifted to the Polo Grounds, Chesterfield—the local radio and TV sponsor for regular-season Giant games—paid the bill for the coast-to-coast hookup over NBC. WPIX, the *New York Daily News*-owned station, originated the broadcast. Russ Hodges and Ernie Harwell were the broadcasters, switching off between radio and TV. Jack Murphy directed.

Hodges would be calling the game on radio when Thomson hit his home run. A lone Brooklyn fan, thinking that his team would wrap up the win, taped the inning on a crude home tape recorder, forever preserving Hodges's excited call: "The Giants win the pennant! The Giants win the pennant!" ◆

Eventually, everyone went home. The fulfilled Giant fans, the desperate Dodger fans, a bleary-eyed Branca, a burning Newcombe, an injured Mueller, a dumbfounded Thomson. The darkness that descended on the park at the Polo Grounds gave way to the lit-up streets of New York. And the molecules of every moment of that day still exist. We are still breathing the air of that home run. The very air.

On the Record: Bobby Thomson

Valenti: You had good luck against Branca all year, including the playoffs. Did that enter into your mind as you came to the plate in the ninth inning of Game Three?

Thomson: No. One of the key aspects of this whole thing was the fact that Mueller hurt himself at third base. I walked down there, still with the bat in my hand, instead of walking up to home plate and getting in the batter's box. I was down there (at third) for quite awhile, because Don was hurt, and he's a good guy, and I had a concern for him. But it helped me, because it took my mind off the game, off the situation. In the meantime, Dressen changed pitchers. I wasn't even aware of it. You've got to realize, we were kind of numb at the time, in this dead-serious situation. You're all wrapped up in it, completely. You could be standing in the middle of a million people, and you wouldn't know it. You're just so wrapped up in what you're doing, following your instincts. You know what you have to do. So they carry Mueller off the field. Durocher (coaching third) is right there. He put his arm around me. He's got his version of it, and I've got mine. My version is that he put his arm around me, which he had never done before, and said, "Bobby, if you ever hit one, hit one now." And I thought, "Leo, you're out of your mind." I didn't even talk to him, didn't answer him. But on my way to home plate,

I started talking to myself, calling myself names, saying, "You son of a bitch, get up there and give yourself a chance to hit. You son of a bee, wait and watch." I kept telling myself "Wait and watch. Wait and watch, you SOB. Give yourself a chance. Do a good job."

Valenti: When did you realize that Dressen had made a pitching change, and that Branca was in there?

Thomson: When I got to home plate. By that time, Branca was done warming up. He's on the mound, ready to go. Even at that point, my mind's a blank. First of all, when I got into the dugout after the top of the ninth inning, I thought, "We're dead." It's the last of the ninth. Newcombe had looked so good in the eighth. He blew us away. That was it. I walked 90 feet from third base to the box. I was never in a situation like that before. Nothing even close to it.

Valenti: You mentioned talking to yourself on your way to the plate. Was that unusual for you to give yourself a pep talk?

Thomson: Sure. As I was saying before, going into the dugout for our last at bat, I thought we were dead. I felt terrible. I felt totally dejected. I felt we just weren't good enough to go beyond this point; we weren't good enough to beat the Dodgers. Then the rally started. I'll tell you one thing that ran through my mind. On the way to the ballpark that day, I got thinking, "Gee. If I can get three hits today, it's gotta help us." That ran through my mind as we started getting guys on base. "I've got two hits so far." That ran through my mind, quickly in and out, as I stood in the box looking at Branca. There's so much excitement, and you're tense. I was tense, but when it was time for me to get a bat, I was telling myself, "Hey buddy, don't get overanxious. Give yourself a chance."

Valenti: Branca's first pitch was a called strike.

Thomson: Right down the middle, a perfect strike. I was waiting and watching. I was concerned about being overanxious, because as soon as you start moving too fast, you're out of it. You gotta sit back and wait for that thing, a la Ted Williams. You know, he's the greatest example of a guy that could wait as long as anybody before pulling the trigger. So I don't know why I took it right down the middle. But there it is: "Wait and watch." I watched it right down the middle. And then he came in with the second pitch. I got a glimpse of it coming in high and inside and, boom! I jumped on it. I was quick with my hands.

Valenti: Did you know it was gone immediately?

Thomson: I really made good, solid contact. It took off, and I immediately thought, "Home run!" But then I watched that damn thing start sinking. I didn't get on top of it a whole lot, but just enough to put overspin on it. I'd seen those low line drives. Johnny Mize was pretty good at hitting those low liners that sink right through the infield. They bounce just on the outfield grass. But this was a high sinker, and when it started falling, I thought, "It's just a base hit." Then it disappeared in the seats. I never hit a ball like that in my life, before or since. I didn't know what happened next, until I saw the films. I was only halfway to first base when the ball disappeared in the stands. I should have been running, but I was watching. I then jumped in the air and kind of jumped around the bases.

Valenti: As you made your tour of the bases, Jackie Robinson, competitor that he was, made sure you touched every one of them.

BOX SCORE: The Polo Grounds, 10•3•51

Game Three, 1951 Playoffs
Attendance: 34,320
Time of Game: 2:28

BROOKLYN DODGERS

Name	AB	R	H	RBI
Furillo, RF	5	0	0	0
Reese, SS	4	2	1	0
Snider, CF	3	1	2	0
Robinson, 2B	2	1	1	1
Pafko, LF	4	0	1	1
Hodges, 1B	4	0	0	0
Cox, 3B	4	0	2	1
Walker, C	4	0	1	0
Newcombe, P	4	0	0	0
Branca, P	0	0	0	0
Totals	34	4	8	3

NEW YORK GIANTS

Name	AB	R	H	RBI
Stanky, 2B	4	0	0	0
Dark, SS	4	1	1	0
Mueller, RF	4	0	1	0
Hartung, PR	0	1	0	0
Irvin, LF	4	1	1	0
Lockman, 1B	3	1	2	1
Thomson, 3B	4	1	3	4
Mays, CF	3	0	0	0
Westrum, C	0	0	0	0
Rigney, PH	1	0	0	0
Noble, C	0	0	0	0
Maglie, P	2	0	0	0
Thompson, PH	1	0	0	0
Jansen, P	0	0	0	0
Totals	30	4	8	5

Team	1	2	3	4	5	6	7	8	9		
Dodgers	1	0	0	0	0	0	0	3	0		4
Giants	0	0	0	0	0	0	1	0	4		5

Name	IP	H	R	ER	BB	SO
Newcombe	8⅓	7	4	4	2	2
Branca (L)	—	1	1	1	0	0

Name	IP	H	R	ER	BB	SO
Maglie	8	8	4	4	4	6
Jansen (W)	1	0	0	0	0	0

Thomson: Yeah, he stood there watching that I touched the bases. Anything could have happened, I suppose, even missing a base. I was hyperventilating. I had never been through anything like that before. It was just a onetime thing in my lifetime in baseball. There have obviously been a lot of big home runs in history, but it's not for me to ask why this happened to me. The clubhouse was wild. Buddy Kerr called me on the clubhouse phone. He had been the shortstop with the Giants when I first joined them. Durocher had traded him to Boston with other players for Dark and Stanky. He called me and was whooping it up. We were laughing. Oddly enough, the locker room was almost empty when I first got there. The cameras and everything were on the other side, the Dodger side, because it looked like they would win.

Valenti: When did it finally sink in, that is, the magnitude of what had happened?

Thomson: The first inkling I got was when I was asked to go on "The Perry Como Show" that night. Then, when I got home to Staten Island, my brother Jim was the first one I talked to. We looked at each other, shaking our heads. And he said, "Do you realize what you did?" I said, "Now, what a dumb question. Of course. I was there." He said, "No, Bobby. You don't realize. Something like this might never happen again." That was the first time I felt it was bigger than just beating the Dodgers for the pennant. Then from there, wherever I went, people were telling me where they were. I guess I was pretty naive about the whole thing. I was surprised so many people were listening. It had meant so much to so many. People ran out in the streets of New York, like it was the Fourth of July. Even now, I hear about it. I hear people telling me the films were on TV, that they heard Russ Hodges's call.

Valenti: Do you still think about the home run? Do you dream about it?

Thomson: I don't recall dreaming about it, but people bring it up all the time. My son has a photo of the home run on his bedroom wall, a panorama of the swing. I've felt a little funny getting all this attention over one home run. What the heck. And I also think about the Giant team. Like Whitey Lockman. If he hadn't hit that double, I wouldn't even have been there. Dark and Mueller. And Mays was on deck. Those guys should be a big part of the picture.

I'm too happy to think.

BILL MAZEROSKI
October 13, 1960

3

Pittsburgh 10,

New York 9

"The last time I checked the rule book, they were still settling the World Series on games won or lost, not on total runs," Danny Murtaugh cracked. The Pirate skipper spoke to a group of writers before Game Seven of the 1960 World Series.

Murtaugh's deadpan remark was in answer to a question laced with skepticism, something along the lines of, "Do you really think you have a chance today?" The question, in turn, needed to be asked because of the strange proceedings in the Classic's first six games. It had been one of the oddest World Series on record, a roller-coaster series of games that sounded in New York and Pittsburgh as mysterious as a wind whistling through the broken battlements of a closed amusement park. That's it: these games had a sound to them. The sound of incredulity in the Big Apple. The sound of whistling through the graveyard in Pittsburgh.

In New York in October 1960, Nikita Khrushchev blustered menacingly at the United Nations, but Yankee fans hardly noticed. They were wondering how the Bucs were still alive, why the formality of a seventh game was even necessary. Pirate fans, on the other hand, looked through the black smoke of the steel city and saw Game Seven as a blessing, a grace that held one slim, last chance for the city's first world title since 1925.

The Pirates had won by scores of 7–4 (Game One), 3–2 (Game Four), and 5–2 (Game Five). The mighty Yankees steamrolled to victory by scores of 16–3 (Game Two), 10–0 (Game Three), and 12–0 (Game Six). It was this third Yankee victory in Game Six (Whitey Ford's second shutout of the Series) that made the result in the finale seem inevitable. The baseball world wondered how the Pirates could shake off the brutal pummeling. Sure, the Bucs had won three, but these were dismissed as flukes, aberrations that were the result not of superior talent but of some combination of Dame Fortune, sunspots, and collective off-days by the gods of Metropolis.

Yankee manager Casey Stengel, however, had been around baseball too long to take anything for granted. He hid his plans for Game Seven from the writers. Asked before the deciding contest about his lineup, the platoon master would reply with a bit of Stengelese: "I've got to build up my defense. Who's gonna be in my outfield, and who's gonna be in my infield? What about catcher? I'm not saying. Now if you ask me position by position, you'd know. But I ain't gonna tell you."

Besides, Stengel knew full well that during the regular season, the Pirates had demonstrated a remarkable comeback ability. That was the team's key to approaching their tall order for Game Seven.

"We came back and won a lot of ball games that year. Going into the last game, we still thought we would win. We just had a bunch of guys that were confident they would win," says catcher Hal Smith, one of Game Seven's heroes.

Center fielder Bill Virdon agrees:

> I think the Series was basically like the Pirates' regular season. We won a lot of close ball games. We always seemed to win when we had to, to come back when we had to. I remember the feeling in the clubhouse before Game Seven. We knew we were going to win. We felt confident. We weren't favored to win the World Series. The Yankees were favored, I think justifiably. On paper, they had the best ball club. But there was something about the makeup of our club.

That "something" was a resiliency, an amazing ability to overcome the odds, a will to win that was hard to explain but easy to quantify with the number of clutch wins. Perhaps the most overlooked ingredient of the so-called "something" was the managing style of Murtaugh. The square-jawed Irishman wove magic throughout the season, winning with just two reliable starters, Vernon Law and Bob Friend, Roy Face in the bullpen, and a solid defense anchored by Bill Mazeroski. Murtaugh, moreover, knew how to handle people.

"Murtaugh was excellent at working personalities," says Smith. "Like [Roberto] Clemente. Danny found out that Clemente would have days when he didn't feel real good, and he might not want to play...He would have a slight bruise, or maybe a little pulled muscle, or a cold. And he wouldn't want to play. But Danny got to know him and his ways, and he just put his name down in the lineup every day. He didn't even talk to him [about his ailments]. Another example was Don Hoak, a real rah-rah guy on the bench. Danny kind of let him go and do his thing because it helped the team spirit. He handled Dick Stuart that way, too. Stuart was temperamental, but Murtaugh just let him play his own game.

"The one thing I remember about Danny was this: he was on *your* team, and if you got into it on the field, he was right there with you. If you had any personal problems, he would always be willing to talk with you. He was just a man's man. A good guy. He kept you pretty loose. And he knew baseball. He knew when to take pitchers out and when to pinch-hit. Of course, that year, everything he did was right."

For Game Seven, Murtaugh went with his ace, Vernon Law. Stengel countered with his 1958 Cy Young Award winner, Bullet Bob Turley, who found out he was starting when he reported to the locker room and saw a new ball in his shoe. With the right-hander in for the Yanks, Murtaugh went with his left-handed hitting lineup, putting Rocky Nelson at first in place of Stuart, Bob Skinner in left, and Smoky Burgess behind the plate. With Burgess catching, Smith was on the bench, a move that would have staggering meaning as events unfolded.

The Pirates got out fast, scoring two in the first on Nelson's two-run home run into the right-field seats and two in the second in Virdon's clutch two-out single to right center with the bases loaded. Law started sharp. Through five innings, he had given up just three hits and one run, that coming on a fifth-inning leadoff homer into the lower right-field seats by Bill "Moose" Skowron.

But in the sixth, Law tired. Bobby Richardson led with a single, and Tony Kubek worked him for a walk. Despite the protesting Pirate fans, Murtaugh went for a quick hook, yanking Law in favor of Face. The move backfired; by the time the inning was over, the Yanks had pushed across four runs, three coming on a home run along the foul line into the upper right-field seats by Yogi Berra.

Bobby Shantz, meanwhile, had strung together five innings of shutout relief. He gave up just one hit, a leadoff single in the bottom of the seventh by Smoky Burgess.

At that stage, the Bucs trailed 5–4. Murtaugh sent in Joe Christopher to run for Burgess. The move seemed totally irrelevant, as Shantz got Hoak on a liner to left and Mazeroski on a double-play grounder, Kubek to Richardson to Skowron. But the runner meant that Hal Smith would come on in the top of the eighth to catch. And just as major events of life sometime hinge on unbelievably chancy insignificancies, so the game would change with this substitution. For the Bucs, it looked bad and then worse. The Yanks got two more in the top of the eighth to take a 7–4 lead going into the bottom of the inning. They were six outs from the championship.

But what a Pirate eighth. Freaky. Simply freaky.

After his team had come off the field and before the inning began, Murtaugh held an impromptu meeting with his team, telling them what a great year they had had and that the game was not over yet.

Gino Cimoli led off with a pinch-hit single. Up came Virdon.

Virdon set himself at the plate. Shantz had given him trouble the whole series, and Bill thought about that. He wasn't thinking about a hit, only about getting wood on the ball, making contact. He did—a perfect double play ball to Kubek. It looked like the one Mazeroski had hit to end the seventh. Some fans turned their heads in grief. Virdon put his head down and ran as hard as he could toward first base.

> I hit the ball well, but I hit the ball right at Tony. Fortunately, there was a clump of dirt out of place, a pebble, or something, and just as he got ready to field the ball, it took a quick, short hop that wasn't expected, and it hit him in the throat, directly in the Adam's apple. Instead of the double play, I ended up getting a single, and we had two runners on and nobody out. There's no question that it would have been a double play.

Kubek went down in a heap, backward and to his right, fighting in a panic for air. The ball squirted to his left, where Richardson retrieved it and yelled for time. Kubek was down, clutching his throat, in obvious pain. He was unable to continue and was taken to a hospital, his bruised larynx leaving him speechless. Without doubt, the play turned the World Series 180 degrees. The Forbes Field crowd screamed. The Pirate bench was up. They could sense what had happened so often during the regular season: a late-inning rally.

Dick Groat obliged with a single past third, scoring Cimoli, making the score 7–5. Stengel yanked Shantz, going with sidearming Jim Coates. The move looked good.

Bob Skinner sacrificed the runners to second and third, but Coates got Nelson on a fly to shallow right. The inning seemed over when Clemente, who was swinging wildly at Coates's pitches, hit a weak chopper toward first. Skowron fielded it, picked it up, then turned to throw to first. But Coates had failed to cover. Virdon scored, and Groat went to third.

"Coates was probably so busy trying to figure out what his share of the winners' purse would be that he forgot to cover the bag," wrote Arthur Daley in the *New York Times*.

That set the stage for Smith, who in the top of the inning had, without fanfare, replaced Burgess behind the plate. Smith worked Coates to 2–2. He blasted the fifth pitch over the left-field wall.

"I knew it was gone as soon as I hit it," Smith recalls. "A couple of steps out of the batter's box, I was thinking, 'That should win the ball game.' And as I rounded first going into second, it dawned on me what was happening. The fans were going crazy, just absolutely crazy. They were standing on the dugouts, jumping in the stands...As I circled the bases, the Yankees didn't say a word. They were hung. They looked like dogs with their tails between their legs. They just couldn't believe it. Their mouths were open and they were just staring at me. Clemente and Groat, the runs on base, were jumping up and down around home plate as I rounded third. It was *wild*. It was pandemonium!"

With one swing, it was a 9–7 Pirate lead, and seemingly the championship. Stengel came out to get Coates, bringing in Ralph Terry, who got Hoak on a fly to Berra in left to end the incredible inning. It seemed over. All the Pirates had to do was hold the Yanks in the ninth, and they'd have their first world title since 1925.

But the Yankees would not die. In the top of the ninth, they rallied against Bob Friend and Harvey Haddix. Improbably, they tied the game at 9–9 on singles by Richardson, pinch hitter Dale Long, and Mickey Mantle, plus a bizarre groundout by Berra.

With the score 9–8, Yogi came up against Haddix with one out, Gil McDougald on third (running for Long), Mantle on first. Berra hit a looping liner off the end of his bat toward first. Mantle thought Nelson might catch the ball in the air, so he stuck close to the bag. Nelson came in, just missed it in the air, and made a difficult pickup of a short hop to his backhand. Expecting Mantle to be breaking for second, he stepped on first for the out, taking off the force play, then looked to second for a possible throw. Mantle wasn't near second; he dove back to first. Nelson dove as well, but Mick beat the tag, and McDougald scored. It was a brilliant bit of base-running by Mantle, and it tied the game 9–9. Haddix got out of further trouble as Skowron forced Berra, Groat to Mazeroski.

The Yankee rally deflated the Pirates. The bench was demoralized. Hal Smith would have been the hero if his team had held on: "I felt down and disappointed. I thought we might get beat, that it was in the books that we weren't supposed to win that game. We had it won and didn't hold it, and usually when that happens, you end up losing."

Mazeroski was first up against Terry. Though he was the number eight hitter, Maz was enjoying a fine series at the plate. He had driven home the winning runs in the first game (a two-run homer) and fifth game (a two-run double). He took a Terry fastball for ball one. At 3:36 P.M., Terry came in with his next pitch. Mazeroski waited, then turned on the ball, a high fastball, and drove it deep to left. Berra gave chase, ran out of room, and continued running off the field. The game was over. It was the only time a World Series had ended on a home run. The celebration began.

Mazeroski did a wild dance around the bases, taking his helmet off as he touched second base, and windmilling it around in his hand. The entire team was waiting for him at home as the stands emptied onto the field. He fought his way to the plate, touched it, and felt the blows of people eager to touch him. He had become a relic, a holy object.

In the clubhouse, champagne mixed with beer, water, soda, wet towels, parts of uniforms, and papers. Murtaugh went around the room repeating, "What a finish! Did you ever see such a thrilling finish? What a finish! This club never gives up!"

Reporters were yelling questions at the skipper.

"When did we know we had it? When I saw Yogi give up chasing Mazeroski's home run in the ninth."

Mazeroski was mobbed by everyone. A writer asked for his thoughts.

"I'm too happy to think," he shouted.

"This is the greatest ballclub in the world," bellowed Dick Groat.

"I think I took a shower sitting down," Virdon remembers. "I don't think I was able to stand up. We consumed a great deal of champagne."

Into the wild scene, fourteen-year-old Andy Jerpe shyly walked. Andy was out from school, and waiting in the vacant lot behind the left-field wall when Mazeroski unloaded. He retrieved the ball. When he tried to give it to Mazeroski in the locker room, Maz gave it back saying, "You keep it, son. The memory's good enough for me."

By this time, the city of Pittsburgh had become unglued. Workers poured out into the street. The business district was soon ankle deep in paper. Streets were blocked, bridges were closed, and no one could get in or out. Streetcars were pushed off their tracks; cars had no room to move. In the middle of the streets, people were drinking, dancing, yelling, laughing. The city stopped, frozen in the Highest of Highs, New Year's Eve, Mardi Gras, Christmas Day, Armistice Day, the Fourth of July, and everyone's birthday rolled into one.

And in proportionate measure to this glee, so was the somberness of the Yankee dressing room.

Berra sat in front of his locker, stripped to his shorts, head hung, repeating to himself, "I can't believe it."

Terry—young, educated, analytical—wallowed in a deep depression. Stengel came over, put his arm on his shoulder and said, "As long as you tried your best and threw the pitch you wanted, I have no complaints."

"I don't know what the pitch was. All I know, it was the wrong one," Terry said, biting off the words.

Looking back on the pitch, Terry recalls: "I thought that was the end of my world. I felt I had let everyone in the world down. I wasn't thinking of myself. The remorse came later, and it was plenty bad. My wife told me to forget, but I never thought I would."

The strange Series was over. The totals were incredible. The Yankees outscored the Bucs 55–27, outhit them 91–60, hit 10 home runs to the Pirates' 4, 4 triples to their none, and hit .338 to Pittsburgh's .256. New York's team ERA was 3.54 to Pittsburgh's stratospheric 7.11.

Supreme Reaction

On October 13, the U.S. Supreme Court listened to arguments in a patent case. Ralph S. Spritzer, assistant to the solicitor general, was making his case, saying at one point that "Yankee ingenuity" was a common characteristic of inventors.

Chief Justice Earl Warren, an avid baseball fan, had aides keep him up to date on the seventh game. Shortly after the court rose at 4:20 P.M., someone handed Warren a slip of paper. Warren said, "Mr. Spritzer, you spoke earlier of 'Yankee ingenuity.' According to the information I have just received, you should have spoken of 'Pirate ingenuity.'" ◆

The Yankees charter flight flew back to New York without Kubek, who was hospitalized for his throat injury. Team physician Dr. Sidney Gaynor refused permission for Tony to talk. A writer asked him if Virdon's ball in the eighth would have been a double play. Tony nodded yes in a sad pantomine.

Before the week was up, the Yankees fired Stengel.

"I'll never make the mistake of being seventy again," the Ol' Perfesser remarked.

For Pittsburgh and Bill Mazeroski, defeat had been annihilated in the face of victory, and had become an unqualified pure savoring. There was nothing left to do but enjoy it.

On the Record: Bill Mazeroski

Valenti: Bill, going into Game Seven, did it bother you that the Yankee wins were so lopsided? You were shut out 12–0 in Game Six.

Mazeroski: Well, it's tougher to lose by a close score than getting walloped. We came back an awful lot that season, in the seventh, eighth, and ninth innings. So I didn't worry going into that seventh game. They had scored 12 runs the game before, but I figured they couldn't keep scoring that way, although they did score 9 in Game Seven (*laughs*). I didn't prepare any differently for Game Seven. No change at all, either the night before, or at the park that morning. I always got to the park before I had to, to relax, sit around, chew tobacco, and sit on the floor of the clubhouse.

Valenti: Were you concerned when the Yankees went ahead 7–4 in the eighth?

Mazeroski: Oh, yeah. That was the point in the game where Danny Murtaugh had a meeting in the dugout and said, "Boys, don't be ashamed of anything. You've played a heck of a World Series. Hold your heads up. It's not over yet."

Valenti: Then Virdon hit the ground ball to Kubek, and things turned around. What do you remember about that?

Mazeroski: I watched it from the dugout. We were down, feeling low. The ball would have been a certain D.P. But after it hit Tony, we were excited about getting a couple of guys on base. We didn't know if it was going to help or not, but we did know that we had come back all year and that it was going to help in some way. Later in the inning, Coates didn't cover first on Clemente's ball, and we really got excited. We came back to life.

And it came down to Hal Smith. He was never expected to hit a home run, just like I was never expected to. When he hit the home run, we went crazy. We thought we had it made at that point. It was hit well, but it was 430 feet to that part of left field, and I wasn't sure it was going out. Especially with someone like Mantle in center. He made center field at Forbes Field look like it was 150 feet, he covered so much ground. But sitting in the dugout, I could tell by the crack of the bat that Smith got it all. It brings you off your seat when a guy hits one like that. I thought the game was over. I thought we had it won.

Valenti: So the Pirates head onto the field with a 9–7 lead, only to have the Yankees tie it up in the ninth. How did that feel?

Mazeroski: After they tied that game up, I was probably as low as I was the whole series. I grew up being a Yankee hater, rooting for the Cleveland Indians all my life. But the Yankees always had a way of coming back to beat you. They were always "The Great Yankees." Nobody ever beat them, it seemed. So coming into the dugout, I thought, "Gee whiz, here we go. Now they're gonna come back and beat us, too." Coming off the field, it never entered into my mind that I would be leading off in the bottom of the ninth. Once I got back into the dugout, though, reality took hold. I knew I was leading off.

Valenti: Had you ever hit against Terry?

Mazeroski: No, I don't think so. That could have been the first time I ever faced him. I never really thought about that. In the dugout, nobody said much. We were all down. I got my bat and went to the plate. All I'm thinking is that I'd like to hit the ball hard somewhere and get on base. That's all I was thinking about. Get on base and get an inning started. Terry came in with a fastball that I took high for a ball. After that pitch, Johnny Blanchard went out in front of the plate and yelled to Terry, "Keep it down. He's a high-ball hitter." The next pitch was the one I hit out. I thought it was another high fastball. I saw Ralph a couple of years later, and he said it was a high slider that didn't slide. I got a good look at the ball coming in, swung, and knew that I hit it good. But it was 410 feet to left field, and you had to really blast it to get it out of there. I didn't know for sure if it was high enough to get over the left-field wall, which was 12 feet high.

I had a good feeling it was over Berra's head...so I had it in my mind I was going to end up at second, but if he fumbles it a bit, that I'm gonna go hard and try for third, where we would have two shots at scoring me on a fly ball.

Valenti: When did you realize it was gone?

Mazeroski: Well, I was running hard down the first-base line. But as I was heading into second, I saw the umpire down the left-field line waving his arms in a circle, and I heard people screaming. That's when I first knew it was out—as I was going into second. As soon as I hit the bag and took another step or two, I took my helmet off and started waving it. All I could think about was, "We beat the Yankees! We beat the Yankees!" It came as a surprise. I was in kind of a daze. All I knew was that we had won, that we had beat the great Yankees.

Valenti: So complete your tour of the bases.

BOX SCORE: Forbes Field, 10•13•60

Game Seven, 1960 World Series
Attendance: 36,683
Time of Game: 2:36

NEW YORK YANKEES

Name	AB	R	H	RBI
Richardson, 2B	5	2	2	0
Kubek, SS	3	1	0	0
DeMaestri, SS	0	0	0	0
Long, PH	1	0	1	0
McDougald, 3B	0	1	0	0
Maris, RF	5	0	0	0
Mantle, CF	5	1	3	2
Berra, LF	4	2	1	4
Skowron, 1B	5	2	2	1
Blanchard, C	4	0	1	1
Boyer, 3B, SS	4	0	1	1
Turley, P	0	0	0	0
Stafford, P	0	0	0	0
Lopez, PH	1	0	1	0
Shantz, P	3	0	1	0
Coates, P	0	0	0	0
Terry, P	0	0	0	0
Totals	40	9	13	9

PITTSBURGH PIRATES

Name	AB	R	H	RBI
Virdon, CF	4	1	2	2
Groat, SS	4	1	1	1
Skinner, LF	2	1	0	0
Nelson, 1B	3	1	1	2
Clemente, RF	4	1	1	1
Burgess, C	3	0	2	0
Christopher, PR	0	0	0	0
Smith, C	1	1	1	3
Hoak, 3B	3	1	0	0
Mazeroski, 2B	4	2	2	1
Law, P	2	0	0	0
Face, P	0	0	0	0
Cimoli, PH	1	1	1	0
Friend, P	0	0	0	0
Haddix, P	0	0	0	0
Totals	31	10	11	10

Team	1	2	3	4	5	6	7	8	9		
Yankees	0	0	0	0	1	4	0	2	2		9
Pirates	2	2	0	0	0	0	0	5	1		10

Name	1P	H	R	ER	BB	SO
Turley	1	2	3	3	1	0
Stafford	1	2	1	1	1	0
Shantz	5	4	3	3	1	0
Coates	⅔	2	2	2	0	0
Terry (L)	⅓	1	1	1	0	0

Name	1P	H	R	ER	BB	SO
Law	5	4	3	3	1	0
Face	3	6	4	4	1	0
Friend	0	2	2	2	0	0
Haddix (W)	1	1	0	0	0	0

Mazeroski: I can still see myself almost floating between second and third. But when I hit the bag at third, I saw all these people. I wondered if I were going to get to home plate or not. People were coming out of the stands toward me. One of them grabbed my neck; another scratched my back. I was worried about not getting to the plate and made up my mind to get there any way I could. When I got to the plate, there was like a vee in there, a pocket of humanity. I stepped on the plate, and that's as far as I got. Everybody collapsed on me. I had to carry a bunch of people into the dugout. I felt like I had gone about ten rounds with the heavyweight champ, my legs were so weak from carrying people. I could barely get up the ramp to get to the dugout, I was so weak. Once I got into the dugout, I dashed into the clubhouse. It was empty.

Valenti: What do you remember immediately after, in the locker room?

Mazeroski: Bob Prince was our announcer. He always said this was his most embarrassing moment. He was doing a live broadcast from the clubhouse. He was waiting inside for the game to end, so he didn't see what happened. He didn't know I had hit the home run. All he knew was that we had won. I had just run off the field, my bat still in my hand, and I was the first person they stuck up there with Bob. He asked me how it felt to be a World Champion, patted me on the back, said, "Congratulations," and sent me away. When he found out later what I had done, it was too late.

The locker room was bedlam. The press was twenty-five deep around me. I couldn't move. After I finally dressed and got out of the clubhouse, I drove up to the old public park outside of Forbes Field with my wife. There wasn't a soul there. Everybody was downtown celebrating. We just sat there for an hour or two, looking over the city. No one knew we were there.

Valenti: Do you have any artifacts from the home run?

Mazeroski: I still have the bat. That's about it. Of course, part of the left-field wall is still up. When the Pitt campus took over the site and put up buildings, they left that part of the wall standing. And in one of the buildings, they still have home plate marked. But that home run really didn't change my life. I hit it shortly after I had turned twenty-four. I still had twelve, thirteen years to play. You can't live off of one hit. You know, for me, that home run didn't start to get big until I was out of baseball. People didn't talk about it much when I was playing. Then after I quit baseball, it seemed to become bigger and bigger.

TED WILLIAMS
September 28, 1960

4

Ted Williams, the greatest hitter of his age and probably of all time, sat in the Red Sox locker room, getting dressed. He had just done the nearly impossible (an AP story said it "bordered on the uncanny"): he had hit a home run in his last at bat. A writer asked him why he didn't tip his hat.

"I felt nothing. Nothing, nothing, nothing." And so Teddy Ballgame sealed the stone over his brilliant, turbulent career. Many runs, many hits, many errors, no apologies.

To swing a baseball bat is a deceivingly simple act, even assuming a more than generous amount of dexterity, coordination, and overall athletic ability. It is at once delicate and crushing, a tantalizing alloy of timing and motion, a perfect proportion of innate ability and rote practice. The swing consists of many separate actions, each of which must blend seamlessly into connected movement. The bat foot digs in; the stance is assumed. Above all, the stance must be comfortable. Then the batter begins an internal rhythm, both psychic and physical, timed with the pitcher's motion. Every aspect of the swing predicates itself on this motion. The great lefty Warren Spahn gave the most succinct description of it: "Hitting is timing. Pitching is upsetting timing."

As the ball comes in, the batter strides, shifting his weight from back foot to front. The hips open. The wrists explode. The bat buggy-whips around, and anywhere from seven to eight times out of ten, the result will be an out. With a round ball and bat, even a fraction of an inch will make a huge difference.

Consistent solid contact is so difficult that hitting's greatest student (and consequently its most accomplished master) calls it the single most difficult thing to do in all of sports. Few argue with Ted Williams.

As a boy, Williams wanted to be the best. He wanted to grow up with people saying, "There goes the greatest hitter who ever lived." As Williams has said, no boy could grow up with more of a desire to play baseball, to hit.

Living in San Diego, young Ted could play baseball all year. By day, he would hit against anyone who would throw to him. At night, he would over and over and over swing a bat, until his hands blistered, bloodied, and then formed calluses. In his professional career, Ted estimates he faced some 200,000 pitches. The information from each would be stored in his computer-like mind for future reference. It was this scientific approach to hitting that set Williams apart from every other hitter in the game, before or since. Even when he was on the bench waiting for his turn, Ted would study the pitcher, looking to see what he used in certain situations. He'd even grill his teammates when they'd come back to the bench. If they couldn't answer his questions, he'd grumble.

"I never could understand how a guy could go up there to hit, come back dragging to the bench, and not know how the pitcher got him out. 'For Crissakes,' I'd yell, 'he's taking money right out of your pocket and you don't even have a clue.' I tell you, any hitter who does that is one stupid SOB," Ted says.

In his twenty-two year career with the Boston Red Sox, he hit .344 lifetime, with 521 home runs, 1839 RBIs, 1798 runs, six batting crowns, two MVP awards, and two Triple Crowns. He hit .406 in 1941, the last man to top .400. He was named to 18 All-Star teams. But numbers tell very little about this complicated man.

His offensive statistics are made even more incredible when you consider the five prime years he lost serving in two wars; the bronchial condition he picked up in Korea that would stay with him the rest of his career, especially in cold weather; the injury to his left elbow (shattered in thirteen pieces) suffered in the 1950 All-Star Game, which nearly ended his career; his lack of speed, especially in later years, to take away many infield hits; and the weak lineups he played in for the last seven years of his career.

Ted was more than a hitter. He was like Ruth, in his time, one of the pivotal figures on the American scene, as much a part of sociology as baseball. Maybe more. He was a *Life* magazine cover boy, an endorser of products. His views on politics and politicians were front-page news. He was a hero to children, a champion of charity. He spit at fans and intimidated writers.

Much of this stems from his dominant personality. Ted is the kind of man who could walk into a roomful of strangers, where nobody knew him, and a few minutes later, all the attention would be on him. There is something about him that draws attention out of people, almost like drawing energy. If such a machine could be built, I'm sure this energy would register physically.

Ted is like a vortex, the eye of a storm, self-contained, evincing waves of sheer presence—even in his later, mellower years. It was such a man who found himself thrust into the middle of Boston, the Hub, with more newspapers per square foot than anywhere else except the reading room of the New York Public Library.

At one time, there were nine newspapers in Boston, each trying to outscoop the other in Ted Williams stories. Under such a magnifying glass, anyone would seem larger than life, let alone someone as enigmatic, alluring, and volatile as Ted. As the writer Franz Kafka remarked, if enough people start pointing their fingers at you, sooner or later you'll start to feel guilty. And so went the feud between Williams and the Boston press. They had papers to sell. He had privacy to keep. Immovable object versus irresistible force.

He was a walking page-one story. As such, he was fair (but often unfair) game to a pack of hunters, led by such men as Dave Egan of the *Record*, Austen Lake of the *American*, and Hy Hurwitz of the *Globe*. It's true that he also had great friends in the press, such as Bud Leavitt ot the *Bangor Daily News*. But too often, his life was a tale told in screaming "Second-Coming" type, such as his divorce in 1955 or his outspoken comments in 1957 against Harry Truman, Senator Taft, and the Marines.

Ted described himself this way: "A guy who could not reach an armistice with his environment." The battle affected the fans as well. People packed Fenway not so much to see the Red Sox but the spectacle of Williams, who became an easy target for the leather-lunged, beer-soaked reptiles who inhabited the left-field grandstand.

It was against all this that the forty-two year old slugger prepared for his last game on Wednesday, September 28, 1960. The Boston weather was dismal, with cold, drizzle, muck, fog, and a continual threat of heavy rain.

Ted arrived in the clubhouse in the late morning, time enough to blast a writer who requested an interview and chew out a photographer, ordering the clubhouse boy to throw him out of the room. The rest of the team filed in, dressed, and went to the field for batting and fielding practice, which Ted declined. He remained in the empty locker room. He caught a break; the Red Sox had selected that day to announce Jackie Jensen's return from a year of self-imposed retirement. The writers were up in owner Tom Yawkey's office for this, leaving Ted alone with his thoughts.

Williams slowly put on his uniform, then sat alone in the trainer's room with the memories of a lifetime cascading in his head. Finally at 1 P.M., about half an hour before game time, he left the locker room and popped into the dugout. As he did, a horde of photographers crowded around. They had it a little better than the writers. They could bring Ted up close with their telephoto lenses. To do their job, writers had to be within earshot. Ted cursed, "Geezus, they've had twenty-two bleeping years to take my picture. Isn't that enough?" It was clear that Williams was not about to mellow, to give into the sentiments of the day.

Fans straggled into the park. Their first glimpse of Ted came as he was filmed in an on-field interview with a Boston TV station. The crowd cheered, as they would his every move that day. Williams grumbled about the interview, doing it only at the request of league president Joe Cronin, Ted's mentor and manager in Boston in the forties. After the interview was over, Ted sauntered back to the dugout, yelling out to Marlan Coughtry, a young third baseman recently called up from the minors, "Stay on it today, Bush." Williams had been helping Coughtry with his swing.

With the warmups over, the pregame ceremonies began, emceed by Red Sox broadcaster Curt Gowdy.

"As we all know, this is the final home game for—in my opinion and most of yours—the greatest hitter who ever lived. Ted Williams." During the ceremony, Ted received several awards, as well as donations to his favorite charity, the Jimmy Fund. While listening to the speeches of Gowdy and Mayor John Collins, Williams fidgeted, looking down at the ground, shuffling from one foot to the other. He took his cap off, crushing it in his hands. He seemed almost embarrassed to be on the field.

Gowdy concluded the ceremonies: "He can be summed up in one word: pride. Because of it, he has worked harder than anyone in baseball to get where he is. . . He's a champion." Gowdy than asked for a standing ovation. He needn't have. Ted approached the mike, and the crowd was on its feet, cheering a genuine cheer of love.

For the first time in the day, Ted warmed up and smiled sincerely. But he could not resist one last jab at the press:

> Despite some of the terrible things written about me by the knights of the keyboard up there [*points to the pressbox*], and they were terrible things—I'd like to forget them, but I can't—my stay in Boston has been the most wonderful part of my life. If someone should ask me the one place I'd want to play if I had to do it all over again, I would say Boston, for it has the greatest owner in baseball and the greatest fans in America.

He then walked back to the dugout to another ovation. The game began. Aside from Williams, it was meaningless. The Orioles were playing for a chance at second place, and the Sox were stumbling their way to a seventh-place finish, 32 games out. Williams came up in the first against lefty Steve Barber, one of the O's Kiddie Korps. The youngster walked Ted on four pitches. Ted eventually scored on Lu Clinton's sacrifice fly to give the Sox a 2–0 lead. He even slid home.

In the third, he led off against another Baltimore youngster, twenty-one-year-old Jack Fisher (Barber had been chased after a third of an inning). On a 1–1 pitch, he flied to medium-deep right center. The crowd jumped to its feet when he hit the ball, even though it was a routine play for center fielder Jackie Brandt. They badly wanted a home run.

In the fifth, facing Fisher with two outs and the Orioles leading 3–2, he came close. Ted jumped on a fastball, sending it to deep right. It had a chance, a real chance. The crowd jumped up, screaming. Right fielder Al Pilarcik raced to the bullpen wall and made the catch right up against it, nearly 400 feet from home. The heavy air held up the ball just enough. The crowd groaned, then cheered Ted's effort. Ted himself just stood in the base paths between first and second, hands on hips, shaking his head. Shortstop Pumpsie Green brought Ted's glove out. Ted jogged to his position in left, thinking his last chance for a final home run had just disappeared. He remembers: "I thought that ball was gone. I was right on it. I couldn't have hit a ball harder than that. I remember telling [Vic] Wertz, 'If that didn't go out, then nothing's going out today.' "

In the top of the eighth, Mike Fornieles came on in relief of starter Billy Muffett for the Sox. His seventieth appearance set an American League record. Three boys ran onto the field to shake hands with Ted. After Fornieles set the Orioles down, the Sox trotted in, and a buzz of excitement rippled through the park. Ted was due up second, for his final at bat.

Center fielder Willie Tasby led off, but all eyes were on Ted in the on-deck circle. He was kneeling, his right knee on a couple of white towels. He took measured swings with his bat, biting his bottom lip in determination. Opening-act Tasby wasted no time, bouncing softly to Ron Hansen at short on Fisher's first pitch. Fisher had done well in long relief, going seven shutout innings. He wasn't about to let up for Williams. Williams wouldn't have it any other way.

As Ted walked to the box, the crowd cheered once more. Again, it was a cheer of heartfelt affection, a there's-nothing-to-forgive-because-we-loved-you-all-the-time cheer. And they kept cheering. Louder. Louder. Home-plate umpire Ed Hurley called time. The ovation continued for about three minutes. Ted just stood in the box, pretending to ignore it. The press box was quiet.

Finally, time was signalled in, and Fisher went to work, missing with a curve low and inside for a ball. Then he cracked a slider past Williams, who took a vicious cut. Fisher, feeling lucky, tried to blow a fastball by the relic (youth having a go at old age). The ball came in belt high, slightly to the outside edge of the plate. Ted was ready, figuring the kid would come in with that exact pitch. He swung. The photo of the follow-through shows Ted with his eyes closed, almost in ectasy, that other-worldly state that is at once extreme pleasure and pain. It is a transfigured expression. He knew the ball was gone. So did the crowd. They just knew.

Fisher wheeled around to watch the ball, his left cheek swollen with tobacco, his shoulders stooped, his hands helpless at his side. Brandt and Pilarcik raced back as the ball sliced the thick, soupy air. Brandt was the closest. He went to the left corner of the bull pen. He could do little more as the ball landed on the bull-pen roof, bounced into the wire screen in front of the bleachers, then returned into the bull pen.

It was the last thunderbolt of an ancient god. He had *willed* a home run.

Williams jogged quickly around the bases, head down. He thought briefly about tipping his cap but said later that when he reached second base, he decided he wouldn't. He couldn't. It would have been forced and false; Williams could not be phony if his life depended on it. Oriole catcher Gus Triandos offered his congratulations to Ted as he came home. Ted smiled. He shook hands with the on-deck batter, Jim Pagliaroni. Pagliaroni was smiling, but Ted still had his head down. Before he reached the dugout, a fan vaulted over the dugout roof and grabbed Ted's hand. In the right corner of the dugout, Del Baker, Manager Mike Higgins, and Tasby greeted him. Ted ran into the runway to get some water. He then went back to the bench, put his jacket on, and just sat there, head down, smiling to himself.

The fans were on their feet. The home run had brought the Sox to within a run, 4–3. But that hardly mattered.

"We want Ted! We want Ted!" Over and over, the chant rang throughout hallowed Fenway. Despite the fact that two seats in three were empty, the 10,454 made a deafening din. The umpires called to him, Higgins called to him, his teammates called to him to acknowledge the crowd. Ted continued to sit, head down. He would not budge, defiant to the end. Play finally resumed. As Clinton struck out to end the inning, Higgins made perhaps the only brilliant move of his sleepy career at the Sox helm. He called out, "Williams, left field." Ted cursed, then ran out to his position.

The crowd hadn't expected to see him again and erupted all over. Higgins then sent Carroll Hardy—the only man ever to pinch-hit for Williams—out to replace him. The Kid had one last chance to tip his cap. Instead, he jogged in, head down, touching the first-base bag, ducking into the dugout, heading up the runway, and straight into the locker room. Five hundred twenty home runs after he hit his first off Philadelphia's Bud Thomas on April 23, 1936, at Fenway, Ted Williams peeled off No. 9. It was immediately retired by the Red Sox. He hung it in his locker ("WILLIAMS–9. DO NOT PUT WET STUFF IN DRYER. NO SADDLE SOAP," the hand-printed legend above the locker warned).

When the game was over (Boston winning 5–4 on two ninth-inning runs), the Red Sox announced that Williams would not go on to New York for the final three games. The photographers were allowed directly into the locker room. Writers had to stay out for fifteen minutes. When one tried to sneak in with the camera crews, Williams pointed a menacing finger at him and yelled, "You're not supposed to be in here!" Finally, the writers were let in, and he talked to all who came over. Some wouldn't go near him.

"Everything was with me today," he said. "I was gunning for the big one. I let everything I had go. I really wanted that one."

An hour after the game, a big crowd surrounded the players' parking lot, waiting for Ted. The home run was the talk of Boston. Miles away, a ten-year-old boy stuck his head out of a car window and yelled, "Hey, mom, did you hear? Williams hit one." It was a typical reaction. Ted hung around the locker room longer than usual, sipping beer, moving from his locker room to the trainer's room. A writer from *Sport* magazine asked Ted if he felt anything.

"I felt nothing."

"No sentimentality? No gratitude? No sadness?"

"I said, nothing. Nothing, nothing, nothing."

Of course, it wasn't true, as Ted admitted in his life story, *My Turn At Bat*, even going so far as to say that maybe he should have tipped his cap.

A couple of hours after the game ended, with most everyone gone, Ted Williams snuck out of Fenway through a side entrance and went back to his hotel room. He was alone.

On the Record: Cliff Keane

Cliff Keane, one of the deans of the Boston press, started at The Boston Globe as a copyboy in 1929 and left forty-seven years later in 1976. Keane began in the sports department in 1942, the year after Ted hit .406.

Valenti: What kind of man was Ted during his playing days?

Keane: Ted's a hard man to explain. He could be so nice and generous at times, and five minutes later, he could be something else, just the opposite. So you never really knew what to expect from him. But it was good being around him because he was such a great ball player. So if someone asks me, "What do you think of Ted Williams?" I'd say, "Well, I was glad to watch him play, but I don't know about living with him." He wasn't very pleasant.

Valenti: How did Fenway Park affect Ted as a hitter?

Keane: One thing about Ted playing at Fenway Park. It isn't really a great ballpark for a hitter [like him]. It's a fun ballpark. But it's pretty hard to play [half your games] there, then try to go out on the road and try to play well, too. You get adjusted to your home park and you don't play well on the road, which was typical of the Red Sox, especially in the 1950s. With the short wall and unusual geometry, it's an altogether different game in Fenway than it is in other towns. It's fun for the fans. But I was with Williams one day last year [1987], and we were talking about Fenway Park, and he said, "You know what a lousy ballpark that is?" I said, "It *is* a lousy ballpark." You like to see the game played well, and you can't in Fenway Park.

Welcome Back, Jack

Despite the clamor associated with Ted Williams's last game at Fenway Park, before the game Ted's story actually took a back seat to the return of Jackie Jensen.

The Red Sox held a press conference in Tom Yawkey's office to announce the slugger's return to the team. He had quit baseball following the 1959 season because of his morbid fear of flying. In doing so, he had walked away from a brilliant career, leading the American League in RBIs three times, including 1958, when he was named MVP.

Jensen told the press that his problems were ''still there,'' but that they wouldn't interfere with playing ball. He credited hypnotist Arthur Ellen for helping him control his fear of airplane flights.

After the announcement, Jensen joined other dignitaries at home plate for pregame ceremonies honoring Williams. Jensen signed his contract when his name was officially taken off the voluntarily retired list on October 31. He played in 1961, hit just .263 with diminished production, and then quit again. ◆

On the Record: Bobby Doerr

Hall of Fame second baseman Bobby Doerr played with Ted from Ted's rookie year to the dawn of the fifties. He probably knows Ted as well as any man does.

Valenti: What was Ted like to be around?

Doerr: He was a very compassionate person, when you were just one-on-one with him. He was a loner. I can remember especially when we'd make trips on the train from Cleveland to Detroit, or Detroit to Cleveland. We'd get into town at 9:30 at night. And he'd always say, "Come on, Bobby. Let's take a walk." In those days, you could walk around window-shopping at night. We'd do a lot of talking about fishing. I can remember a few times where guys would say, "What are you gonna do?" But Ted would want it one-on-one. Walking about like that with me seemed like a relaxation for him. We'd go to the movies. Ted was a big movie fan. In those days, they would have live vaudeville in the movie houses, people like Ted Lewis. We used to like Westerns. I guess that was another thing we had in common besides fishing. We'd always look to see where there was a Western playing and go take it in. But he was a very compassionate person, a very generous person. At times, he would get uptight. But he wouldn't say anything to the players. He'd just go off by himself. He didn't stay around and bother anybody. He'd just go off by himself and want to be left alone.

Valenti: What essential point would you make about Ted as a hitter?

BOX SCORE: Fenway Park, 9•28•60

Attendance: 10,454
Time of Game: 2:18

BALTIMORE ORIOLES

Name	AB	R	H	RBI
Brandt, CF	5	0	0	0
Pilarcik, RF	4	0	1	0
Robinson, 3B	4	1	1	0
Gentile, 1B	3	1	1	1
Triandos, C	4	1	2	2
Hansen, SS	4	1	2	0
Stephens, LF	4	0	2	0
Breeding, 2B	2	0	0	0
Woodling, PH	1	0	0	1
Pearson, PR	0	0	0	0
Klaus, 2B	1	0	0	0
Barber, P	0	0	0	0
Fisher, P	4	0	0	0
Totals	36	4	9	4

BOSTON RED SOX

Name	AB	R	H	RBI
Green, SS	3	0	0	0
Tasby, CF	4	1	0	1
Williams, LF	3	2	1	1
Hardy, LF	0	0	0	0
Pagliaroni, C	3	0	2	0
Malzone, 3B	3	0	0	0
Clinton, RF	3	0	0	1
Gile, 1B	4	0	0	0
Coughtry, 2B	3	1	2	0
Muffett, P	2	0	0	0
Nixon, PH	1	0	0	0
Fornieles, P	0	0	0	0
Wertz, PH	1	0	1	0
Brewer, PR	0	1	0	0
Totals	30	5	6	3

Team	1	2	3	4	5	6	7	8	9		
Baltimore	0	2	0	0	1	1	0	0	0		4
Boston	2	0	0	0	0	0	0	1	2		5

Name	1P	H	R	ER	BB	SO
Barber	⅓	0	2	2	3	0
Fisher (L)	8⅓	6	3	2	3	5

Name	1P	H	R	ER	BB	SO
Muffett	7	9	4	4	0	4
Fornieles (W)	2	0	0	0	0	2

Doerr: He was so much sharper and more knowledgeable than anyone else about what he was going to do at the plate, all the time. If there was a young pitcher that came into the league that he didn't know too much about, he would go seek somebody who had played with this fellow or against him in the minor leagues, and Ted would find out everything he could about that pitcher. Everything. Delivery, motion, pitches. Then Ted would study the pitcher warming up. So that when he walked into the box, he had a darn good idea what he was going to be looking at. Whereas the majority of us, it would take us two or three times watching a guy and hitting against him to realize what was happening. So the one thing I would point out is Ted's scientific approach to hitting. It was genius. There's no other way to put it.

5

BABE RUTH
September 30, 1927

New York 4,

Washington 2

*U*nique is an overused word, except in the case of Babe Ruth. He was the most uninhibited, dramatic, fun-loving, dynamic, free spirit ever to play baseball. The nostrils of his nose were large, as if to take in as much life-giving breath as possible. His powerful physique was a pure abandonment to action. He was as giving as a child, and almost as innocent.

His magnitude and largesse captured the imagination of a country still feeling the alienating effects of World War I and, without knowing it, psychically preparing for a world depression by plunging into a ten-year bash known as the Roaring Twenties. He was the right man, in the right time, at the right place. Personality, time, and space converged in some mystic way to produce George Herman Ruth. If Babe hadn't existed, it's likely that no one could have invented him.

Ruth grew up a tough kid on the streets of Baltimore. He didn't know right from wrong, but he wasn't the hoodlum that legend makes him out to be. So many of the facts of Babe's childhood are lost that historians recreate it with each telling. Suffice it to say that his youth, while not defined by squalor, was on the low side of lower middle class. His parents ran a saloon seven days a week and had little time for young George, who took advantage of the freedom to get into scrapes, roaming Baltimore streets, hiding in its alleys, throwing eggs at trucks, stealing.

He was out of control, and at eight and a half years old, they sent George to St. Mary's Industrial School for Boys. St. Mary's was part vocational school and part reformatory run by the Catholic Xaverian Brothers. Babe was enrolled on Friday the 13th, in June of 1902. He was listed as "incorrigible." The brothers were tough but caring. Babe prospered under their guidance, especially that of Brother Matthias, a strapping man six feet six inches tall and 250 pounds, who became like a father to Ruth.

It was under the brothers that Babe learned the trade of shirtmaking (specifically, attaching collars to shirts). He also learned baseball. The school, like most of the country, was baseball crazy. Baltimore itself was a hotbed, with hundreds of amateur and semipro teams. St. Mary's fielded forty teams, and Babe became the school star. Eventually, he attracted the attention of Jack Dunn, owner of the Orioles, at that time in the International League. Shortly after his twentieth birthday, Ruth signed a contract, which soon was purchased by the Boston Red Sox. By 1914, Babe was in the majors and the Greatest Baseball Story Ever Told began unfolding.

To this day, everyone remembers Ruth the slugger, as well they should. But they sometimes forget his incredible career in Boston as a pitcher. He regularly outdueled Walter Johnson, he was the top left-hander in baseball, and he helped the Red Sox to World Championships in 1915, 1916, and 1918. He was 89-46 with the Sox, pitched twenty-nine consecutive scoreless innings in the World Series, and led the league with an amazing 1.75 ERA on 324 innings pitched. But by 1919, he was moved to the outfield to take advantage of his booming bat. The year before, as a part-time hitter, Babe led the League with eleven home runs.

Boston was baseball paradise. The Red Sox had established themselves as baseball's first dynasty. But every Eden has its snake, and Fenway Park was no different. Theatrical producer Harry (*No, No Nanette*) Frazee bought the team from Joe Lannin in 1916. Frazee financed a string of failing stage productions by selling his players to Yankee owner Jake Ruppert. On January 5, 1920, he sold Ruth to New York ("I can't help it. I'm up against the wall.").

Ruth felt bad about leaving Boston, but in New York, he arrived in his element: a town that would never shut down, a town ready to build up its heroes into Leviathan proportions. With Ruth, though, no buildup was necessary. This idol thing, it was all show to Babe anyway. His message to New York was basically this: don't tell me to do anything, anywhere, for anyone, at any time, because I'll do it all on my own anyway. Just get out of my way and watch.

The stories were numerous. When writers asked his 1920 roommate Ping Bodie what it was like rooming with Ruth, Bodie replied, "I don't room with him. I room with his suitcase." When the Yankees were playing the Senators one hot day in Washington, President Cal Coolidge came out to the park. A reception line was set up. Everyone gave polite and respectful greetings to Coolidge. When he met Babe, Coolidge shook his hand.

"Mr. Ruth."

"Hot as hell, ain't it, Prez?" Babe replied in front of his aghast manager, Miller Huggins.

With a collection of ex-Boston stars (courtesy of Frazee) led by Ruth, the Yankees shook their identity as losers, going from doormats to dynasty.

People began noticing his bat in Boston, but once in New York, Ruth's hitting changed the very structure of the game itself. Before the Babe, no manager really counted on the home run as part of an offensive strategy. After Ruth, all that changed. In 1920, Babe topped his major league record of 29 homers, set with the Red Sox in 1919, by clubbing the astounding total of 54. Going along with his .376 average, 158 runs, 137 RBIs, and .847 slugging percentage (still an all-time mark), Babe had one of the great seasons of all time in 1920.

It was the kind of first year that made him a fixture and a draw beyond belief in New York and the rest of the country. He packed the parks. People flocked to see him, were desperate to read about him. Soon he was everywhere—on film, on the radio, in the papers, in ads. His popularity grew, and the homers continued; his home run totals for the next six years: 59, 35, 41, 46, 25, 47. Everyone wanted a piece of him, in Gotham and everywhere.

In May 1923, Ruppert unveiled the new theater in which Babe would perform for his wide-eyed audience: Yankee Stadium. Babe homered in the first game. Babe was a fever, baseball the patient, made delirious.

The culmination of Ruth's march through New York and baseball came in 1927, when he hit 60 home runs. That year, the fates conspired to bring together a most amazing collection of baseball talent: the '27 Yankees, generally considered to be the greatest team ever. They were in first place from coast to coast, crushing early, token attempts at competition from the Washington Senators and the Philadelphia A's, who finished in second place, 19 games behind. The juggernaut went 110-44 and swept the Pirates in the World Series. The team batting average of the '27 Yankees was .307. They blasted 158 home runs, tripling their nearest rival. Writers dubbed the lineup "Murderers Row."

At first base, Lou Gehrig hit .373, with 47 homers and 175 RBIs. At second, Tony Lazzeri, a cold, intense man (said one writer, "Interviewing him is like mining coal with a nail file") who hit .309 and 18 homers. Mark Koenig at short and Jumpin' Joe Dugan at third provided airtight defense on the left side. Bob Meusel was in left with a .337 average and 103 RBIs. Earle Combs handled center and also leadoff in the batting order, hitting .356 with a league-leading 231 hits.

In 1927, the pennant race was, in effect, over by the middle of July. Led by the electric Babe Ruth, the '27 Yankees was the team everyone wanted to see. It got to the point where the team played in exhibition games during the regular season, when the schedule called for an off day. The nation couldn't get enough of Ruth, and Jake Ruppert couldn't say no to easy money. They would play local teams or minor league clubs in cities like St. Paul, Buffalo, Scranton, Toronto, and Dayton. One exhibition in Toronto had to be held up when a bunch of young boys went out to right field, surrounding Babe. They rode on his shoulders, tackled him. Babe good-naturedly put up with it—like a father happily wrestling with his sons.

Everything else about the season was decided: no one was going to catch the Yankees for the title. They led the league in just about everything. The only item of suspense was Ruth's home run total. He had been hitting them at a, well, Ruthian, pace, which meant, once again, he was in competition with himself. Ruth had set the major league record for home runs four times, with 11 in 1918, 29 in 1919 (both seasons with the Red Sox), 54 in 1920, and 59 in 1921. But the 60th home run had eluded him. It seemed to be the sound barrier, the four-minute mile, the line that no mortal could cross. Ruth had badly wanted to hit 60, for he felt it would be the one record no one would ever touch.

Broken down by month, Babe's totals looked like this: April, 4; May, 12; June, 9; July, 9; August, 9. Going into September, Ruth had 43 home runs. In the early part of the season, Gehrig matched Babe, and as late as August 10, actually led him, 38 to 35. But the Bambino put on an incredible finish, outhomering Gehrig 25 to 9 the last fifty days of the season.

When Babe hit number 50 on September 11 against Milt Gaston of the St. Louis Browns, the pressure started to build. He needed 10 home runs with 17 games to play. A tall order even for Ruth. But then, in one of the great displays of clutch hitting, he began hitting them in bunches. He hit two on September 13, and one each on

Ruth's 60: Homer by Homer

◆

Home Run No.	Team Game No.	Date	Pitcher, Team	Place
1	4	Apr. 15	Ehmke, Philadelphia	home
2	11	Apr. 23	Walberg, Philadelphia	away
3	12	Apr. 24	Thurston, Washington	away
4	14	Apr. 29	Harriss, Boston	away
5	16	May 1	Quinn, Philadelphia	home
6	16	May 1	Walberg, Philadelphia	home
7	24	May 10	Gaston, St. Louis	away
8	25	May 11	Nevers, St. Louis	away
9	29	May 17	Collins, Detroit	away
10	33	May 22	Karr, Cleveland	away
11	34	May 23	Thurston, Washington	away
12	37	May 28	Thurston, Washington	home
13	39	May 29	MacFayden, Boston	home
14	41	May 30	Walberg, Philadelphia	away
15	42	May 31	Quinn, Philadelphia	away
16	43	May 31	Ehmke, Philadelphia	away
17	47	June 5	Whitehill, Detroit	home
18	48	June 7	Thomas, Chicago	home
19	52	June 11	Buckeye, Cleveland	home
20	52	June 11	Buckeye, Cleveland	home
21	53	June 12	Uhle, Cleveland	home
22	55	June 16	Zachary, St. Louis	home
23	60	June 22	Wiltse, Boston	away
24	60	June 22	Wiltse, Boston	away
25	70	June 30	Harriss, Boston	home
26	73	July 3	Lisenbee, Washington	away
27	78	July 8	Hankins, Detroit	away
28	79	July 9	Holloway, Detroit	away

continued on next page

the 16th, 18th, 21st, and 22nd. With that 56th home run off Detroit's Ken Holloway, Ruth carried the bat with him around the bases so it wouldn't be a target for souvenir hunters. By the time the season's final series with the Senators got under way at the Stadium, Babe needed three homers. He got the first two on the 29th. So on September 30, Ruth stood tied with himself at 59.

His first three times up on the 30th against screwballing lefty Tom Zachary, Ruth had walked and had two base hits. It all came down to one shot, in the eighth inning. Ruth stepped in with the score tied 2–2. Mark Koenig, who had just tripled, was at third with one out. Zachary's first pitch was a fastball in for a called strike. The crowd booed. The second pitch, a screwball, was high. On the next one, Zachary

Home Run No.	Team Game No.	Date	Pitcher, Team	Place
29	79	July 9	Holloway, Detroit	away
30	83	July 12	Shaute, Cleveland	away
31	94	July 24	Thomas, Chicago	away
32	95	July 26	Gaston, St. Louis	home
33	95	July 26	Gaston, St. Louis	home
34	98	July 28	Stewart, St. Louis	home
35	106	Aug. 5	Smith, Detroit	home
36	110	Aug. 10	Zachary, Washington	away
37	114	Aug. 16	Thomas, Chicago	away
38	115	Aug. 17	Connally, Chicago	away
39	118	Aug. 20	Miller, Cleveland	away
40	120	Aug. 22	Shaute, Cleveland	away
41	124	Aug. 27	Nevers, St. Louis	away
42	125	Aug. 28	Wingard, St. Louis	away
43	127	Aug. 31	Wingard, Boston	home
44	128	Sept. 2	Walberg, Philadelphia	away
45	132	Sept. 6	Welzer, Boston	away
46	132	Sept. 6	Welzer, Boston	away
47	133	Sept. 6	Russell, Boston	away
48	134	Sept. 7	MacFayden, Boston	away
49	134	Sept. 7	Harriss, Boston	away
50	138	Sept. 11	Gaston, St. Louis	home
51	139	Sept. 13	Hudlin, Cleveland	home
52	140	Sept. 13	Shaute, Cleveland	home
53	143	Sept. 16	Blankenship, Chicago	home
54	147	Sept. 18	Lyons, Chicago	home
55	148	Sept. 21	Gibson, Detroit	home
56	149	Sept. 22	Holloway, Detroit	home
57	152	Sept. 27	Grove, Philadelphia	home
58	153	Sept. 29	Lisenbee, Washington	home
59	153	Sept. 29	Hopkins, Washington	home
60	154	Sept. 30	Zachary, Washington	home

◆

delivered another fastball, low and inside. Babe pulled away from the plate slightly, then stepped into the ball with a gigantic cut. He made solid contact. As the *New York Times* put it, bat met ball "with a crash that was audible in all parts of the stands." The ball rose into the air, deep to right, but near the foul line. The *Times* said it started out "about ten feet fair, but curving rapidly to the right."

It looked like it might hook foul. The crowd waited nervously as it landed—about a foot fair, halfway up the top of the bleachers. A triumphant Ruth watched the ball land, then began a slow, regal jog around the bases. Hats were tossed in the air, and the small crowd (about 10,000) went crazy. The Yankees all rushed out onto the field, gathering at the plate to greet the Babe.

As the ball landed, Zachary screamed to umpire Bill Dineen that it was foul. When the ump ruled fair, Zachary tossed his glove in the air in rage, muttered angrily to himself, and stood staring out at nothing in center field. Author Robert Creamer, in his biography of Ruth, relates a story that occurred in 1947. Babe and Zachary shook hands during a ceremony at Yankee Stadium. Ruth could barely talk because of the cancer in his throat, but he still told Zachary, "You crooked-arm son of a bitch, are you still claiming that ball was foul?"

The ball was caught by forty-year-old Joe Forner of 1937 First Avenue, Manhattan. When the game was over, Forner gave the ball to Ruth in the locker room. Ruth gave him a bat in return. In the locker room, Ruth bellowed at the top of his lungs, "Sixty, count 'em, sixty! Let's see some other SOB match that." Ruth and mates celebrated well into the night. The next afternoon at the Stadium, Ruth, well covered by the hair of the dog that bit him, went 0-for-3 in the game number 155, the season's finale (the Yankees played 155 games because of a tie on April 14).

The following year, Babe hit 54, and he was never again to come close to 60. He dipped to 22 in 1934 with a .288 average, and the Yankees sent him back to Boston, this time with the Braves. The lowly Braves were only too eager to have Ruth's name in the lineup (truth be told, they didn't want his bat). It was a mistake, and Babe hit an embarrassing .181 in 72 at bats. It was fitting, however: six of his thirteen hits were home runs. It all came to an end on June 2, 1935. Ruth could no longer do it. He quit.

On the Record: C.E. "Pat" Olsen

Pat Olsen roomed with Babe Ruth in 1924. Olsen never made it into a big league game, but after leaving baseball, he became a millionaire in business. He is noted for his philanthropic work for baseball and retired old-timers.

Valenti: When did you room with Babe Ruth?

Olsen: I was there in 1924, early in the season. I roomed with him on the road, and at home we lived on the same floor, the fourth floor of the Concourse Plaza, up there on the hill right by Yankee Stadium. That was less than a year after the Stadium opened. Of course, that area around the Stadium, in the Bronx, was just country then. You could hunt rabbits right outside the park. Yeah, I knew Babe pretty well. He was indescribable as a person. Totally unique. Being on the same floor with him and next to him for all those months, was quite an experience. He could never remember my name. He couldn't remember anyone's name. Even after living right next to him for months, Babe never remembered anybody for more than two days. He'd just yell out, "Hi, boy." Or he'd call you "kid." That's all he ever knew. He was a great guy, and he loved kids, always stopping to sign autographs for them.

Valenti: When did you join the Yankees?

Olsen: I was sold to New York in August of '23. With the Yanks, I didn't play, but hung around on the bench. I went to my first spring training with the Yankees in 1924. And Lou Gehrig and I roomed together on trips. Earle Combs, Lou Gehrig, and I were the only three rookies that they took north that year.

BOX SCORE: Yankee Stadium, 9•30•27

Attendance: Not available from
  box score (approximately 10,000)
Time of Game: 1:38

WASHINGTON SENATORS

Name	AB	R	H	RBI
Rice, RF	3	0	1	0
Harris, 2B	3	0	0	0
Ganzel, CF	4	0	1	0
Goslin, LF	4	1	1	1
Judge, 1B	4	0	0	0
Ruel, C	2	1	1	1
Bleuge, 3B	3	0	1	0
Gillis, SS	4	0	0	0
Zachary, P	2	0	0	0
Johnson, PH	1	0	0	0
Totals	30	2	5	2

NEW YORK YANKEES

Name	AB	R	H	RBI
Combs, CF	4	0	0	0
Koenig, SS	4	1	1	0
Ruth, RF	3	3	3	3
Gehrig, 1B	4	0	2	1
Meusel, LF	3	0	1	0
Lazzeri, SS	3	0	0	0
Dugan, 3B	3	0	1	0
Bengough, C	3	0	1	0
Pipgras, P	2	0	0	0
Pennock, P	1	0	0	0
Totals	30	4	9	4

Team	1	2	3	4	5	6	7	8	9		
Senators	0	0	0	2	0	0	0	0	0		2
Yankees	0	0	0	1	0	1	0	2	X		4

Name	1P	H	R	ER	BB	SO
Zachary (L)	8	9	4	4	1	1

Name	1P	H	R	ER	BB	SO
Pipgras	6	4	2	2	4	0
Pennock (W)	3	1	0	0	1	0

Valenti: Is there a Babe story that stands out in your mind?

Olsen: Babe was an interesting character. One of the things I'll never forget was one
day, when we were coming out of Philadelphia into New York on the train. Babe
was in one of his fun-loving moods, and he picked Miller Huggins up, had him by
the ankles. He had him hanging over the back of the observation car, with Huggins'
head about six inches off the rails! That was in 1924. Another thing I remember
was the way Babe was with names. To show you how forgetful he is, he was sitting
on the bench, talking to a fellow for about 30 minutes before a game at Yankee
Stadium. When he left, Babe turned to me and said, "Who's that son of bitch?"
Of course, everyone was a "son of a bitch" when he didn't know their name, that's
all he knew. "I said, 'Babe that's the same fellow you just got done spending two
weeks with up in Albany on his estate.'" That's how quick Babe would forget a
name.

6

ROGER MARIS
October 1, 1961

New York 1,

Boston 0

Hell is many things to many people. To some, it's viscerally repelling, like a room full of spiders or an eternity of slow torture. To others, it can be more cerebral but no less awful. Writer Jean Paul Sartre said, "Hell is other people." This was closer to the hell Roger Maris found in 1961 when he went up against the ghost of Babe Ruth. It was a hell defined not by nine circles (unless they were innings), but by an asterisk, a little mark that marred what should have been—both for Maris and baseball—a wonderful season. But should-have-beens and could-have-beens weren't what Maris faced that season. Instead, he smacked into the reality of a stodgy baseball hierarchy, a relentless press, and misunderstanding fans.

Why did this go sour? It should have been one of baseball's great times. Maris should have had fun. Why the absurdity? The answer to that begins with Maris himself.

Maris was a country boy, one who loved his privacy, his family, and the freedom to live his life without compromising absolute honesty. He hated phonies—something the phonies themselves can't stand. He said little, but the little he said was straight from the hip. He spoke his mind, no words minced. That would come back to haunt him in New York.

Maris signed with the Cleveland Indians in 1956 for $15,000. He worked his way up through the system, arriving in the big leagues in 1957. In the minors, he developed a reputation of a hard nose, someone difficult to get along with. This may have been the result of Maris's total dedication to baseball. He took the game seriously and never let up on himself. Many saw him as aloof. When he was platooned or played out of position, he griped. As a result, he had problems with his managers, Dutch Meyer in Tulsa and Kerby Farrell in Indianapolis. He even had trouble with Frank Lane in Cleveland. Lane, the kind of autocrat Maris detested, wanted him to play winter ball in the off-season of 1957. Maris refused, preferring to stay home with his family. The next year on June 15, Maris and his .225 average were traded to Kansas City. When the subject of Lane would come up, Maris had no apologies: "I can't stand

Lane's guts—not because of what he did to me, but what he did to others. He thinks nothing of people's feelings. Talks big. Thinks he's a big deal. Who's he kidding?"

In Kansas City, Maris bought a home and put down roots. He was well liked by the fans, and genuinely happy playing ball and raising his family in the Midwest. He had the best of both worlds: playing big league baseball, but doing so virtually in private. The A's had just one or two writers covering them, and the fans put no pressure on him. Maris responded by hitting 19 home runs the rest of the '58 season. The next year, he hit .273, with 16 HRs and 72 RBIs. Not spectacular, but steady and solid, especially since his season was interrupted by an emergency appendectomy in May. Maris had found a home.

But in those years, Kansas City was the Kissin' Cousin of the New York Yankees. The trades were suspiciously numerous. Players tagged it the Underground Railroad. K.C. would develop some players the Yanks could use; then, presto! a deal would be made. Maris worried about this when he came to Kansas City, and his worst fears were realized on December 11, 1959. He had been traded to New York.

He heard the news on the radio at home in Raytown, Missouri. He felt dread and anguish, and reported to New York only reluctantly. He had no choice other than to quit. He made a statement that he wasn't happy about the trade, that he wanted to stay in K.C., that the fans were better there. New York fans took it as a slap in the face.

Besides, the Big Apple had a hero: Mickey Mantle. Mantle himself had already run the Gauntlet of Gotham. Like Maris, he had country roots, coming to New York from the zinc mines of Commerce, Oklahoma. He arrived with explosive, breathtaking skills, a once-in-a-lifetime combination of speed, power, and raw ability. But the star-making machinery, designed to feed New York's insatiable desire for manufactured idols, took its toll on Mick.

For ten years, Yankee fans booed him unmercifully, despite some fantastic seasons. For a decade, from 1951 to 1960, New York jeered Mickey Mantle ("I've got to have a reason?"—fan in bleachers in 1958). They saw him as immature, a walking advertisement for unfulfilled potential. It wasn't rational, but it was real.

But by 1961, things were changing. More people became aware of his leg problems and the daily pain he had to play through. Fewer cared that he had replaced the great Joe DiMaggio in center field. He no longer sulked after a bad day. He no longer destroyed water coolers after striking out. He was civil with the fans and the press. It had taken ten years, but peace was at hand for the new, relaxed Mantle. The fans and writers went looking for another patsy.

In 1960, Maris dueled Mantle for the home run crown, finally losing, 40 to 39. But he came first in the MVP balloting, which enraged many Mantle supporters. It's hard to understand why. Maris led the league in RBIs with 112 to Mantle's 94, and outhit Mick .283 to .275. Maris was most bitter not at the fans, but at Yankee manager Casey Stengel. Casey spent the last month of the season on the stump for Mantle, pleading Mick's case for MVP and clearly trying to influence the writers. In the process, he sold a lot of fans on the idea. These same fans were angry that Maris won the award. They also said he didn't deserve his huge pay raise, going from $19,000 in 1960 to $37,500 in 1961.

After the debacle of losing the 1960 World Series to the Pirates, Stengel was fired as manager and replaced by Ralph Houk. The American League had a new look as well in 1961, expanding to ten teams (adding the Los Angeles Angels and the

Minnesota Twins). Immediately there was discussion on the watering down of talent, particularly of pitchers, and how this might inflate the offensive performance of the new year. This, too, would come back to haunt Maris.

In spring training, Maris hit poorly with one home run and a .235 average. His slump continued into the regular season. He went ten games without a home run. By mid-May, he was hitting .218 with three home runs. Ruth was resting quietly in his grave.

The fans were all over Maris for his slow start. He became moody, reticent, sullen. Even when things were going well, Maris had always been a "yes/no" type with the writers. He wasn't one for elaborating or volunteering information. But with the slow start, the monosyllables gave way to no syllables. Maris was still the outsider, not considered a "true" Yankee. Which was just fine by him.

With Maris struggling, Yankee president Dan Topping told him to forget about hitting for average. Just go for the home runs and RBIs. It was welcome advice for Maris, and that's just what he did. On May 17, he hit his fourth home run off Pete Burnside of the Senators. By the end of the month, he had upped his total to 12. Then the homers came in bunches. He hit 15 in June, giving him 27 in 66 games. It was about then, the beginning of July, that the press started picking up on the home runs. Maris was ahead of Ruth's pace. Mantle was keeping pace with Ruth and Maris. The press called them the M&M Boys, a myth in the making. Or was it a monster ("It's moving. It's alive, it's alive!")?

The outline of Maris's long, grueling summer looked like this: by the end of July, 40; going into September, 51. The pressure mounted each day.

The subplot was Mantle. He stayed with Roger all year. On September 2, when Maris had 53, Mick had 50. The increased attention, the writers, the pressure, were easier for Mantle. He'd been through it all for a decade. Besides, the press gave him kid-glove treatment. Mantle was written up as the legitimate contender, a proven superstar who had earned the "right" to go ghost-busting after Ruth. When he sulked after a bad day, the press ignored it. Maris, however, was the outsider, the fluke, the pretender. Each Freudian aspect of his moodiness made headlines. Mantle enthralled the press with his colorful stories of womanizing and drinking. Maris regurgitated a bland diet of yeses and nos, clichés, chilly silence, and icy stares.

The writers, cut cold by Maris's icicles, retaliated by trying to brew up a feud between him and Mantle. Their Yankee teammates knew better, but the fans only know what they read. They bought the notion that Mantle and Maris hated each other.

Their relationship may have been delicate, but in truth it was never divisive (or derisive). Not counting Mantle's ten-year edge in dealing with the pressures of New York, they had much in common. Each came from the country, with a natural suspicion of cities. Each was shy, introspective, moody. Each was driven by an intense desire to succeed. Each had a good sense of humor. Mantle just had ten years of polish on Maris. But the two men got along.

In fact, they even shared an apartment with outfielder Bob Cerv that summer. Ever since their families had moved back home after the start of the season, each had been living in Manhattan hotels. When the home runs started, Mantle and Maris were constantly bothered by writers and fans. They decided to get a place together. A mutual friend, Julie Isaacson, rented it for them, using his own name to preserve the anonymity of Mantle and Maris. He also kept its location a secret from the press. The apartment was in Queens, about a twenty-five minute drive from Yankee Stadium.

The $251-a-month apartment was a refuge, a lifeboat, a sanctuary. They played cards, used the living room as a putting green, cooked their meals, listened to Mantle's stacks of rock and country records. But most of all, it was quiet, "normal." They got away from the attention, the Crush, which to Mantle was a minor annoyance but to Maris was an Iron Maiden, a rack, a red-hot poker pressed into his stripped flesh.

Maris and Mantle thought the idea of a feud was a joke. They would make fun of it by yelling at each other in mock anger, "I hate your guts."

But it was no joke in New York. By July, New York (and the rest of the country) realized they were both chasing Ruth. Fueled by the press, they would have to take sides. "Give us Mantle!" they yelled. And what of this man, what of Maris? "Crucify him!" they screamed.

Behold, the man.

The writers quickly pointed out that Maris had never hit .300, and that Mantle had a lifetime .307. In discussing Maris, they pointed out that expansion had put twenty pitchers in baseball who wouldn't normally have been there. With Mantle, it was his heroic playing through pain. Even a poll taken on the team indicated that eighty percent of them believed Mantle, not Maris, would catch Ruth. Mantle received more fan mail. Maris received mostly hate mail.

In mid-July, the home run chase had taken on a life of its own. To make matters worse, on July 17, Commissioner Ford Frick ruled that Ruth's record would stand unless broken within 154 games. Thus, the asterisk was born. If the record were to be topped beyond 154 games, it would not be the same. It would be diluted, qualified, incapable of standing on its own without crutches, without a footnote, almost an apology. Thus, in one stroke, Frick incredibly emasculated the quest.

Many questioned his motives. In his newspaper days, Frick had been close to Ruth. Ruth's widow, Claire, had Frick's ear and publicly stated she hoped Maris wouldn't get the record. Most of baseball's old guard wanted Ruth's record to remain intact, and in Frick they had the right man. It was a ridiculous ruling. No other records set after the schedule had expanded to 162 games (in 1961, by the way) needed a qualifier. Why this one? Because Frick had his own interests to protect and his cronies to please.

The ruling created more pressure on M&M. To really beat the Babe, they were expected to do it in 154 games. By the time September arrived, the atmosphere was like a circus. Writers from all over the country were following the race. Most of the New York papers sent four writers to the park: one to do a game story, three to report on Mantle and Maris. Just when Maris thought it couldn't get worse, Mantle developed a virus he couldn't shake, that left him weak and tired. He was out of the lineup for most of September.

Maris was alone.

Instead of three deep, the media were now six deep in front of his cubicle. Writers did stories on his meals, what movies he watched. With his every move being reported to hundreds of millions of people worldwide, Roger Maris may have been the most isolated person on the face of the earth.

For Maris, it was truly horrific. He had trouble sleeping. When he did sleep, he had nightmares. The questions never ended, each one seemingly of no consequence, like the individual drops in a Chinese water torture. But in aggregate, they were maddening.

"Do you fool around on the road?" Drip.

"Does Houk ever give you a home run signal?" Drip.

"How are your kids taking this?" "Does all this make you excited?" Drip, drip.

In the face of all this, Maris became sarcastic and surly. Once, after he had hit a home run, a writer asked what he hit, trying to get a comment on the type of pitch. "A baseball," Maris snapped.

"Even the clubhouse attendants think I'm tough to live with," Maris commented at the time. "I guess they're right. I'm miffed most of the time, regardless of how I'm doing. I'll never take abuse from anybody—big or small, important or unimportant—if I think it's unfair."

The barrage continued. Hundreds of writers. Thousands of questions. Millions of words. Photographers shouted at him for poses, flashbulbs constantly exploding. Autograph hounds and hecklers shadowed him. Writers wrote that the Yankees had private detectives trailing Maris; he made the gossip columns along with Hollywood celebrities. "How can they write stuff like that?" he would fume. If he was asked a question like, "How can a hitter like you hit 60 home runs?" he would say something like, "You've got to be a damned idiot."

In Detroit, someone threw a chair out of the upper deck. It landed a couple of feet away from Maris. The hate mail continued. His hair started falling out in clumps. He developed a bad skin rash. He detested coming to the park. He went in, crying, to Manager Houk's office, saying he couldn't take it anymore. "I need help. I need help." What could Houk say?

Everything else was rendered invisible—the pennant race with Detroit, Whitey Ford's great year (he would end up 25-4). Mantle observed it all from the sidelines, in the unfamiliar but immensely enjoyable position of being overlooked, overshadowed.

After hitting number 56 at home on September 9 off Cleveland's Jim "Mudcat" Grant, Maris went dry for the next eight games. Writers said he was choking.

"Mick, it's driving me nuts, I'm telling you," Maris told Mantle.

"And I'm telling you, you've got to get used to it," Mantle shot back.

Maris bounced back to hit homers on September 16 and 17, leaving him with 58 home runs after 154 games. Frick seemed to have won. The commissioner's ruling made Maris look like a failure. His teammates were angry. To the fans, who booed him every time he did not get a home run, and the press, who portrayed him as a man who'd come up short, Maris was now an impostor after a pseudorecord.

He hit number 59 in game 155 (the Yanks clinched the pennant, but who cared?). Home run number 60 came off Jack Fisher of Baltimore, two days short of a year after Fisher gave up a home run to Ted Williams in his last at bat. Waiting at the plate before hitting number 60, Maris said to catcher Gus Triandos, "Don't think my collar isn't tight." After he hit the ball, he just stood there watching.

"If it was fair, I had plenty of time," he explained. "If it was foul, I'd save my strength." That's how exhausted he was. In the locker room, he slumped in his chair, saying to no one in particular, "Nobody knows how tired I am." He sat out the next game, gearing up for the final series in Yankee Stadium against the Boston Red Sox. It finally came down to the last game, Maris locked at 60.

The Red Sox started rookie right-hander Tracy Stallard, a hard-throwing pitcher who came in at 2-6. Stallard got the nod over Gene Conley, who was a late scratch because of arm trouble. The Yanks started Bill Stafford, 12-9. Because of the Frick

Maris's 61: Homer by Homer

◆

Home Run No.	Team Game No.	Date	Pitcher, Team	Place
1	11	Apr. 26	Foytack, Detroit	away
2	17	May 3	Ramos, Minnesota	away
3	20	May 6	Grba, Los Angeles	away
4	29	May 17	Burnside, Washington	away
5	30	May 19	Perry, Cleveland	away
6	31	May 20	Bell, Cleveland	away
7	32	May 21	Estrada, Baltimore	home
8	35	May 24	Conley, Boston	home
9	38	May 28	McLish, Chicago	home
10	40	May 30	Conley, Boston	away
11	40	May 30	Fornieles, Boston	away
12	41	May 31	Muffett, Boston	away
13	43	June 2	McLish, Chicago	away
14	44	June 3	Shaw, Chicago	away
15	45	June 4	Kemmerer, Chicago	away
16	48	June 6	Palmquist, Minnesota	home
17	49	June 7	Ramos, Minnesota	home
18	52	June 9	Herbert, Kansas City	home
19	55	June 11	Grba, Los Angeles	home
20	55	June 11	James, Los Angeles	home
21	57	June 13	Perry, Cleveland	away
22	58	June 14	Bell, Cleveland	away
23	61	June 17	Mossi, Detroit	away
24	62	June 18	Casale, Detroit	away
25	63	June 19	Archer, Kansas City	away
26	64	June 20	Nuxhall, Kansas City	away
27	66	June 22	Bass, Kansas City	away
28	74	July 1	Sisler, Washington	home

continued on next page

ruling, interest wasn't all that great in New York. Only 23,154 came out. Two-thirds of the park was empty, but every seat in right field was taken. Sam Gordon, a Sacramento, California, restaurant owner, offered $5000 for the ball should there be a 61st home run.

In the first, Stallard worked Maris well, getting him to fly to Carl Yastrzemski in left field. Maris got up again in the fourth, the game still at 0–0. Stallard missed with his first pitch, a fastball high and away. The second pitch was low and inside. The crowd booed. The rookie came in with a fastball that got a lot of the plate. Maris turned on it, sending it deep to right. He stood transfixed at the plate, watching.

Home Run No.	Team Game No.	Date	Pitcher, Team	Place
29	75	July 2	Burnside, Washington	home
30	75	July 2	Klippstein, Washington	home
31	77	July 4	Lary, Detroit	home
32	78	July 5	Funk, Cleveland	home
33	82	July 9	Monbouquette, Boston	away
34	84	July 13	Wynn, Chicago	away
35	86	July 15	Herbert, Chicago	away
36	92	July 21	Monbouquette, Boston	away
37	95	July 25	Baumann, Chicago	home
38	95	July 25	Larsen, Chicago	home
39	96	July 25	Kemmerer, Chicago	home
40	97	July 26	Hacker, Chicago	home
41	106	Aug. 4	Pascual, Minnesota	home
42	114	Aug. 11	Burnside, Washington	away
43	115	Aug. 12	Donovan, Washington	away
44	116	Aug. 13	Daniels, Washington	away
45	117	Aug. 13	Kutyna, Washington	away
46	118	Aug. 15	Pizarro, Chicago	home
47	119	Aug. 16	Pierce, Chicago	home
48	119	Aug. 16	Pierce, Chicago	home
49	124	Aug. 20	Perry, Chicago	home
50	125	Aug. 22	McBride, Los Angeles	away
51	129	Aug. 26	Walker, Kansas City	away
52	135	Sept. 2	Lary, Detroit	home
53	135	Sept. 2	Aguirre, Detroit	home
54	140	Sept. 6	Cheney, Washington	home
55	141	Sept. 7	Stigman, Cleveland	home
56	143	Sept. 9	Grant, Cleveland	home
57	151	Sept. 16	Lary, Detroit	away
58	152	Sept. 17	Fox, Detroit	away
59	155	Sept. 20	Pappas, Baltimore	away
60	159	Sept. 26	Fisher, Baltimore	home
61	163	Oct. 1	Stallard, Boston	home

◆

Right fielder Lu Clinton went back to the wall. The ball came down amid a bunch of jumping fans. Someone threw his jacket up, trying to catch the ball. The ball bounced off the jacket and into the hands of Sal Durante, a nineteen-year-old truck driver from 1418 Neptune Avenue, in the Coney Island section of Brooklyn.

Mantle watched from his hospital bed (in for his virus infection and abscessed hip—"I got goosebumps"). Stallard kicked the mound and paced it, looking down. Maris briskly circled the bases, shook hands with on-deck batter Yogi Berra, and disappeared into the dugout. The crowd was on its feet, cheering. Maris stood on the dugout steps, smiling, but not really acknowledging the crowd. When he tried to sit down again, the Yankee bench wouldn't let him. They told him to wave to the crowd. Then Hector Lopez ("Roger seemed sort of in a daze"), Moose Skowron, and Joe DeMaestri pushed him onto the field. He waved his cap four times, went back into the dugout, sat down, and let out a great sigh. It was finished.

Maris left the dugout in the fifth inning, met Durante in the clubhouse, and posed for pictures. The kid said he didn't care about the money. He just wanted Maris to have the ball. That impressed Maris immensely. When he came up again in the eighth, he said to Red Sox catcher Russ Nixon, "What do you think of that kid? The boy is planning to get married, he has bills, but he still wanted to give me that ball for nothing. It shows there are some good people in the world after all." Sal eventually got his money from Gordon.

After the game, Maris calmly and politely answered questions for almost five hours. He sipped beer. The pressure was off. He praised Stallard for being "man enough to pitch to me."

Stallard said he didn't feel bad. He had pitched his best game of the year, with Maris's run being the only run of the game. "I'll tell you this," he said of the home run, "My price on the banquet circuit just went up."

When he finally got out of the locker room, Maris and his wife ducked into a Catholic Church on 47th Street for evening Mass. Five minutes later, he left. Surprised friends asked him why. The priest wanted to talk about the home run, Maris said.

On the Record: Tracy Stallard

Valenti: How aware of the situation were you that day in Yankee Stadium?

Stallard: I was aware of it as much as anyone else. You don't give it that much thought. I don't think the players do. I was more worried about doing well in the game itself. In that Yankee club, there were a lot of hitters to worry about, not just Maris. But I was certainly aware of the situation, yes.

Valenti: What were your thoughts before the game?

Stallard: Well, I didn't know I was starting until I got to the clubhouse. It would have been me or Gene Conley. Mike Higgins gave me the ball, and the main thing for me was winning the ballgame, pitching well. I was young and still trying to earn my spot on the club. I'm sure the fact that Maris had 60 home runs went through my mind, but I tried to treat it like just another game. I think the Yankee team worried you more than any individual player. The Yankees had a lineup full of guys who were capable of hitting home runs. There was a lot of media attention, so I stayed in the clubhouse until about twenty minutes before game time. Then I went out and started warming up. I knew it would be a little hectic. I didn't want to answer questions before the game, so I stayed away from the press.

Valenti: So you faced Maris in the first, and he flew out.

Stallard: Yeah, he popped out to Yaz [Carl Yastrzemski] in left. Then he hit his home run in the fourth. He was trying to pull the ball. And we were trying to keep the ball away from him. And I got behind, two balls and no strikes. I didn't want to walk him, so I had to throw a strike. I don't remember the position of the ball, if it was up or down or where it was. But you don't hit many good pitches for

BOX SCORE: Yankee Stadium, 10•1•61

Attendance: 23,154
Time of Game: 1:57

BOSTON RED SOX

Name	AB	R	H	RBI
Schilling, 2B	4	0	1	0
Geiger, CF	4	0	0	0
Yastrzemski, LF	4	0	1	0
Malzone, 3B	4	0	0	0
Clinton, RF	4	0	0	0
Runnels, 1B	3	0	0	0
Gile, 1B	0	0	0	0
Nixon, C	3	0	2	0
Green, SS	2	0	0	0
Stallard, P	1	0	0	0
Jensen, PH	1	0	0	0
Nichols, P	0	0	0	0
Totals	30	0	4	0

NEW YORK YANKEES

Name	AB	R	H	RBI
Richardson, 2B	4	0	0	0
Kubek, SS	4	0	2	0
Maris, CF	4	1	1	1
Berra, LF	2	0	0	0
Lopez, LF, RF	1	0	0	0
Blanchard, RF, C	3	0	0	0
Howard, C	2	0	0	0
Reed, LF	1	0	1	0
Skowron, 1B	2	0	0	0
Hale, 1B	1	0	1	0
Boyer, 3B	2	0	0	0
Stafford, P	2	0	0	0
Reniff, P	0	0	0	0
Tresh, PH	1	0	0	0
Arroyo, P	0	0	0	0
Totals	29	1	5	1

Team	1	2	3	4	5	6	7	8	9		
Boston	0	0	0	0	0	0	0	0	0		0
New York	0	0	0	1	0	0	0	0	0		1

Name	1P	H	R	ER	BB	SO
Stallard (L)	7	5	1	1	1	5
Nichols	1	0	0	0	0	0

Name	1P	H	R	ER	BB	SO
Stafford (W)	6	3	0	0	1	7
Reniff	1	0	0	0	0	1
Arroyo	2	1	0	0	0	1

home runs, so obviously, it was in his powerhouse. I didn't know it was gone at first. Maris hit the ball pretty hard, but he hit it real high, and it's not a long ways down the right-field line in Yankee Stadium. I saw Lu Clinton go back to the warning track still looking up. But it ended up in the seats. There was no possible way for Lu to make the catch. After he hit it, I just looked down. I knew I'd have to wait a little bit to pitch to the next batter, with all the commotion.

Valenti: What were things like after the game?

Stallard: Everything was crazy. But most of the press was in the Yankee clubhouse. I showered, answered some questions, but got out before they got to me. There might have been a couple of writers in the Red Sox clubhouse, probably because they couldn't fit in the Yankee locker room (*laughs*). After the game, Gene Conley and I took a train back to Boston, and we went fishing up in Maine. And that winter, I worked for the Red Sox doing community relations. Everybody wanted to know about the home run, but it didn't bother me, I think because I was so young [twenty-four years old]. I don't know. It might have affected me if I had been older. But I was young enough to give it my best shot and then say, "To hell with it." That was my attitude. I gave it my best, and every record that's set in baseball, it takes two people: a pitcher and a hitter or whatever. Actually, I felt good about the game itself. It was a 1–0 game, probably the best game I pitched all year, or probably ever. And I felt good about ending the season leaving a good impression on the Red Sox brass. But I didn't realize the impact of the home run for quite a while.

Valenti: And twenty-seven years later, here you are, still talking about it.

Stallard: I think there were 23,000 people there, and I think I've met at least 700,000 people who say they were there. I'll say one thing. It made people remember me. As a matter of fact, I was in the coal fields today [Stallard owns a mining company in Wise, Virginia] on a strip job, and a guy brought it up. It was somebody I never met before. We were just going to look at some coal property. He recognized my name. We were about the same age.

Valenti: Did you ever talk to Maris about it?

Stallard: I talked to him next year in spring training, but we didn't talk about the home run. I mean, what can you say? I liked Roger. He was a good guy. I attended his golf tournament in North Dakota. I'm going back this year [1988]. It's a nice event for a good cause.

7

CARLTON FISK
October 21, 1975

Who was the most important Beatle? How do you account for the continuing popularity of the Three Stooges? Or ask any mother: which child do you love the most? These questions are unanswerable, of course. The most you can ever offer is an opinion. That's the way of mystery.

So it is when someone asks: what was the greatest single game of major league baseball ever played, the most exciting, breathtaking, heart-stopping? Unanswerable, right? Wrong. The answer is Game Six of the 1975 World Series. Consensus would have it this way, as well as the result of both careful analysis and full reign of the emotions.

This was a game with everything: lead changes, clutch defensive plays, crushing errors, hallelujah home runs. Some seventy million people witnessed this event on television, and it's because of television that everyone so vividly remembers the stunning coda: Carlton Fisk's game-winning blast, history's first made-for-TV home run.

For nine years, Fisk, and not Carl Yastrzemski, was the soul of the Boston Red Sox. He came up in 1972 as something new, on two counts. First, he became baseball's best catcher, Boston's answer to Yogi Berra or Johnny Bench. This was unheard of in Boston, where catching had forever been one big headache, a chain of weak links like Pete Daley, Ed Sadowski, Lou Berberet, Russ Nixon, Jim Pagliaroni, Bob Tillman, Mike Ryan, Russ Gibson, Tom Satriano, Joe Azcue, Gene Oliver, Don Pavletich, and Duane Josephson. Guys like Sammy White and Elston Howard could provide only occasional relief.

Second, Fisk was a different kind of rookie. He was tall, handsome, articulate, fiery—"patrician," *Sports Illustrated* called him. Traditionally, Boston rookies were expected to do their jobs and keep their traps shut, meekly fitting in somewhere deep south on the club's totemic pecking order. For Fisk, that meant ignoring (thereby tacitly accepting) the team's "twenty-five men, twenty-five cabs" mentality of the early seventies.

This was a troubled club. In 1971, a feud involving Yastrzemski, Billy Conigliaro, and Reggie Smith tore the Sox in two. Players criticized manager Eddie Kasko for playing favorites. They bickered themselves out of contention, finishing 18 games out.

In 1972, the cliques continued, and a serpentine tangle of clubhouse politics once again threatened to strangle any spark of life. They got off to a somnambulant start, and soon it seemed as if some players were just going through the motions. This puzzled Fisk, a man with a burning desire to win but—at this stage in his career—not concerned with clubhouse etiquette. So it was on August 7, 1972, when Fisk gave an interview in which he questioned the team's attitude, specifically accusing Yaz and Smith of lack of leadership. New England was abuzz, and almost overnight, the Red Sox began to play ball. By Labor Day, they were back in contention. They came within twenty-four hours of a pennant, finishing a half game behind Detroit because of the one less game they played in the strike-shortened schedule.

All of a sudden, Boston felt itself on the verge of achievement. In '73, and '74, they again contended, but were a couple of players away. They were Fred Lynn and Jim Rice away. On opening day in 1975, Rice was on the bench, and Lynn went 0-for-4. By the time the year was over, they had respective batting totals of .331, 21 HRs, 105 RBI and .309, 22, 102. Fisk broke his arm in the first spring-training game, and was out until June. But he came on to hit .331 over the last half. Luis Tiant, Rick Wise, and Bill Lee combined for 54 wins, and Boston had a flag. Meanwhile, in Cincinnati, the Big Red Machine won 108 games with a lineup that included Bench, Pete Rose, Tony Perez, George Foster, and Joe Morgan.

In the playoffs, the Sox swept Oakland, three-time World Champions. The Reds dumped the Pirates, also in three games. The Reds went into the series heavily favored, but were soon to realize differently. Tiant shut them out in Game One, 6–0. The next three games were decided by a run, with Cincy taking two and three, the Sox coming through in the clutch behind Tiant again, this time on the road, in Game Four. The Reds went up 3–2 in the series with a 6–2 victory at Riverfront Stadium in Game Five. Then the rains came.

Maybe it was God's way of getting everyone to take a deep breath for what was to follow. For seventy-two hours, the fog drifted in, and the rain fell upon the place beneath, the Fenway pitch. Boston hotels, restaurants, and shops got an extra three days of World Series business.

Finally, the sun pierced the fog and drizzle. Commissioner Bowie Kuhn ruled the game would be played at night. At game time, the weather would rally from earlier forecasts of chill to a pleasant 64 degrees. Kuhn could shed his topcoat without forfeiting his self-respect.

Red Sox manager Darrell Johnson took advantage of the days off to come back with Tiant, who hadn't lost since September 20 and who had a string of 36 consecutive innings without giving up an earned run in Fenway Park. Bill Lee, who had been originally scheduled, voiced his displeasure.

"It's unfair to me," Lee protested. "Like I always say, the whole world is insane. I'm insane, therefore I'm normal...What the heck, I decree forty-eight hours of rain and darkness so Tiant can get an extra day's rest and pitch the sixth game."

Tiant shook off tiredness and back trouble to take up the challenge:

"All my life, I wanted to pitch in the World Series, so it's a great honor. My back's been bothering me, but I'll do what I can."

The other change had Carl Yastrzemski returning to left, with Cecil (1-for-13) Cooper playing first. The move paid off immediately. In the top of the first, leadoff hitter Pete Rose hit a sinking liner to left. Yaz charged and made a sliding one-hand grab.

In the bottom of the first, the Red Sox wasted no time off righty Gary Nolan. With two outs, Yaz and Fisk singled. Both rode home on Lynn's three-run shot into the bleachers in right center for a 3–0 advantage.

Tiant continued his magic, giving up two harmless singles through four. Boston, meanwhile, let two good chances slip by. In the third, they left the bases loaded. In the fourth, they put runners on second and third with one out and again came up empty. The crowd got edgy.

This nervous edge may have Fu Manchu'ed its way into the mustachioed Tiant's right arm in the fifth. With one out, the Reds had runners on the corners. For a month, Tiant had found a way to rumba out of this kind of spot. But not this time, as Ken Griffey obliged by driving a pitch deep to right center. Lynn, playing Griffey to pull, had a long run. He loped to the 379-foot mark, leaped high in the air, but the ball sailed just over the top of his glove. Two runs came home, but the crowd really didn't care. All eyes were on Lynn.

In attempting the catch, Lynn crashed into the cement wall with his lower back. He fell to the warning track in a heap, like a scarecrow without enough stuffing, and remained motionless. His head hung down; his torso was propped up against the base of the wall at a scary angle, as if he had been snapped in two. Yaz rushed over from left. Trainer Charlie Moss rushed to Lynn's aid while 35,205 stood silent. After a couple of minutes, Lynn moved.

"I wasn't knocked out. I just laid there because I felt numb," he said later. "I didn't feel anything. It lasted only a minute, but it seemed like an eternity."

Finally, Lynn struggled to his feet. He loosened up a bit and told Moss he could continue. The crowd cheered the display of true grit.

With Griffey on third and one out, Tiant got Morgan to pop to Petrocelli, but Bench delivered a ringing single off the Green Monster in left, knotting the game at 3–3. It stayed that way until the seventh, when the Reds pushed across two runs on Foster's double off the center-field wall.

In the eighth, the struggling Tiant gave up a leadoff homer to light-hitting Cesar Geronimo. He had fought the good fight and could go no more. The crowd gave him an appreciative cheer. He trudged off the mound, the soft ground giving way to heavy footsteps. Lefty Rogelio Moret came in to get the next three batters. But by then, the outlines from Tiant's steps had vanished...as had any realistic hopes for a Boston win.

Actually, the seemingly insurmountable 6–3 lead was just the backdrop for a bigger drama, which finally began to reveal itself, a ribbon at a time.

Lynn started the Boston eighth with a single off of Pedro Borbon's leg. Rico Petrocelli walked. Reds manager Sparky "Captain Hook" Anderson replaced Borbon with his sixth pitcher, Rawley Eastwick. The move looked good as Eastwick got Evans on strikes and Rick Burleson on a fly to left. With Moret scheduled, Johnson went to his bench, sending up Bernie Carbo to hit. Carbo, an accomplished free-swinger (and free spirit), had already had a pinch home run in the series. But surely, it could not happen again.

Eastwick ran the count to 2-2, then came in with a pitch that should have ended the inning. It was a biting fastball that snapped in on the hands. Carbo was completely fooled. In self-defense more than anything else, he swung the bat late, just managing to tick the smallest part of the ball to stay alive. Fisk, who later said it was the sorriest swing he could ever remember, braced for the worst. The next pitch was different.

Eastwick went with the fastball again. But pitching is like real estate. The three most important things are location, location, and location. The ball was slightly up and away, but over the meat of the plate, right in Carbo's "sweet spot." Bernie jumped all over it. The ball floated into the center field seats. The game was tied, 6–6, and Fenway literally shook from the cacophonous din that rose into the night sky, heavenward. Carbo flew around the bases, clapping his hands, laughing, and cheering.

"I was just trying to get a piece of it for a single," he said, "But when I hit it, I knew it had a chance to go out."

Carbo's hit not only tied the score; it also gave him a piece of a series record, tying Chuck Essegian's two pinch home runs in the 1959 classic. It was the twelfth pinch homer in World Series history. But Boston could have cared less. Carbo was mobbed in the dugout, where spirits were soaring.

In the bottom of the ninth, the Sox were ready for the kill. Denny Doyle drew a leadoff walk, and Yaz singled him to third. With the winning run 90 feet away with no outs, Anderson went to work, putting Fisk on with an intentional pass, and bringing in both the infield and outfield. The game seemed over. "Seem" was to be quite an operative word this October night.

"I went into the dressing room when we had the bases loaded," said Bill Lee. "I thought it was all over and got ready to shower. I just got there, and the first thing I know, the game wasn't over."

What transformed the inning from sure score to deadly dud? A simple misunderstanding. Lynn lofted a soft fly to shallow left, clearly not deep enough to score Doyle. But to everyone's shock, Doyle broke desperately for the plate, where he was an easy out on Foster's egg toss home. The double play had killed the inning.

Everyone wondered why third-base coach Don Zimmer had sent Doyle on his suicide mission. He hadn't.

"I never sent Doyle home," Zimmer explained. "I told him not under any conditions [was he to tag up]. It wasn't a gamble. It was suicide. I yelled at him, 'You can't go. No! No! No!' I saw where the ball was. There were no outs, and I knew he couldn't make it...I ran back to the bag, where he could hear me, and yelled, 'You can't go. No! No! No!' But I guess he thought I said 'Go! Go! Go!' "

When Will McEnaney got Petrocelli to bounce to third, it meant extra innings. In the tenth, the Reds got Dave Concepcion to second with one out but couldn't score. When Rose came up, he said to Fisk, "This is some kind of ball game, isn't it?"

"Yeah, it sure is," Fisk replied.

In the eleventh, it looked like *they* had it won. Dick Drago hit leadoff man Rose with a pitch. Griffey then laid down a bunt in front of the plate. Fisk eschewed the certain out at first and took a major gamble. It would be all or nothing. He gunned a perfect strike to Burleson to nip the sliding Rose by an instant. The play revealed a lot about Fisk, his instincts, his competitive drive, his controlled abandon. The fans gasped when they saw him going to second, then let out a sigh of relief when the out was made. What followed would be even more breathtaking.

Joe Morgan, the little second baseman with coils in his wrists, whipped his bat into a Drago offering, driving the ball toward the right-field seats, well over Dwight Evans's head. Evans turned around, ran full speed to the short wall in right. At the last instant, totally on instinct, he flicked up his glove and speared the ball as it was heading into the seats. He banged into the three-foot-high wall, actually colliding with the fans in the front row. The fans were pretty heady about it, backing away so the off-balance Evans would have room to right himself. He wheeled a throw toward the general vicinity of first base.

Yastrzemski, who took over at first in the ninth, scooped the ball up about 15 feet into foul territory, just up the line from the bag. With Doyle out in short right for a possible relay, Burleson rushed over to first, and took Yaz's toss to double up Griffey. Evans's play stunned Griffey as much as anybody. He was near second base when Dwight made the grab, and he momentarily froze in his tracks. So the Red Sox had *their* improbable double play. Sparky Anderson called it the greatest catch he had ever seen. "We'll never see one any better," he said.

"I knew about where it was going to be," Evans explained, "so I ran to the wall and saw it. I had a good chance, knew it, and made a leap. The fans were good. They moved back a little for me, and I was able to make the catch. I looked back and saw a lot of scrambling around first. My throw was off the mark, but I guess it got to Yaz all right...I could feel (the ball) going over my shoulder when Morgan hit it. So I got going. It wasn't the best catch I've ever made, but I never made one that meant more."

Pat Darcy, the eighth Cincy pitcher, retired the Sox 1-2-3 in the bottom of the eleventh. There was a slight tremor in the top of the twelfth when the Reds put two aboard with one out. But Rick Wise got Concepcion on a fly to Evans and blew a fastball by Geronimo for a called third strike.

And in the bottom of the twelfth, Carlton Fisk dug into the box against Darcy.

Fisk took the first pitch for a ball. Darcy grooved the second pitch. Fisk took a huge cut, and made the kind of contact that's so solid you can't feel the ball meet the bat. The ball had legs, that was certain. But it was perilously close to foul territory. The high, arcing ball, illuminated by the stadium lights, gleamed virginally against the black sky. The ball was hit so high it almost looked disassociated from the events taking place on verdant Fenway below.

It's interesting how such peak moments in life often seem unreal as they are actually taking place. Such moments *feel* different. As the ball came down, everyone knew what it meant. But however much they invested it with meaning, no one could do anything but watch helplessly. They were along for the ride. Time had stopped, and the ball behaved in a totally predetermined way. Whatever the result, fair or foul, it would be the right one. There were no participants at this moment, only witnesses.

Would it be fair, or end up as a strike against Fisk? As the ball began to spin foul, Fisk halted his run from the box, stopping a few feet down the line, single file with the foul pole, 315 feet away atop the 37-foot-high Green Monster. He hopped on both feet, applied body English, and feverishly waved his arms in the direction of fair territory.

"Don't go foul! Don't go foul!" he screamed.

The ball came down, kissing the yellow neon of the foul pole. An electric kiss. A shiny, unarmored joy. A home run. Another inch to the left, and it would have been foul.

"I knew it was gonna go out," Fisk said later. "It was just a question of it being fair or foul. The wind must have carried it 15 feet toward the foul pole. I just stood there and watched. I didn't want to miss seeing it go out."

"The Rains Fall Mainly on the Game"

The rains that came between Games Five and Six of the 1975 World Series put Commissioner Bowie Kuhn on the spot. As commissioner, he had sole authority to make decisions regarding postponements and starting times. A minor feud developed between members of the press and Kuhn as a result.

On Monday, October 20, Kuhn went to Fenway to inspect the field. After walking around, consulting with the grounds crews, the umpires, the managers, and local weather reports, he decided that Fenway Park was not playable Monday night. He ruled the game would be played, weather permitting, the next day—or, rather, the next night. The confusion stemmed from this: Kuhn said that if rain was forecast for the night, they would try to squeeze the game in during the afternoon. But if clear skies were on tap, the game would be played at night.

The press wanted day games so the writers could make their newspaper deadlines. NBC-TV wanted the games played at night, when there would be a much larger viewing audience. The press viewed Kuhn's decision as a cave-in to TV, since forecasts called for a clearing trend. They cited it as proof, once and for all, that TV really called the shots. ◆

Fisk ran the bases in unrestrained delirium. First-base coach Johnny Pesky met him with open arms. Zimmer followed him to the plate, shouting his congratulations. Fans ran out onto the field. As he hopped on the plate with both feet, Burleson, Reggie Cleveland, Wise, Zimmer, and Pesky led the rest of the team in the celebratory rites. Fans were everywhere.

"This is a great crowd, and I knew they would go sky high," Fisk said. "I made sure to touch everything that was white. I didn't want to miss a base. I was going to make certain I stepped on every little white thing out there, even if I had to straight-arm or kick somebody to do it."

Organist John Kiley broke out with "Stouthearted Men." The fans remained either in their seats or on the field, cheering, kissing, hugging, crying, laughing, staring.

Meanwhile, NBC had isolated its left-field camera on Fisk, and came away with the greatest, most dramatic sports sequence ever televised. They kept replaying Fisk's home run, his waving, his dance around the bases. It was an unforgettable image that even today remains etched in the minds of millions upon millions of fans. It's now probably the single most famous, recognized baseball image.

It was well past midnight, approaching one in the morning. Writers struggled with the task of making deadlines while trying to convey the quality, the feel, of this game.

"I'm supposed to write a piece about the game's hero, and I've already crossed off nineteen heroes. Maybe they should play a tiebreaker, like tennis," wrote Bud Collins in the *Boston Globe*.

Another *Globe* writer, Ray Fitzgerald, started his piece this way: "Call it off. Call the seventh game off. Let the World Series stand this way."

All to follow would be an irrelevance.

On the Record: Bernie Carbo

This interview is taken from conversations with Carbo conducted at various times, specifically, in Boston, April 1976; in Florida, February 1986; and in Boston, May 1987 at Old-Timers' Day. Also included are some public comments Carbo made in October 1975.

Valenti: You seemed to have a lot of fun playing in Boston. How do you rate the fans and the organization?

Carbo: I think the fans in Boston are fantastic. I always said, and I still feel it to this day, that I'm a Boston Red Sox fan. I was drafted No. 1 by the Cincinnati Reds, and played throughout their minor league system. I was rookie of the year for them in 1970, [with] 21 home runs. I hit .310. But I still consider myself a Boston Red Sock. But the fans? Fantastic. When I first came here in 1974, I didn't know the fans were this way, the organization was this way. I had no idea. I had just left the Cardinal organization, which was a good organization. I went from the Reds to the Cardinals to here. And I would say if I had my choice of where I wanted to play, it would be in Boston.

Valenti: What are your feelings on your famous home run in the 1975 World Series.

Carbo: The easiest way to put it is like this: it was the worst swing in baseball followed by the best swing in baseball. The pitch before was a slider in on me. I just barely fouled it off. Then he [Eastwick] came back with a fastball. It was over the plate, outside. I was just trying to make contact. All I was trying to do was just put the ball in play someplace. Funny, when I hit the ball, my hand came off the bat. I didn't know it was gone until [center fielder Cesar] Geronimo turned his back. As soon as he turned his back, I knew the ball was in the stands. I knew I had a home run. Rounding third, I yelled to Pete Rose, "Don't you wish you were as strong as I am?" It was just in fun. He laughed.

Valenti: Let's go back to that pitch you fouled off.

Carbo: The ball was in on me. There wasn't much I could do with it, but I had to do something because it was in the strike zone. So I swung late. If it had gone fair, it wouldn't have made it to the pitcher. The ump [Satch Davidson] actually called it a strike. That's how late I swung. I learned a lot about pinch hitting from Matty Alou when I was with St. Louis. He was a great pinch hitter. He taught me to go up there swinging. You can't take too many because you need the hit. You only get that one chance at the pitcher, so you've got to make the most of it. You won't see more than one mistake.

Valenti: What were your thoughts after the home run?

Carbo: Happy. Just very happy. Almost too excited. I was terribly thrilled. I never thought of hitting a home run. All I wanted was a single. You can't ever go up there thinking you're going to hit a home run. I'll bet you Hank Aaron never thought he was going to hit any of his. But it kept rising, and I knew it had a chance. When I saw Geronimo standing there looking up, the first thing I thought of was that I had tied a record (for two pinch-hit home runs in a World Series). Then I realized I'd also tied the score. The dugout scene was unbelievable. The fans were going crazy. It's a once-in-a-lifetime feeling.... Of course, that home run wouldn't have meant much if we didn't eventually win. But Fisk took care of that, didn't he? I was just the set-up guy.

BOX SCORE: Fenway Park, 10•21•75

Attendance: 35,205
Time of Game: 4:01

CINCINNATI REDS

Name	AB	R	H	RBI
Rose, 3B	5	1	2	0
Griffey, RF	5	2	2	2
Morgan, 2B	6	1	1	0
Bench, C	6	0	1	1
Perez, 1B	6	0	2	0
Foster, LF	6	0	2	2
Concepcion, SS	6	0	1	0
Geronimo, CF	6	1	2	1
Nolan, P	0	0	0	0
Chaney, PH	1	0	0	0
Norman, P	0	0	0	0
Billingham, P	0	0	0	0
Armbrister, PH	0	1	0	0
Carroll, P	0	0	0	0
Crowley, PH	1	0	1	0
Borbon, P	1	0	0	0
Eastwick, P	0	0	0	0
McEnaney, P	0	0	0	0
Driessen, PH	1	0	0	0
Darcy, P	0	0	0	0
Totals	50	6	14	6

BOSTON RED SOX

Name	AB	R	H	RBI
Cooper, 1B	5	0	0	0
Drago, P	0	0	0	0
Miller, PH	1	0	0	0
Wise, P	0	0	0	0
Doyle, 2B	5	0	1	0
Yastrzemski, LF, 1B	6	1	3	0
Fisk, C	4	2	2	1
Lynn, CF	4	2	2	3
Petrocelli, 3B	4	1	0	0
Evans, RF	5	0	1	0
Burleson, SS	3	0	0	0
Tiant, P	2	0	0	0
Moret, P	0	0	0	0
Carbo, PH	2	1	1	3
Totals	41	7	10	7

Team	1	2	3	4	5	6	7	8	9	10	11	12	
Reds	0	0	0	0	3	0	2	1	0	0	0		6
Red Sox	3	0	0	0	0	0	0	3	0	0	0	1	7

Name	1P	H	R	ER	BB	SO
Nolan	2	3	3	3	0	2
Norman	⅔	1	0	0	2	0
Billingham	1⅓	1	0	0	1	1
Carroll	1	1	0	0	0	0
Borbon	2	1	2	2	2	1
Eastwick	1⅓	2	1	1	1	2
McEnaney	⅔	0	0	0	1	0
Darcy (L)	2	1	1	1	0	1

Name	1P	H	R	ER	BB	SO
Tiant	7	11	6	6	2	5
Moret	1	0	0	0	0	0
Drago	3	1	0	0	0	1
Wise (W)	1	2	0	0	0	1

What a nightmare this has been.

8

HENRY AARON
April 8, 1974

There was no asterisk, but there was controversy.

What could one expect? No one, it seems, could go after Babe Ruth unmolested. Ruth had been baseball's perpetual backdrop, a constant piece of scenery against the profound changes sweeping through the game in the sixties and midseventies: expansion, the 162-game schedule, a bunch of younger players who wouldn't think twice about criticizing a manager, impinging free agency. One could not challenge Ruth without consequences. Look at Roger Maris.

Yet here was Henry Aaron, poised atop Everest, one step away from shoving the Bambino himself off the hallowed summit. This black man from Mobile, Alabama, was telling it to the mountain, one flick of the wrists from home run number 715.

It had been a long climb, starting in Milwaukee in 1954. He was a skinny twenty-year-old who hit 13 home runs his first year. He couldn't even eat in many of the same hotels as his white teammates. No one could seem more ill-suited to challenge what was always considered one of baseball's most untouchable records. But even depressingly long journeys begin with a single step. So did Aaron's. He wasn't big like Ruth. He wasn't fast like Mantle. He wasn't exciting like Mays. But he had an acute sense for the game, played with extreme intelligence, and possessed strong wrists, wrists that could send baseballs jumping off a bat as if they were whipped out of a catapult.

He also had hitter's eyes. All the great hitters have them. It means something more than just good vision. It means eyes that can see angels dancing in the air, eyes that see baseballs differently from the rest of us—not as small, white, intimidating pills, but more like large, unhinged possibilities. The great hitters may not expect to hit home runs, but they do expect to hit.

On April 8, 1974, Aaron sat in the home dugout on a windy, breezy, misty night in Atlanta. His eyes focused all the way across the field, on the right-field bull pen, where Al Downing of the Dodgers warmed up resolutely. Seen at eye level from the dugout, the expanse of lawn and dirt between dugout and bull pen blazed under the brilliant lights like a mirage. Maybe it was all a dream.

Atlanta 7,

Los Angeles 4

Aaron commented on how long it had taken him to reach this point and how long the previous week had been. He was worn out, tired of carrying the weight of Ruth's legend on his shoulders, a weight that kept shifting, that kept him off balance. It had rained all day, and was easing up now. The old wives' tale seemed true: it always rains before a battle. Henry looked around the stands at the gathering crowd, and let out a long, deep sigh. "I just hope I can get this thing over with tonight."

This thing. He had spoken of his noble quest as "this thing," as if it were a curse, a spooky shadow, some hovering spirit which he had initially approached with great success, but now from which—with no success at all—he tried to take flight. Maybe these early April days, with their swift dawns, would have been more placid, or at least less draining, if Aaron had not finished the 1973 season with 713 home runs. But he had. After his last at bat in '73, he was one home run short of Ruth's 714. So he lived with it the entire off-season, all the spring training, and now in the beginning of the new year. It was the old Maris Treatment, the relentless hounding by the press, the what-did-he-have-for-breakfast obsession with minutiae.

In 1974 spring training, the media and fans paid almost no attention to the Braves ballclub, only to Aaron. All talk centered on the Braves' opening series in Cincinnati on April 4, 6, 7. With Hank's ability to hit in the clutch, and with his intense desire to end this madness as soon as possible, Braves fans openly worried that they might miss out on history, that Hank would tie or even break the Babe's record on the road. Braves owner Bill Bartholomay, sensitive to this, declared that Aaron would not play in those first three games in Cincinnati.

When Commissioner Bowie Kuhn heard this, he stated the Braves had an obligation to field their best lineup possible, and that included Aaron. For the integrity of the game, he ordered the Braves to play Aaron in no less than two of the three contests (about the same frequency that the Braves employed Aaron in 1973). The decision angered Bartholomay, enraged manager Eddie Mathews, and infuriated Braves fans. At first, the club threatened to ignore the order. But when Mathews made out his lineup card on opening day, he had Aaron in left field, batting cleanup.

After making the concession, Mathews and the Braves tried to arrange a meeting with Kuhn to discuss the matter. Kuhn refused, further aggravating the situation. For his part, Aaron avoided comment, but clearly he felt like a pawn.

Mathews blasted Kuhn's ruling, saying that he was the manager, and it should be his decision on who plays and who sits. Kuhn wasn't pleased with the reaction, wanting the Braves to accede quietly, in the interest of the game. Some reporters and fans questioned whether Aaron would play well. They suspected the Braves would try to get around Kuhn by taking Aaron out of games early or convincing him to deliberately avoid making good contact, thereby not "risking" a home run. In other words, they implied that Hank might take a dive.

Such suggestions betrayed a monumental ignorance of Aaron's nature. Aaron never "went down." He never played ball without trying his hardest. So when he came up in the first inning on opening day, he did so determined to silence these rumors. Ralph Garr led off against Jack Billingham and drew a walk. Mike Lum followed with a single. Following a fly out by Darrell Evans, Aaron stepped into the box. On his first swing, No. 44 hit home run 714 on 4/4.

The 52,154 applauded respectfully (their team had just started the season getting down, 3–0). It was Hank's 96th home run against the Reds (more than he hit against any other ball club)—his 54th in Cincinnati (43 at old Crosley Field, 11 at Riverfront Stadium). NBC interrupted its soap opera "Another World" to show the replay. The U.S. Senate adopted by voice vote a resolution of congratulations introduced by Hubert H. Humphrey of Minnesota. Mrs. Babe Ruth, who thirteen years earlier publicly rooted against Maris, said she had expected it for a long time, that it came as no shock.

The game itself (the Reds would eventually win, 7–6 in eleven innings) was halted for about six minutes for a tribute to Aaron. Teammates, officials, and family members offered congratulations. On the mound, Billingham seemed bewildered ("It seemed like fifteen minutes to me. . .it made me uneasy"). Despite the glory of the moment, Aaron himself was feeling uneasy toward the Reds' management.

They had refused his request to have a moment of silence before the game in honor of Martin Luther King, Jr. who had been assassinated on that day four years earlier. The Reds gave him some story about how tight and well timed the pregame ceremonies were, and how they couldn't be interrupted. It sounded like a convenient excuse. To his credit, Hank didn't make an issue of it. After the game, he would only talk about the home run, which, interestingly enough, he played down somewhat. He said he had only tied the record. The next one would be the big one. For that, he joked, he might run the bases backward.

The next day was an off day spent in the relative quiet of his hotel room. But on Saturday, April 6, the controversy flared up again. Mathews kept Aaron on the bench. The Reds won, 7–5. Mathews went to his bench four times for pinch hitters, each time bypassing Aaron. After the game, Mathews openly admitted that he didn't play Hank because he wanted him to get number 715 at home. When Kuhn heard this, he hit the roof.

Kuhn immediately dispatched his aide John Johnson to Cincinnati. In a hastily arranged meeting with Mathews, Bartholomay, general manager Eddie Robinson, and Aaron, Johnson repeated Kuhn's order: play Aaron Sunday or face "serious penalties." Mathews got Kuhn on the phone to protest, but Kuhn directly ordered him to play Aaron Sunday. Kuhn reminded Mathews that the commissioner had "unlimited power" that could be used not only against individuals, but also against the franchise itself. In other words, "My way, or the highway."

The Braves found religion and played Aaron on Sunday. It was an uneventful appearance. In six and a half innings, Aaron struck out twice and bounced to third. Some Cincinnati fans booed, saying Aaron wasn't trying. But in Atlanta, they felt on the verge of the biggest happening since the premiere of *Gone with the Wind*.

The Braves came home. On Monday, Aaron spent the day in his southeast Atlanta home, watching soap operas. He then took a two-hour nap from 1–3 P.M., as was his habit for night games. Outside, it rained, heavily at times. He made the drive to Atlanta County Stadium, arriving at 4 P.M. The rain eased up, and the crowd started to pour in. Nearly 54,000 would be on hand. Millions more would be watching on ABC's "Monday Night Baseball."

The home crowd was different for this game. Atlanta is a football town; its baseball fans are laid back at best, indifferent at worst. But these fans were on edge. They were excited, like row after row of unsupervised kids at a Saturday matinee. Hundreds of media members were on hand from across the world. Aaron ducked into the trainer's room for some privacy, then showed up for his daily pregame press conference, to answer more of the same questions.

Then there were the balls. Clubhouse manager Bill Acree helped the umps load up with specially numbered "Aaron balls." Since he had hit number 710, a special set of baseballs was used each time Aaron came to the plate. Each of these balls was marked with a series of numbers; the ink could only be seen under ultraviolet light. Each time Aaron fouled a ball off, or one had to be tossed from the game, another special ball would be given to the pitcher by the umpire closest to the Braves dugout. The numbering system would insure the authenticity of the record-setting ball; Sammy Davis, Jr., had made a standing offer of $25,000 for the ball that Hank would hit for his 715th.

The pregame atmosphere was a combination carnival, Super Bowl, "Monty Python's Flying Circus" TV episode, and used-car commercial. There were 5000 balloons, fireworks, a choir, a 140-foot by 84-foot map of the United States painted on the outfield grass, dancing girls, speeches, birds let aloft, marching bands; sixty-three security guards instead of the usual seventeen. In other words, the atmosphere was exactly the antithesis of the quiet, gentlemanly, reflective Hank Aaron.

Aaron's parents and family members sat in the lower field boxes. His father told a story of seeing Babe Ruth play in an exhibition game in Mobile. He said Ruth hit a long home run into an open boxcar and that the ball ended up in New Orleans. Pearl Bailey was there to sing the national anthem. Governor Jimmy Carter was there. Sammy Davis, Jr., was there. Atlanta mayor Maynard Jackson was there. National League President Chub Feeney was there. John Mullen, the man who signed Aaron, was there. Charlie Grimm, his manager during his rookie year, was there. Bowie Kuhn, commissioner of baseball, was not there.

Kuhn cited a "previous commitment" that required him to be in Cleveland. Kuhn had dispatched his assistant Monte Irvin to attend the game. The Listerine and Lavoris people combined could not make enough mouthwash to get the sour taste out of the mouths of Braves officials, players, and fans.

Finally, the game began. After a 1–2–3 first, Aaron came up for the first time, leading off in the bottom of the second. Downing fed Aaron mostly curves. Aaron took five pitches, four of which were balls. He trotted down to first as the crowd booed Downing. He later scored on a Dodger error and a double by Dusty Baker. As a footnote to history, it was the 2063rd run of his career, breaking Willie Mays's National League record.

Aaron got his second chance in the fourth. Darrell Evans led off by reaching on shortstop Bill Russell's error. A fine, almost invisible, misty rain floated down from the sky. Aaron walked to the batter's box as he usually did, carrying his helmet in his hand. He placed it on his head, then stepped into the box softly. He always entered the box gingerly, like a man stepping on the surface of an ice-covered lake, careful of thin spots, or maybe like an infantryman wary of mines. Brightly colored umbrellas sprinkled the stands like confetti candy on an angel food cake. The crowd was mostly quiet and tense. Downing stared in.

His first pitch was in the dirt for a ball. That ball was tossed from the game, a new one entered, one with the secret markings of two 12s and two 2s. The crowd booed. Downing rubbed up the new ball on the mound. He peered at the white surface. Faint letters like ghost writing could be seen, as if at a distance: "Drink it as the fates ordain it." Well, not really. But he was out there, wondering if he felt particularly lucky.

Ruth and Aaron: Milestone Home Runs

The following shows the timetable of milestone home runs in the careers of Henry Aaron and Babe Ruth.

	Ruth			Aaron	
No.	Date	Versus	No.	Date	Versus
1	5-6-15	Yankees*	1	4-23-54	Cardinals
50	5-1-20	Red Sox	50	7-6-56	Cubs
100	9-24-20	Senators	100	8-15-57	Reds
200	5-12-23	Tigers	200	7-3-60	Cardinals
300	9-8-25	Red Sox	300	4-19-63	Mets
400	9-2-27	Athletics	400	4-20-66	Phillies
500	8-11-29	Indians	500	7-26-68	Giants
600	8-21-31	Browns	600	4-27-71	Giants
700	7-13-34	Tigers	700	7-21-73	Phillies
714	5-25-35	Pirates**	714	4-4-74	Reds
			715	4-8-74	Dodgers

*Hit as a member of the Boston Red Sox.
**Hit as a member of the Boston Braves.

On the 1-0 count, he came in with a fastball. It got up in the strike zone, in Aaron's wheelhouse, right down the middle. Downing knew immediately the pitch was a mistake. At 9:07 P.M., Aaron swung a bat for the first time all night.

The ball rose high in the air after contact. Left fielder Jim Wynn and center fielder Bill Buckner raced to the fence in left center. Buckner was closer. Just to the right of the 385-foot sign, Buckner started a frantic climb up the six-foot wire-mesh fence. Before the game, Buckner had practiced going up the fence. He got to the top, reached out with the glove, but the ball traveled too far. It came down just over the fence in the Braves bull pen, with Buckner straddling the fence top.

The bull-pen members had been lined up in the pen from left to right, according to seniority. More senior members got what was thought to be the choicest locations, more toward left field. Tom House got the low man's position next to Buzz Capra, at the end of the line toward center field. As the ball came down, two things happened that proved fortuitous for House: a kid with a butterfly net took a swipe at the ball from the stands, missing, and Capra pushed House while trying to get into position. Capra pushed him right under the ball. House stuck up the glove, and made a nice one-hand catch in front of a sign advertising a bank credit card with the appropriate headline: "Think of It as Money." House held the ball aloft, then started for the infield.

Aaron jogged slowly down the first-base line, looking at the bag. He didn't see the ball go out, but the reaction of the coaches and the crowd told him it had. First baseman Steve Garvey and second baseman Dave Lopes shook his hand as he ran by. Between second and third, Hank was startled by two Georgia Tech students, Britt Gaston and Cliff Courtney. They had run onto the field and were now completing the trot with the new home run king. As Aaron, Gaston, and Courtney reached third, there was another strange sight, this one in the outfield. Wynn and Buckner—the opposition—were applauding. Aaron got third-base coach Jim Busby's hand, then headed the remaining 90 feet for home with a broad smile on his face.

At the plate, catcher Joe Ferguson shook his hand, his teammates were all congratulating him, and the cops were waiting for Gaston and Courtney. House rushed into the pack with the ball and gave it to Hank. A tearful Aaron embraced his parents. The game was halted for eleven minutes for ceremonies. Monte Irvin, representing Kuhn, was booed. The crowd let loose an even louder expression of derision at the mention of Kuhn's name. But the jeering became cheering as Irvin introduced Aaron as "the greatest ballplayer, the finest gentleman."

Aaron stood before the microphone and said, "I would like to say to all the fans here this evening that I just thank God it's all over with."

When the game resumed, Downing got wild and was taken out. He left the stadium while the game was in progress. He ducked out of the park and stood in a runway waiting for a cab. A photographer spotted him and came over. He asked Downing to pose with a souvenir card commemorating number 715. The annoyed Downing refused. Also during the game, President Richard Nixon called the Braves clubhouse to speak to Aaron, but an attendant, thinking it was a joke, hung up on him (Nixon later got through).

After the Braves had come off the field with a 7–4 victory, Mathews closed the clubhouse so the team could have a private celebration. Mathews toasted Aaron with champagne, calling him the best player of all time. The clubhouse was opened up. At his press conference, Aaron repeated his relief that the ordeal was over.

"I have never gone out on a ball field and given it less than my level best," he said. He went on to say that the only thing on his mind was to touch all the bases. He said the home run felt like any other home run, but that in time the impact would hit him. And he offered this assessment: "Now I can consider myself one of the best. Maybe not the best, because a lot of great ones have played this game—DiMaggio, Mays, Jackie Robinson. But I can fit in there somewhere."

The ball and the bat (34 ounces, 34½-inch Louisville Slugger) were given to Magnavox as part of a deal Aaron had signed with them in 1973. At home that night, Aaron got almost no sleep. The phone didn't stop ringing, and family and friends came by at about 2 A.M. and stayed until dawn. When the exhausted Aaron arrived at the park that afternoon, some 700 telegrams (the total would reach 2000) waited for him. They included wires from Joe Louis, Bill Cosby, Ted Williams, Roy Campanella . . .and Bowie Kuhn.

"The average person can't realize what a nightmare this has been . . . I'm just tired. Not let down—tired," Hank said.

On the Record: Walt Hriniak

Walt Hriniak was signed by the Milwaukee Braves in 1961. He played in the Braves system and was a teammate of Hank Aaron in Atlanta, where he was an astute observer of Aaron's hitting style. Hriniak went on to become one of the most influential batting coaches in baseball with the Boston Red Sox.

Valenti: What's the most important factor in generating power, in hitting home runs?

Hriniak: That depends on the hitter. Even among power hitters, there are differences. There are guys who hit home runs mainly on strength, where they muscle the ball out of the ballpark. And there are guys who hit the ball out of the ballpark with a little more technique, a little more weight shift. They don't rely upon their strength, because they are not as strong as, say, a Reggie Jackson, who had tremendous upper-body strength. Harmon Killebrew was the same way. People like Henry Aaron and Stan Musial used more of a technique and a weight shift.

Valenti: Should home run hitters be coached any differently as far as hitting goes?

Hriniak: I don't believe so. No. I think if a guy has the capabilities to hit home runs, he's going to hit them. I don't think you should try to teach someone to try to specifically hit home runs. As a coach, you look at a guy and learn what he can and can't do. Then you try to perfect the things he's capable of doing and maybe improve him on the things he can't do quite as well.

Valenti: How important are the hips in the swing?

Hriniak: They're very important. By emphasizing the hips, however, hitters have a tendency to come off the ball. So I get at it another way, by emphasizing a high finish in the swing. With a high finish, the hips work at the right time. They don't work too soon. If the hips open too soon, you get hitters coming off the ball. And I know you can't hit the baseball by coming off it. Aaron never came off it. But if we make hitters finish their swings high, or swing through the ball—whatever you want to call it—the hips seem to work at precisely the right time.

Valenti: Let's talk about the swing. What do you teach?

Hriniak: I teach hitters to start the bat down. By doing that, you're able to get the bat out in front a lot quicker, instead of starting up and getting too much of an upswing. If you start your swing with your hands down and hit the ball out in front, by the time you hit the ball, your bat is going to be level, or maybe slightly up, and you're going to be able to get the head of the bat out in front. If you start up too quick [and uppercut], the bat has a longer arc to travel...and it's harder to get the head of the bat out in front.

Valenti: So that's a function of bat speed.

Hriniak: Absolutely. You're shortening the swing. They say you can't teach bat speed. I believe that you can. A shorter swing is a faster swing. A longer swing is a slower swing. You can teach bat speed by shortening the length of the stroke. Again, Aaron had that short, quick swing and a very quick bat.

Valenti: And does quicker bat speed translate into greater distance, and in fact, more home runs?

Hriniak: Yes. If you can't get the bat out in front, you're not going to hit. That's the first thing you have to be able to do: be able to get the barrel of the bat out in front, so you can extend your arms, and so you can get the maximum weight shift and hit the ball out of the park. If you're constantly late, you'll never get the bat out in front to pull the ball and hit a home run.

Valenti: Are home-run hitters harder to coach?

Hriniak: Some of them are. The only guy in the last forty years that was able to hit home runs and still maintain a high batting average was Ted Williams. He did it by pulling everything. All the rest of the great home run hitters that maintained a high average, such as Hank Aaron and Jim Rice, utilized the whole field. The

Attendance: 53,775
Time of Game: 2:27

LOS ANGELES DODGERS

Name	AB	R	H	RBI
Lopes, 2B	2	1	0	0
Lacy, PH, 2B	1	0	0	0
Buckner, LF	3	0	1	0
Wynn, CF	4	0	1	2
Ferguson, C	4	0	0	0
Crawford, RF	4	1	1	0
Cey, 3B	4	0	1	1
Garvey, 1B	4	1	1	0
Russell, SS	4	0	1	0
Downing, P	1	1	1	1
Marshall, P	1	0	0	0
Josua, PH	1	0	0	0
Hough, P	0	0	0	0
Mota, PH	1	0	0	0
Totals	34	4	7	4

ATLANTA BRAVES

Name	AB	R	H	RBI
Garr, RF, LF	3	0	0	1
Lum, 1B	5	0	0	1
Evans, 3B	4	1	0	0
Aaron, LF	3	2	1	2
Office, CF	0	0	0	0
Baker, CF, RF	2	1	1	0
Johnson, 2B	3	1	1	0
Foster, 2B	0	0	0	0
Correll, C	4	1	0	0
Robinson, SS	0	0	0	0
Tepedino, PH	0	0	0	1
Perez, SS	2	1	1	0
Reed, PH	2	0	0	0
Oates, PH	1	0	0	1
Capra, P	0	0	0	0
Totals	29	7	4	6

Team	1	2	3	4	5	6	7	8	9		
Dodgers	0	0	3	0	0	1	0	0	0		4
Braves	0	1	0	4	0	2	0	0	X		7

Name	1P	H	R	ER	BB	SO
Downing (L)	3	2	5	2	4	2
Marshall	3	2	2	1	1	1
Hough	2	0	0	0	2	1

Name	1P	H	R	ER	BB	SO
Reed (W)	6	7	4	4	1	4
Capra (S)	3	0	0	0	1	6

trouble you can get into by trying to hit home runs is that the hitters will commit themselves a lot sooner, try to pull the ball too much. And to do that, you have to hit the ball further out in front and commit much sooner. So you're wide open for mistakes. But if you can make sure that a guy who has the capabilities of hitting home runs will use the whole field—hit the ball to left center as well as right center—now you have an all-purpose hitter, not just a guy who can go over the fence 35 times a year and hit .240.

Valenti: What's your theory on footwork?

Hriniak: Hitting starts in the feet. You have to have a certain amount of balance. And balance starts in the feet. You have to have the weight on the balls of your feet in your stance to maintain your balance as you swing. The other thing I feel that all good hitters do in their feet or in their bodies is that they start to go back before they go forward. There has to be a weight shift, a cocking action. Some hitters do it by sitting on the back foot. Dwight Evans sits on his back foot. George Brett does. Rod Carew did. That was their way of getting back. Other hitters such as Wade Boggs and Ted Williams, they did it with an inward rotation of the hips, or a front leg cock. And their weight also came back before it went forward. It's the same principle as anything else in sports, where you project an object forward: you have to go back first for maximum power. Throwing a baseball, swinging a golf club: you go to your back side and then transfer your weight to the front side.

Valenti: What don't you like to mess with in a hitter, especially in the matter of style?

Hriniak: That's a thing that takes time. You want to take each hitter as an individual and find out what he can and can't do, and what he feels comfortable with. So it's a learning process for the coach. He has to get to know the hitter. You don't want to take anything away from a hitter that he has a positive feeling about, that he really believes in. But at the same time, you want to lead him maybe in a slightly different avenue so he can get even better. . .The one thing I try and teach all my hitters is keep the head down on the ball, or lower the head, or keep the head in place, whatever you want to call it. After that, I teach a high finish. They can fill in the rest of it as they go along.

Valenti: Why is it so important to keep the head down?

Hriniak: It gives you a longer look at the ball. Most hitters will realize it's important to be able to see the ball as long as they can. If you pick your head up a little bit too soon, you lose the ball over the last two or three feet. Aaron, all the great hitters, they kept their heads down. The best guy to watch to try and explain this, or to try to visualize it for yourself, is Wade Boggs. Wade's head will stay down and over the baseball. Even after contact. This is the reason why I feel he's the greatest hitter I've ever seen.

It's a dream. That's what it is. A dream.

9

DICK SISLER
October 1, 1950

Pascal said it, or something like it. In life, it's best to measure a person's virtue not by his extraordinary achievements, but by the quality of his everyday life. It usually happens this way in baseball. A .235 lifetime hitter may spend enough nondescript years in the majors to earn a pension, but he'll be remembered—if at all—for his dependable mediocrity. On the other hand, we can measure a great hitter like Ted Williams and find him exceptional because he "ordinarily" hit so well.

But every so often, again like life, a player will do something so unusual that it alone becomes his measure; he is associated not with his career, but with that one specific moment. The normal yardstick is thrown out. Such a player doesn't have a career; he has an instant. The question of his worth thus becomes much more philosophical: is one crucial hit more valuable than 2000 hits that never mean, say, a pennant? All of which leads us to Dick Sisler and the 1950 Philadelphia Phillies.

The Phillies Phold. Ask any Phils fan about it, and you'll hear about 1964, when Philadelphia and Gene Mauch blew a six-game lead with ten to play. Mention 1950, and they'll give you that snappy nickname that always seems forever young, a name that conjures up visions of streaking jet exhaust, of energetic movement: the Whiz Kids. They won't think of a collapse. But for Sisler, they might have.

The 1950 Phillies were a talented ball club, moving into first place by sweeping a doubleheader at home on July 25th against the Cubs on twin shutouts by Bubba Church and Robin Roberts. The regular lineup provided a nice balance of hitting, pitching, and defense that seemingly made the club immune to any lengthy slump. Eddie Waitkus, recovered from gunshot wounds inflicted by an obsessed female fan, played first. Mike Goliat and Granny Hamner formed the keystone combination, with Willie "Puddin' Head" Jones at third. The outfield from left to right included Sisler, Richie Ashburn, and Del Ennis. Andy Seminick was behind the plate, with Roberts and MVP Jim Konstanty anchoring the pitching staff.

As late as September 19, the Phillies led the Brooklyn Dodgers by nine games. They were cruising to their first pennant since 1915. But then things began to unravel. They lost talented lefty Curt Simmons, and his 17 wins, to the Army on September 10.

Philadelphia 4,

Brooklyn 1

Pitchers Bob Miller and Church went down with injuries, Miller with arm problems and Church when he was struck in the face by a line drive on September 15. Sisler badly sprained his right wrist sliding into third, missing three weeks. With five days left in the season, Seminick sprained an ankle in a collision with Monte Irvin of the Giants. To top it all, the team went into a batting slump.

The losses mounted, their deflating impact felt like a darkening of the heart, like a lengthening shadow creeping over self-confidence. Necks weren't getting bigger. Collars were tightening. Going into the last game, the Phillies dropped 12 of 15, including 5 straight losses in the previous three days. The Dodgers, meanwhile, never gave up, winning 13 of their last 16, and whittling a 7-game deficit down to one game in just nine days.

That's where it stood as the two teams squared off at Ebbets Field in the season's last regular game. A Dodger win would force a three-game playoff for the pennant. With the momentum and an intact pitching staff, Brooklyn would be favored in any playoff. Brooklyn forced the one-game, regular-season showdown by winning the day before, 7–3, behind Erv Palica's complete game and home runs by Roy Campanella and Duke Snider.

For the finale, Philadelphia manager Eddie Sawyer penciled in Roberts, his ace. Bert Shotton countered with his big gun, Don Newcombe. For added drama, both pitchers would be after their 20th win, with Roberts at 19–12, and Newcombe at 19–11. Roberts would be looking to become the Phils first 20-game winner since Grover Cleveland Alexander did it on his way to 30 wins in 1917. Some questioned Sawyer's choice. Roberts would be making his third start in five days, working on two days rest. He had been stuck on 19 wins since September 12. Actually, Sawyer had no choice, with his staff decimated by Uncle Sam, injury, and a rash of doubleheaders. When Sawyer gave him the ball on October 1, Roberts said he was ready. Adrenaline alone would be enough to get him through.

Two hours and thirty-five minutes after Newcombe threw the opening pitch to Waitkus, Roberts had delivered an amazing demonstration of raw courage, willpower, and stamina—one of the great clutch-pitching performances of all time. It was also after these 155 minutes that Sisler found himself a hero, and Dodger fans had a galling plate of second-guessing to swallow during the long off-season. It would be an icy off-season indeed, a psychic ground zero of devastation and shattered hope.

Through the first five innings, the last game lived up to its billing, as Newcombe and Roberts threw shutout ball. But in the sixth, the Phillies got on the board on singles by Sisler, Ennis, and Jones. Brooklyn got it right back in their half of the inning on a fluke home run by Pee Wee Reese. Reese hit a drive that landed—wedged, really—between the screen behind the scoreboard and the top of the right-field fence.

Newcombe and Roberts matched each other like two heavyweights even on points. Through eight, the score was still 1–1. Newcombe got the Phils in the top of the ninth, then watched in disbelief as its team ran itself out of a win in its half of the frame. The inning would stay with Dodger fans for a long, long time.

Cal Abrams led with a walk. Reese moved him to second by singling on an 0-2 pitch. Roberts seemed to be tiring. Then came the key play of the entire year.

With Snider up, Sawyer came out to the mound to talk to Roberts. The infield discussed its options. Sawyer then made two decisions: he kept Roberts in the game, and he ordered the Phillies to play for the bunt. It was a gamble. Snider, the number three hitter, might bunt...but then, he might not. Nonetheless, as Roberts came in with his first pitch to Snider, Sawyer had his infield charging. Shotton guessed Sawyer would play it this way and decided to let Snider hit away. It was a fine piece of managing; in fact, it seemed brilliant when Snider, swinging away on the first pitch, lined a hard single to center. The crowd rose to its feet, cheering.

Now a combination of things happened that, when put together, turned Brooklyn elation into disgust. First, Richie Ashburn was playing shallow in center to back up any throw to second on a bunt. Second, the ball was hit sharply, getting to Ashburn in a hurry. Third, Abrams had a short lead, since the Phils were keeping him close in the event of a bunt. Fourth, Abrams, not the fastest of runners anyway, hesitated a split second to make sure the ball got through. And fifth, the ball came up nicely on a gift hop to the charging Ashburn. These five factors should have added up to Abrams's being held at third, leaving the Dodgers with the bases loaded, nobody out, and the 4-5-6 hitters due. Ideal.

But wait. There was a huge however. Its name was Milton Stock, the third-base coach. Milton inexplicably waved home Abrams, who rounded the bag doubting what he saw. But like a good foot soldier, his was not to reason why. He obediently continued home. Ashburn came up throwing and launched a perfect strike to catcher Stan Lopata (in for Seminick, whose bad ankle forced him to leave for a pinch runner in the top of the ninth).

Lopata took the ball about three feet in front of the plate directly up the third-base line. Abrams was about seven feet away—ten feet from the plate! The on-deck batter, Bruce Edwards, signaled for Abrams to slide, but he was too far away from the plate. Instead, Abrams tried desperately to veer around Lopata at the last second. Lopata easily moved with Abrams. Caught dead, Abrams slammed on the brakes and skidded to a halt right into the tag, not even close to the plate.

Later on, the reactions would be varied. Abrams said he should have been held at third, adding that "we all thought he [Ashburn] was playing too close against a long hitter [Snider], but he got away with it."

Ashburn said he was surprised when Stock sent Abrams home. "The ball was hit sharp. It came to me perfectly, and I was all set for a throw."

Sawyer said the throw was the key, pointing out that early in the year, "Ashburn's arm was weak, and runners got in the habit of running on him."

Shotton second-guessed himself. "They were playing for a bunt, holding Abrams close to second, and he couldn't get a good start. I should have bunted. If you don't believe me, look in the newspaper."

And Stock? What did Milton say of paradise lost? "I'd make the play the same way if I had to do it over again." Which, if nothing else, proves that some blunders are so outrageous that they can't be immediately faced and admitted.

When play resumed and the reeling Dodger fans came to their fragmented senses, they surveyed what was still a pretty good-looking scene. Reese was on third, Snider on second (both moved up on the throw home), with one out, and cleanup man Jackie Robinson was due. Sawyer, a former science professor at Ithaca College, ordered Robinson passed intentionally, loading the bases for Carl Furillo. The move paid off as the overanxious Furillo swung at Roberts's first pitch, fouling weakly to Waitkus at first. Dodger fans squirmed. Gil Hodges followed with a long fly to deep right center, which Ennis tracked down in front of the scoreboard. Gil's drive was one out too late. This "must" game would move into extra innings.

Brooklyn had let it slip away. The fans knew it. The players knew it. The momentum shifted. The Phillies, who early in this inning were dying soldiers lying in mud, were now happy children playing in the sand. The stranglehold of defeat now loosened, possibilities lay wide awake. They came back to the dugout light-headed, innocents ready to believe in anything.

Roberts was due to lead off the tenth, leaving Sawyer with another decision. The book said he should hit for his tiring ace; but who could he bring in in the bottom of the tenth? Bull-pen ace Jim Konstanty (with a record 74 appearances) was hit hard the day before. Fact is, Sawyer had no one better than Roberts, so he let Robin bat.

"I considered taking Roberts out for a pinch hitter...I had Dick Whitman ready to hit. I asked Robin how he felt, and he answered, 'Fine.' So I let him bat. It was the luckiest decision I made all year," Sawyer said.

Lucky is right. Roberts promptly singled to center. Waitkus followed with another single, almost to the same spot. With Ashburn up, Sawyer put on the bunt. Richie laid a nice one down the third-base line. Newcombe bounded off the mound, pounced on the ball, never hesitated, and threw a strike to Billy Cox at third. Roberts made a head-first slide, but was out on a close play. On his side, Roberts kicked up the lime of the third-base line and got it in his eyes. He practically groped back to the dugout, his eyes burning and reddening fast. That left Waitkus on second, Ashburn on first, and Sisler up. Sisler was 3–for–4 against Newcombe in the game. Shotton gave no indication of wanting to yank Newcombe. He'd stick with the big right-hander.

Sisler set himself in the left-hander's box. Newcombe came in with a called strike. He reached back for a little extra on the next pitch, and blew a high fastball by Sisler. Newc then wasted a pitch outside. Sisler fouled the 1–2 pitch back into the stands.

In the box seats behind the Brooklyn dugout, a fifty-five-year-old observer sat like a man watching his mother-in-law drive over a cliff in his new Porsche—a classic study in mixed emotions. This man was George Sisler, Dick's Hall of Fame father. George was one of Branch Rickey's top aides in Brooklyn, a man who had helped build the current Dodger team.

On the 1–2 pitch, Newcombe stayed with the fastball. Sisler was right on it, making contact in a tremendous cut. The ball went the other way, toward left. It was hit well, but sinking fast. Sisler raced to first. Abrams dashed to the left-field wall. Waitkus froze between second and third, watching to see if Abrams would have a play. Newcombe waited and watched as the line of the ball traced out an ever-accusing fate.

The ball landed in the third row of seats, 348 feet away, in between and above the "Michaels & Co." and "Griffen" billboard signs and the legend "Disoway and Fisher." Abrams stood against the wall like a man too aware of the sadness of things. Newcombe watched, and George Sisler, in the midst of the somber Brooklyn brass, took his hat and tossed it in the air.

The Philly fans at Ebbets went crazy. Dodger fans sat stunned, their hearts clammy and their hands like cold slate slabs, wondering what more could ever happen to them (they would get their answer one year and two days later, when Bobby Thomson dug in against Ralph Branca).

Sisler flew around the bases, no longer in a baseball game, but in a wedding, a carnival, a dance, a feast. His joyous teammates, led by Roberts, came rushing out to escort him back to the dugout. Just like that, it was 4–1.

"If at First..."

Though it ended in glory, the 1950 season began miserably for Dick Sisler. In the spring, Philly first baseman Eddie Waitkus was battling for a job, trying to recover from gunshot wounds inflicted by a disturbed female admirer. Manager Eddie Sawyer pronounced Sisler the first baseman. In the intrasquad games, Sisler was on a tear; Waitkus slumped. Sisler thought the job was his.

But on March 11, the lineup card taped inside the dugout wall at Clearwater read: Ashburn, cf; Hamner, ss; Waitkus, 1b. Sisler bolted to the clubhouse and angrily threw his glove into his locker. He thought about confronting Sawyer but held off until he cooled down.

The next day, Sisler went to Sawyer and asked him if he could play left. Sawyer agreed to try him there, if Sisler would work hard on his fielding. For four weeks, Sisler was the hardest worker in camp. It paid off; he went north as the Phils left fielder—and went on to become their subsequent all-time hero on October 1. ◆

In the last of the tenth, the red-eyed Robin pitched with new energy, with lightened purpose, with the power of perspective—with a 4–1 lead. Roy Campanella and Jimmy Russell went down. On an 0–1 pitch, pinch hitter Tommy Brown fouled to Waitkus. It was over. Philadelphia had its first championship in thirty-five years.

The clubhouse scene was as it should be: total chaos, a celebration without a ceiling. Sawyer led the team into the locker room, exclaiming, "Well, we didn't back in, did we?"

Players yelled. Flashbulbs and beer cans popped. Writers got their interviews. Coaches Benny Bengough and Cy Perkins cried. Sisler was mobbed by everybody.

"It's a dream. That's what it is. A dream," the hero exhaled repeatedly. He went on to reveal that he almost hadn't come to bat in the tenth. Seems he reinjured his sore right wrist while sliding into second base in the fourth inning. It stiffened, and he thought he had sprained it again. But he was able to loosen it up, and he continued in the game.

Before the game, Sisler had joked to the Brooklyn writers how close the left-field seats looked. Someone reminded him of that.

"How I love Ebbets Field," was his reply. "Have I hit many homers to left? I'd say about half of them this year." Someone asked how he liked hitting against Newcombe. Sisler was diplomatic. "I'd say I hurt him several times in the past, and he's hurt me just as many times."

Over in the Brooklyn locker room, no one would say much. The Dodgers stared at the world as if a thin layer of frost had formed on the inside of their eyes. Brooklyn club secretary Harold Parrott had a brief but fitting epitaph: "We were one fly ball short." George Sisler, asked how he felt when his son hit the home run, said, "I felt awful and terrific at the same time."

On the Record: Dick Sisler

Valenti: Take me back to Ebbets Field, and tell me your feelings when you connected.

Sisler: It's been [sic] a long time ago, but it seems like only yesterday, because there was so much commotion about it and so much publicity over the years. It is an oddity when you do something like that. I was standing in against Don Newcombe. I had already had three hits off him. So this was my fifth at bat. He was an over-powering pitcher. He had a real good fastball, but he was toying with me high and away. Why did he do that? I supposed because he wanted me to go for something bad and strike out.

Valenti: Did he work you differently in that last at bat?

Sisler: Well, I had pulled a couple of balls off him for hits. In fact, one of them (in a previous at bat) I should have hit out, but I didn't. That ball was down, and I hit a hard line drive. He may have remembered that, because in the tenth, he was trying to get me to go for a high-and-away pitch. In fact, the pitch before the home run, I almost did. But I was able to hold up in time. But then on the one that I hit out, I would say it was a high-and-away strike, and I swung just as hard as I could—well, not as hard as I could, but I had a good cut at it. And the ball was going out to left. Now, I didn't know at the time that it was going to be a home run, because it's kind of hard to know on an opposite-field drive just how far it is going to go. Actually, the ball went straight to left. And so I saw the ball go out there. I slowed up my stride a little bit and came down with a home run. But I did not know that it was a home run when I hit it.

Valenti: Running around first base, you saw Abrams running out of room in left.

Sisler: Yeah. He went back but ran out of room, and the ball landed about three rows back into the left-field seats. And of course, all kinds of bedlam tore loose then, all over, all the Philadelphia players and fans.

Valenti: What was going on right after that home run?

Sisler: Well, I think you almost have to know what had happened the last week or so of the season. Because we had a pretty good lead at one time, with just a short time to go. And we lost a lot of tough games on down the way. And it was very enlightening—I don't know if that would be the right word or not—to have us win that ball game, to have us get that lead in the tenth inning, then to win the game and to win the pennant. We had looked forward to it for quite a while, but we just couldn't win that last game, the clincher. I'll tell you, it took a lot out of all of us, losing day after day. We had good pitching, you know. We just couldn't get the big hit at the right time.

Valenti: What was the feeling going into that final ball game? Do you remember feeling nervous in the locker room or anything like that?

Sisler: No. I wasn't actually nervous. Of course, you think of all kinds of things at that time, because you know that this is it. Although we could have tied and gone into a playoff [by losing the final game], by then we had used up our pitching, and chances are we wouldn't have been able to win that playoff. I know on the way out to the ballpark, an interesting thing happened. There were about four or five of us in a cab. And we stopped alongside another car. There was a Catholic priest in the car. And I guess he recognized us. And through the window, he

BOX SCORE: Ebbets Field, 10•1•50

Attendance: 35,073
Time of Game: 2:35

PHILADELPHIA PHILLIES

Name	AB	R	H	RBI
Waitkus, 1B	5	1	1	0
Ashburn, CF	5	1	0	0
Sisler, LF	5	2	4	3
Mayo, LF	0	0	0	0
Ennis, RF	5	0	2	0
Jones, 3B	5	0	1	1
Hamner, SS	4	0	0	0
Seminick, C	3	0	1	0
Caballero, PR	0	0	0	0
Lopata, C	0	0	0	0
Goliat, 2B	4	0	1	0
Roberts, P	2	0	1	0
Totals	38	4	11	4

BROOKLYN DODGERS

Name	AB	R	H	RBI
Abrams, LF	2	0	0	0
Reese, SS	4	1	3	1
Snider, CF	4	0	1	0
Robinson, 2B	3	0	0	0
Furillo, RF	4	0	0	0
Hodges, 1B	4	0	0	0
Campanella, C	4	0	1	0
Cox, 3B	3	0	0	0
Russell, PH	1	0	0	0
Newcombe, P	3	0	0	0
Brown, PH	1	0	0	0
Totals	33	1	5	1

Team	1	2	3	4	5	6	7	8	9	10	
Philadelphia	0	0	0	0	0	1	0	0	0	3	4
Brooklyn	0	0	0	0	0	1	0	0	0	0	1

Name	IP	H	R	ER	BB	SO
Roberts (W)	10	5	1	1	3	2

Name	IP	H	R	ER	BB	SO
Newcombe (L)	10	11	4	4	2	3

handed me a rose, and he said, "Here, Dick. Good luck." And I won't ever forget that because I put it in the only pocket I had. It was in the rear pocket of my uniform, and I had that the whole game. My dad [Hall of Famer George Sisler] was with the Dodgers as the head of their farm system. And so I had been out to his house the night before. I forgot exactly where he lived, but it was over in Brooklyn somewhere. I was walking around the block. I guess I was nervous. He was with the Dodgers, and I was with the Phillies. I went on back to the hotel. We all knew what we had to do. We had to win. We had our best pitcher going for us. And they had their best pitcher going for them. It was going to be one hell of an exciting ball game. So I don't know. It's hard for me to tell you how we actually felt. Being on a such a good ball club and to lose so many darn ball games down the stretch like that, and to get all the way down to the last game, it's hard to explain exactly how we felt.

Valenti: After your home run, you still had to hold them for their last at bat.

Sisler: Well, [Eddie] Sawyer put Jack Mayo in left, in my spot. But as far as Robin Roberts goes, I don't think there was a ball player on our ball club that even *thought* that the Dodgers would come close to scoring, because that's the kind of pitcher he was. If you gave him a one-run lead in the last inning, boy, I don't know how he did it, but he could reach back and get it, and they weren't about to get any runs off him.

Valenti: Has the home run changed your life?

Sisler: It has. I get all kinds of mail, and I get all kinds of recognition in various parts of the country. And it all boils down to that home run.

Valenti: Do you still think about it?

Sisler: Well, I guess when you do something like that, it will come back to you a little bit. Before I did that, I was just another ball player, although I had a good year that year and drove in over 80 runs, and I hit about .300. But that was my best year, and if I hadn't hit that home run, I would have been just another ball player. Maybe a little better than average. But when I did that, it gave me a lot of recognition. I've gone to all kinds of banquets after that, and they always bring that home run up.

This is the greatest thrill of my life.

10

GABBY HARTNETT
September 28, 1938

Hitting a certifiably big home run is a bit like being the subject of one of those Renaissance paintings, the man who holds a mirror into a mirror, triggering an infinite reaction.

The hitter, of course, holds not a mirror, but a bat. The circumstances of the moment reflect off of the home run, like twin mirrors facing each other, producing an everlasting-corridor effect. The home run never ends, really. A day later, a month later, a year later, even fifty years later: the big home run still lives on.

So it is with the home run hit by Charles Leo "Gabby" Hartnett at Wrigley Field on September 28, 1938, the famous "Homer in the Gloaming." Gloaming. It's a Scottish word for twilight or dusk, a derivative of the word "glow." It's such a romantic-sounding word, conjuring up not so much images of baseball as of castle ruins, misty bogs, moonlight reflecting in the depthless waters of a lonely loch. No matter...it is the same *feel* with Hartnett's home run, a home run hit in the nether reaches of Wrigley's ivy darkness.

Hartnett's home run itself did not mean the actual pennant for the Cubs. They clinched over Pittsburgh three days later. But it did give them the lead and the momentum over Pittsburgh from which they never looked back. From the standpoint of the Bucs, it was a backbreaker. It came just before the game was to be called because of darkness.

Hartnett's home run capped a furious stretch drive for the Cubs, in which they won 21 of their last 25 games. The Cubbies started winning 25 of their first 40 games, good for second place behind the New York Giants. But they had made their biggest noise of the early going on April 16, three days before the season started.

That's when they rocked the baseball world by obtaining Dizzy Dean from St. Louis for $200,000 cash, and pitchers Curt Davis and Clyde Shoun. It was a gamble. Dean was still a top box-office draw, but his pitching arm was suspect. The twenty-seven-year-old won 13 games in 197 innings for the Cardinals in '37, a far cry from the 24/306 he averaged his previous five years.

Chicago 6,
Pittsburgh 5

On April 29, Dean pulled a muscle in his throwing arm and was unable to pitch for most of the summer. He tried pitching through the pain, but after his fourth start on May 3, he made only one appearance until August 20. He wouldn't start again for over a month.

Cub fans questioned the trade, especially for that kind of money (in 1938, $200,000 was a fortune). But they had other things on their minds, too. The team started going bad through June and July. At one point, between June 8 and July 12, they dropped 11 of 12 home games. The Pirates, meanwhile, won 40 out of 54 games in June and July. Sinking fast and threatening to disappear from contention, the team axed manager Charles Grimm, replacing him with catcher Hartnett.

To fully understand the hearts of Cub rooters, you must understand that the word "frustration" meant a whole different thing in 1938 than it does to the team's present-day followers. Today, of course, the suffering of Cub fans is legendary, with no pennant since 1945 and no world championship since 1908. In 1938, though, Chicago had actually run up fourteen pennants going back to their first in 1876, the National League's first year. More recent flags came in 1929, 1932 (after another mid-season managerial switch from Rogers Hornsby to Grimm), and 1935 (when they won 21 straight). In fact, since 1876, they finished in first more than in any other single position (second, ten times; third, twelve times; fourth and fifth, eight times; sixth through ninth, eight times). So a pennant was not all that unusual for the Cubs in those years.

For the '38 Cubs, frustration was less epochal and more within rational limits. They had realistic hope for results, and not without cause. The team was solid though not exceptional. They had a weak offense, no one driving in as many as 70 runs. Third baseman Stan Hack led hitters with a .320 average. But they were exceptional defensively, especially Billy Herman at second and Billy Jurges at short. Bill Lee topped pitchers with a 22-9 record; Clay Bryant added 19. After that, no one won more than 10 games. It was hoped that Dean would become dominant once again, though that was not to be.

The change of managers shook up the club. They started winning when it counted, steadily closing in on Pittsburgh. They trailed by 8½ games on September 1, but whittled that down to 1½ on September 26, when they beat the Cardinals at Wrigley Field. That set up the three-game showdown with the Bucs on the 27th, 28th, and 29th. Wrigley Field became the place to be. The papers called it the "September World Series." News of Hitler's meeting with Mussolini, Chamberlain, and Daladier in Munich became a sidebar. Put in its simplest terms, a pennant was on the line.

Hartnett surprised everyone by naming Dean to start the Series opener. It was a roll of the dice: Dean hadn't started since August 20. But sore arm and all, he held his own, throwing a tantalizing assortment of junk and slop over 8⅔ innings to spark the Cubs to a 2–1 win (Lee, normally a starter, came in to wild pitch a run home, then got Al Todd on strikes to end it). The win, before a frenzied 42,223 at Wrigley, pulled Chicago to within a half game of the lead. The next game would be for first place.

Under leaden skies, the Cubs would go on to win the most important game of the year in the most dramatic fashion.

Hartnett started Bryant, 19-11. Pirate manager Pie Traynor countered with Bob Klinger, 12-5. A couple of Pirate errors gave the Cubs a 1–0 lead in the second. But then the Pirates scored three in the sixth, highlighted by Johnny Rizzo's 21st home run of the year. The Cubs came right back in their half of the sixth.

Hartnett led with a double. Another double by Rip Collins scored Hartnett, narrowing the score to 3–2. Jurges then singled Collins to third. Collins scored when Ken O'Dea, batting for pitcher Jack Russell, bounced out. On the play, Jurges took second, but then made a baserunning error. With two outs, Herman hit a ground ball in the hole between third and short. It looked like a sure single. Assuming the ball would go through, Jurges continued on his own around third and toward home. But Pirate shortstop Arky Vaughan made a brilliant backhand stab, then threw out Jurges by plenty at the plate.

In the Pirate seventh, the Bucs went scoreless, but only after a hot dispute. With two on, Rizzo came up against Vance Page, on in relief of Russell, and bounced into an inning-ending double play. But the Pirates argued that Page balked on the pitch. While Page went into his motion, he made an extra foot movement; several Pirates jumped up off the bench in unison and yelled, "Balk!" But the Cubs got away with one. The umps let the play stand. Traynor argued vehemently, to no avail. The fans hooted Traynor as he walked back into the dugout.

In the top of the eighth, the Pirates dampened the mood at Wrigley with two runs. Yet once more, the Cubs came back.

Collins led off the eighth with a single to center. Traynor had seen enough of Klinger, who had gone a respectable seven innings plus. The manager motioned for Bill Swift. The righty worked carefully to the pesky Jurges, who weasled a walk on the 3-2 pitch. With pitcher Lee due up, Hartnett went to the bench once more, coming up with a shadow from the past, Tony Lazzeri.

Lazzeri, of course, was a star second baseman more than a decade earlier for the Yankees. On the fabled '27 team, he hit .309, with 18 homers and 108 RBIs. But time and injury had taken some skill from Tony, who was now a utility infielder with only an occasional pop in his bat. Fortunately for the Cubs, this was one of those occasions.

Hartnett, pushing all the right buttons, put on the bunt. Lazzeri fouled off Swift's first pitch. He bunted and missed the second. The ball got away just enough from catcher Todd for Collins to move to third. Jurges held at first. With two strikes, Lazzeri was on his own. Swift tried to live up to his name by blowing a fastball by the once and past star, but Tony called on some old instincts. He went nicely with the ball, lining a double down the right-field line, Collins scoring, Jurges pulling into third.

Hartnett sent Joe Marty in to run for Lazzeri, who trotted off to a wild hand. Now it was Traynor's turn to manipulate. He ordered an intentional walk to the menacing Hack. This loaded the bases with a 5–4 Pirate lead. But Herman foiled the strategy by singling to right. Jurges scored the tying run easily from third. Marty also tried to score, but right fielder Paul Waner charged the ball like an infielder and pegged Marty out at the plate. This left Hack on second, Herman on first. Traynor went to his pen once more, bringing in relief ace Mace Brown in place of Swift. Brown did his job, getting left fielder Frank Demaree to hit into a 4-3 double play, Tommy Thevenow unassisted to Gus Suhr.

Cub fans felt good about the tie score, but still, the two runners thrown out at the plate in the sixth and the eighth started to gnaw at them. A tie would do them no good, and a tie was a distinct possibility. The skies were darkening rapidly by

"Seems Like Only Yesterday"

In the spring of 1981, while on assignment in Florida, I found myself in Winter Haven, the training camp of the Boston Red Sox. The major league Sox had just finished their morning workout, so I ambled down to the minor league playing fields.

There, on one of the diamonds, stood an old man surrounded by about ten young pitchers. He coached them, talking to them softly and with care, as a grandfather would. Though Mace Brown couldn't throw a competitive curve ball any longer himself, he could tell others how to snap one off the edge of a table.

I watched Brown for about an hour, then talked to him after the coaching clinic was over. We talked about all manner of baseball topics: the Red Sox farm system, the differences between baseball in the 1980s and the 1930s, Jackie Robinson. Finally, the topic of Gabby Hartnett's "Homer in the Gloaming" came up. Almost 43 years later, the home run could still get him fired up.

"They said I threw him fastballs, but it was curves. I threw him three darn nasty curveballs. Only the third one hung a little. But I tell you, it was too dark. He should have swung and missed."

— Dan Valenti ◆

the top of the ninth, and players could not be seen from the press box. There were few grains of sand left in the hourglass, indeed. The umpires conferred, but—for the moment—made no decision.

In the ninth, Charlie Root became the sixth pitcher for the Cubs, following Bryant, Russell, Vance Page, Larry French, and Lee. Lloyd Waner led with a fly to Phil Cavarretta in right. Cavarretta danced alarmingly under the ball, looking for it, then finding it at the last second to make the putout. Brother Paul Waner followed with a single to left. Rizzo, who earlier had the home run, hit Root's first pitch up in the air, behind home plate. Hartnett threw off the mask, wheeled, and made the catch out of the slate-gray sky. This got rid of the dangerous Rizzo and kept Waner out of scoring position.

With the cleanup batter Vaughan up, Waner tried to get to second on his own, breaking to steal as Root came in with his pitch. Hartnett fired a strike to Jurges, who slapped the tag on Waner for the inning-ending out. Hartnett seemed to be setting himself up for his subsequent heroics. He would later say that he had a funny feeling in that ninth, describing it as the way you feel when you're scared, or when something portentous is about to happen.

The skies were darkening by the minute. While the Pirates ran out onto the field, the umpires conferred and made their decision: the game would end after the bottom of the ninth. If the game was still tied, it would be replayed as part of a doubleheader the following day. Both teams knew this was it. The Bucs would settle for a tie and take their chances the next day. The Cubs, with a depleted pitching staff, wanted it to end. Dean couldn't go the following day. Lee was slated for one game, but then who? Five other pitchers had already been used in this game.

Cavarretta led off the bottom of the ninth against Brown and skied a deep drive to center, which Lloyd Waner somehow tracked down in the dark. Carl Reynolds bounced to Thevenow; as he returned to the dugout, Reynolds complained to the bench that he couldn't see the ball as it came in. He saw Brown's motion, and guessed when to swing. That brought Hartnett to the plate as the Cubs' last hope. Gabby was having a good day, with 1-for-3 at the plate, a run scored, and some excellent defensive work.

Brown's first two pitches are disputed. Both were strikes, but frequent reports had Hartnett taking two fastballs. Cavarretta, recalling the at bat almost forty-six years later, insisted that Brown came in with two fastballs, and that Gabby never took the bat off his shoulder. Jurges said Brown told him he threw only curves. Brown himself insists that he threw nothing but curves. He says Hartnett took the first one but fouled off the second pitch.

In any case, Hartnett was in an 0-2 hole. Brown, maybe feeling a bit overconfident, didn't waste a pitch, the common practice with the count 0-2. Instead, he hung a curve in the strike zone (again, Brown denies reports that it was a fastball, up). Hartnett swung and drove the ball deep to left field, where it carried well into the bleachers. Many in Wrigley—fans, players, press—couldn't see the ball. Hartnett said he knew from the contact that it would go out. In any case, the third-base umpire did see it and signaled a home run, giving the Cubs a 6–5 win and putting them in first place by a half game.

When the ump gave his signal, the stands erupted. Hartnett ran down to first as a trickle of fans and teammates came out. The trickle was followed by a stream, then a torrent, then a deluge. By the time he got to second base, Hartnett could not be seen for all the people there.

Between second and third, the crowd lifted him up and started to carry him. Hartnett fought to touch third. The swarm tried to pick him up again. Hartnett fought once more. Home-plate ump George Barr stood sternly, making sure Hartnett touched the base. Screaming for the fans to let him down, Hartnett wrestled his way clear, tagged the plate, and then disappeared into the swallowing mob.

All of a sudden, it dawned on the ushers as well as the cops who were on the field that Hartnett might be in trouble. The ushers and cops rushed to his aid "to save his life," as the *Chicago Tribune* put it.

People were jostling him, patting him on the head, pummeling him on the back. Some tried stripping him of his uniform. The cops started pushing people away. When that wasn't effective, they started throwing punches. Hartnett's teammates rushed over to help out. Finally, utility outfielder Jim Asbell and pitcher French managed to reach Hartnett, and along with several cops and ushers, got him into the tunnel which led from the dugout to the locker room. In the catwalk, there were more fans, but they posed no problem to the heavily chaperoned Hartnett. At long last, he got behind the closed clubhouse doors, out of breath, speechless, disheveled, trying to collect his thoughts.

"This is the greatest thrill of my life," he exclaimed in the jubilant clubhouse.

"When Gabby hit that thing, he was using the Collins stance at the plate," joked Rip Collins.

Attendance: 34,465
Time of Game: N/A

PITTSBURGH PIRATES

Name	AB	R	H	RBI
L. Waner, CF	4	0	2	0
P. Waner, RF	5	0	2	0
Rizzo, LF	4	1	1	1
Vaughan, SS	2	2	1	0
Suhr, 1B	3	2	1	0
Young, 2B	2	0	0	0
Manush, PH	1	0	1	1
Thevenow, 2B	0	0	0	0
Handley, 3B	4	0	2	3
Todd, C	4	0	0	0
Klinger, P	4	0	0	0
Swift, P	0	0	0	0
Brown, P	0	0	0	0
Totals	33	5	10	5

CHICAGO CUBS

Name	AB	R	H	RBI
Hack, 3B	3	0	0	1
Herman, 2B	5	0	3	1
Demaree, LF	5	0	0	0
Cavarretta, RF	5	0	0	0
Reynolds, CF	5	0	1	0
Hartnett, C	4	2	2	1
Collins, 1B	4	3	3	1
Jurges, SS	3	1	1	0
Bryant, P	2	0	1	0
Russell, P	0	0	0	0
O'Dea, PH	1	0	0	0
Page, P	0	0	0	0
French, P	0	0	0	0
Lee, P	0	0	0	0
Lazzeri, PH	1	0	1	1
Marty, PR	0	0	0	0
Root, P	0	0	0	0
Totals	38	6	12	5

Team	1	2	3	4	5	6	7	8	9		
Pirates	0	0	0	0	0	3	0	2	0		5
Cubs	0	1	0	0	0	2	0	2	1		6

Name	1P	H	R	ER	BB	SO
Klinger	7	8	3	2	2	6
Swift	⅓	3	2	2	2	0
Brown (L)	1⅓	1	1	1	0	0

Name	1P	H	R	ER	BB	SO
Bryant	5⅔	4	3	3	5	1
Russell	⅓	0	0	0	0	0
Page	1	1	0	0	1	1
French	—	3	2	2	0	0
Lee	1	1	0	0	0	0
Root (W)	1	1	0	0	0	0

Later, a letter carrier came to the clubhouse door, not to deliver mail, but to deliver the home run ball to Gabby. Hartnett gladly accepted, offering his benefactor an autographed baseball in return.

The gloaming had now turned to black, the homer was on the lips of all of Chicago, and the Cubs were now in first for the first time since June 8. Moreover, it gave them the edge on the demoralized Pirates. The following day, Chicago battered them, 10-1 behind Lee's pitching. It was their tenth straight win and gave them a 1½-game lead. The next day, the Cubs were ironically involved in a tie, their game in St. Louis called after nine because of darkness. The Bucs split two in Cincinnati. The clincher came on October 1 as the Cubs split a pair against the Cardinals, and Pittsburgh lost to Cincinnati. In their amazing finish, Chicago had gone 21-4.

On the Record: Eddie Gold

Eddie Gold is a long-time sportswriter for the Chicago Sun Times. *He grew up an avid fan of the Cubs.*

Valenti: You were only a boy at the time, but do you actually remember hearing the broadcast of Hartnett's famous home run?

Gold: Oh, yeah. I was living in Chicago at the time, and I was six years old. Every day, I'd listen to the radio to all those great shows. Programs like "Little Orphan Annie," "Captain Midnight," and "Jack Armstrong." But that day, every station I turned to had the Cubs game on the radio.

Valenti: What was your reaction when he hit the home run?

Gold: Do you really want to know? Disgust!

Valenti: Disgust? You were not a Cubs fan?

Gold: No, that wasn't it. I was just a six-year-old kid, and I wanted to listen to "Jack Armstrong." But all those shows were cancelled because of the Cubs game. They were on every station. So I had no choice but to listen. You know, hearing that home run come over on the radio was a different experience. There was a magic to radio, almost like a mystery. I remember the description of the pandemonium at Wrigley after Hartnett hit the home run, when he was trying to run the bases. It was totally wild, and to a six-year-old I kind of wondered what was happening. It sounded like they wanted to kill Gabby. Of course, they were only describing the unrestrained happiness from the players and fans.

Valenti: You've written about the home run. What's your assessment?

Gold: It was almost certainly the most thrilling moment in Cubs history. And it became a truly famous homer. I talked to Cavarretta, Jurges, and Herman about it, and they all agree. Although Jurges told me something I didn't know before. In fact, I don't think it ever came out. Like everyone else, I always assumed it was a fastball that Hartnett hit. But Jurges told me that Mace Brown told him that it was a curve. Brown said he threw Hartnett nothing but curve balls. He said the home run pitch was a hanging curve. Another thing that's interesting is the game before. Hartnett really went out on a limb by starting Dizzy Dean. Dean hadn't worked in awhile, and his arm wasn't right. But Gabby played a hunch, and it paid off. Dean almost went all the way. He went 8⅔ before Bill Lee came in. It was one of the last times Dean was on top of his game, because after that, in 1939 and after, he couldn't throw at all.

He's the most powerful hitter who ever lived.

11

MICKEY MANTLE
April 17, 1953

This was a home run ripe for its time, the seminal fifties home run, half past the Korean conflict and quarter after the Cold War. America of the early 1950s was a country rushed into urgency by the haunting shape of a mushroom cloud. The rumblings of the red scare were so pervasive that Cincinnati felt it in the national interest to change its name from the Reds to the Red Legs.

On April 17, 1953, Mickey Mantle would hit The Amazing, Colossal Home Run. The sheer magnitude of this home run would be part science, part fiction, part B movie, part inkblot test. For some reason, the home run struck a resonant chord. Why? Long home runs had been hit before, but never did one sensationalize a nation. So why this one?

The blast would change baseball, ushering in the age of the tape-measure clout, and forever change Mantle. In this urgent, atomic decade, such a mutant home run would be right at home.

Mantle's home run off Chuck Stobbs at Griffith Stadium did not win a World Series. It did not win a pennant. It was not even the decisive run of that meaningless April game. But it would permanently alter New York's perception of the twenty-one-year-old Mantle. It would shackle him with expectations no mortal could long endure and would reshape the career of this supremely gifted but enigmatic young man. But before we get to the details of his famous home run, we must first consider the man himself.

Who was Mantle?

"He had it in his body to be great."

That's how Casey Stengel, Mickey's first manager, would explain his supreme baseball prodigy. Mantle was six feet tall, weighed 190 muscular pounds. He was a boy/man who could hit for high average and with awesome power. He could beat you with a bunt, a stolen base, or a great catch in the outfield. He could get from home to first in 3.1 seconds. He hit from both sides. He was scary.

New York 7,

Washington 3

But Mantle also had in that body the tendency to betray the full realization of his intergalactic talent. And therein lies the germ of his true greatness and his lasting hold as a cultural folk hero: he had the ability to persist, even triumph, despite injury, great pain, and suffering.

Back in the spring of 1951, Mantle must have seemed to the hard-boiled New York writers like a creation of a hack novelist too in love with melodrama. Here was this manchild—this blond, Oklahoma teen-ager named after Mickey Cochrane—who could run like Cobb and hit like Ruth. He was painfully shy; he was a country dirt road bordered by corn rows to Manhattan's paved fast lanes lined with skyscrapers.

Scout Tom Greenwade signed Mantle to a contract for $1150 dollars as a shortstop right after Mick graduated from Commerce High School. The St. Louis Browns and Cardinals bid on Mantle but backed off. Even then, there was concern about his health. In a high school football game, Mantle badly damaged his left leg. The injury got infected, and he contracted osteomyelitis, medicalese for inflammation of the bone marrow. The condition would ravage Mantle for his entire career.

Penicillin saved his life, but when he signed with the Yankees, the organization secretly doubted whether his legs would last five years. But at $1150, he seemed like a reasonable risk. Greenwade based that figure on a $2000 contract, minus what Mantle would have made in the zinc mines if he had stayed on to work there with his father.

He first played D ball in Independence, Missouri, in the old Kentucky-Oklahoma-Missouri League for $140 a month. Later at Joplin, a C league, he hit .383 with 26 home runs. The New York PR staff made a commotion about it, and when Mantle came up to the Yankees for spring training in 1951, the team converted him to the outfield because of his speed, because he had made 102 errors at shortstop in his two years in the minors, and because a place had to be made in the lineup for his bat.

With center fielder Joe DiMaggio playing his last year in 1951, the outfield seemed the perfect place in which to groom Mantle. The only problem was the PR machine. Mantle was billed as the next DiMaggio. It placed on those broad but young shoulders an enormous pressure, one which the New York fans never understood, one which would make the first ten years of Mantle's career in New York all things in between a headache and hell.

He got off to a slow start in 1951. After all, he was learning a new position, a short-stop playing the outfield. The fans booed him lustily. On July 15, he was sent down to the minors. He eventually worked his way back up on August 26 and got into the World Series (he played in the first World Series game he ever saw). But no matter how well he performed, the fans wouldn't let up. In their minds, he was never as great as the hype promised. But who the hell could be?

It was in that 1951 World Series that Mantle suffered another serious leg injury, the worst of his pro career. In the fifth inning of Game Two at Yankee Stadium, the Yankee outfield from left to right was Hank Bauer, DiMaggio, Mantle. Willie Mays hit a sinking fly to right center. It was DiMaggio's play, so Mantle started running over to back up. But the spikes of his right shoe caught in the wooden cover of one of the outfield drain pipes. There was a loud snap in Mantle's leg, and he went down. He remained motionless in the grass, making sure he did not move because he thought he had broken his leg. DiMaggio made the play, then ran over to Mantle. Joe said later that his initial reaction, judging by the way Mantle was supine in the grass, was that he'd been shot.

Intense pain gave way to a numb paralysis. They took Mantle to Lenox Hill Hospital, where the injury was diagnosed as torn ligaments and cartilage in the right knee. Dr. Sidney Gaynor, the Yankee team physician, said it was the worst knee injury he had ever seen in baseball. The good news, if it could be called that, was that the cuts were clean. But it would be a long recovery for Mantle, a notoriously slow healer because of his bone marrow problem.

He recovered during the off-season, but he was still gimpy in 1952 spring training. Mantle said the litany of leg injuries that would plague his career could be traced to that World Series injury. He had managed, before he was twenty, to screw up both legs. But despite the problems, Mick improved from .267 and 13 home runs in '51 to .311 and 23 in '52. New York booed him as much as ever, but he was growing accustomed to it.

In the spring of 1953, his legs were not 100 percent. He could still feel the after-effects of the two traumatic injuries; he also had a charley horse and pulled thigh muscle in his left leg. Nonetheless, there was considerable improvement compared to the previous year.

In an exhibition game on April 9 against the Pittsburgh Pirates at Forbes Field, Mantle would give baseball a preview of what was to come just eight days later. Facing right-hander Bill MacDonald from the left side, Mick put one over the roof of the right-field stands. Only two other times in the history of the old park had that been done, once by Babe Ruth for the Boston Braves in 1935 (the memorable day when he hit the last three home runs of his career), the other by Ted Beard of the Corsairs in 1951. The New York papers played up the home run, as well they should have, whetting New York's appetite to see Mantle do something even more sensational.

The season was but three games old when the 2-1 Yankees met the Washington Senators at Griffith Stadium on April 17. The early spring weather had been cold and wet; there were several postponements. Writers hungry for copy churned out such stories as "Baseball's New Debate: Is Milwaukee Rookie Bill Bruton Faster than Mantle?" Two days before, in Washington, President Eisenhower and Vice President Nixon attended the opener. That was good for some ink, but the writers still hoped for something unusual. On the 17th, they would get it.

New York's Eddie Lopat faced lefty Chuck Stobbs. Before the game, Mantle put on a show in batting practice, driving several balls deep into the left-field bleachers. Lopat remembers one of Mantle's practice drives clearing the bleachers and hitting the football scoreboard. This prompted one of the writers standing around the cage to mention in idle chat how well Mantle hit Stobbs last year, recalling a game in Chicago (Stobbs was with the White Sox in '52) which Mantle won with a long ninth-inning grand slam.

Billy Martin gave the Yanks a 1–0 lead by hitting a wind-blown home run into the left-field bleachers in the third. Washington tied it in the bottom of the third. Wayne Terwilliger singled, went to second on a sacrifice, and scored on a single by Eddie Yost. In the fourth, the Yankees went ahead 2–1 on Bauer's double and a single by Joe Collins. By the time the fifth inning came, Mantle had been up twice. In the first, he was robbed of a hit by third baseman Yost; in the third, he walked and stole a base. In the fifth inning, Stobbs retired Martin and Phil Rizzuto. Yogi Berra drew a walk, bringing Mantle to the plate. He stepped in on the right side against the lefty Stobbs with a bat borrowed from Loren Babe.

Stobbs came in with his first pitch. Some accounts say it was a called strike, others list it as a ball. The second pitch, a fastball high in the strike zone down the heart of the plate, was met with a ferocious cut. The full appreciation of what happened next can only be attained by considering some elemental facts of physics. With a round ball and a round bat, truly solid contact—on the precise core of the sweet spot—is extremely rare.

Even normal solid contact is not, strictly speaking, true contact, which happens when the exact center plane of the ball lines up perfectly straight with the exact center plane of the fat of the bat. This contact can, on minutely rare occasions, be perfect, since a power hitter like Mantle will swing in a slightly upward arc; the ball is coming in off the mound, slightly downward. This was one of those times.

Mantle made *exact* contact, with a tremendous swing. The ball was of a perfect speed, in the perfect location for this perfect swing. In his eighteen-year career, Mantle said he only made contact in that same way one other time: on May 22, 1963, when he powered one almost out of Yankee Stadium off Kansas City's Bill Fischer.

One newspaper account said when the ball met bat, it "sounded like a rifle shot." The ball jumped off Mantle's bat improbably hard and high. It continued to climb toward left center. It went over the bleachers, ticked off the upper-right side of a beer sign atop the old football scoreboard, and disappeared from sight. Confusion reigned in the press box as scribes tried to guesstimate the length of the blast. In both dugouts, players stood silent, shaking their heads. Catcher Les Peden and home-plate ump Jim Honochick watched in awe. Stobbs gave it a cursory glance, then glared in at Honochick, wanting a new baseball. The 4206 fans let out a long *ooo-o-o-o-oh*, but there wasn't much applause as Mantle circled the bases.

Yankee PR man Arthur "Red" Patterson, as astounded as anyone, dashed out of the press box and into the streets and tenements beyond the left-field wall. Here he would uncover the startling truth.

From home plate to the foot of the bleachers was 391 feet. The bleachers were 69 feet deep and 55 feet high. The ball hit the beer sign about five feet above the bleachers, leaving the park 460 feet from the plate. No one knows with absolute certainty what happened next, but the most-agreed-upon version is this.

The ball flew over Fifth Street, which ran directly behind the perimeter of the left-field wall, and landed in the back yard of one Perry L. Cool of 434 Oakdale Street.

By the time Patterson got into the street beyond leftfield, he saw ten-year-old Donald Dunaway of 343 Elm Street holding a baseball. Patterson asked for a look, and there it was. An official American League ball with the cover nearly torn off. It was clearly the home run ball. Patterson then asked the kid how much he wanted for the ball. Dunaway said seventy-five cents. Patterson dug into his pocket, pulling out a one dollar bill and a twenty. He gave Dunaway the buck, then later sent him five dollars and two autographed balls.

He asked Dunaway where he found the ball. The kid took him to the yard at Oakdale Street. Patterson then paced off the distance from the base of the bleacher wall to the point where the ball was found. It came to 105 feet. All added up, it meant Mantle had hit a 565-foot home run.

There was a minor dispute over the final figure. Some held that the distance out of the park was not 460 feet, but the officially posted 457 (a measurement that doesn't allow for the three-foot-thick rear wall itself). They put the blast at 562 feet. Washington vice president Calvin Griffith allegedly measured the distance himself and came up with 562 feet. Some also pointed out that Patterson only had the boy's word for the final resting point of the ball, though one story had a resident of the three-story Oakdale tenement yelling out a window to Patterson, "Yeah, that's where the ball went."

One other controversy revolves around the weather conditions at the time of the home run. Some claim the wind wasn't a factor. However, that goes against the best available information. Sam Diaz, who worked that day as a meteorologist at the Washington Weather Bureau, testified that there was a tail wind of at least 20 mph when Mantle connected.

"Between 3 and 4 P.M. there were gusts up to 41 mph in the direction of the bleachers at Griffith Stadium," Diaz said. "The lightest gusts were at 20. But the wind was blowing that way when the Nats were at bat, too."

And that's really the key point. The wind was blowing out for both teams. In fact, in the nearly thirty years since the bleachers were erected in 1924, wind conditions favored many hitters. But no one ever did what Mantle had done: clear the left-field wall with a batted ball.

DiMaggio had come the closest, six years earlier. He hit one two-thirds of the way up into the bleachers, with the ball caroming into Fifth Street. By the time the stadium was closed after the 1961 campaign, Mantle would remain alone as the only man ever to hit one over the left-field bleachers.

It's interesting to note the ball's brush with the beer sign. The ball ticked off the sign on the old football scoreboard which advertised National Bohemian Beer. The ball grazed the sign just above the close-quotation mark after the word "Beer." The impact was slight, but of enough force that some black paint from the sign rubbed off on the ball's cover. Had it not hit the sign, the ball would have gone even farther. An additional irony is that Griffith Stadium was not a home run park. In 1952, the powerful Yankees only hit two home runs there the entire season.

Clark Griffith, eighty-three-year-old president of the Washington club, said it was doubtless "the longest home run hit in the history of baseball." His manager, Bucky Harris, would not go that far, but did say it was the longest one he'd ever seen. He added that if he hadn't seen it, he wouldn't have believed a ball could be hit that hard.

In the Yankee locker room following the eventual 7–3 Yankee win, Patterson gave Mantle the dented, cover-torn ball. Mantle didn't seem to realize that he'd done anything out of the ordinary. Someone asked him what he would do with the ball.

"If I send the ball home, I know what will happen to it," he said, laughing. "My twin brothers will take it out on the lot, like any twenty-cent rocket." Mantle said that in 1951, he got the ball for his first major league home run, hit in Chicago. He autographed it and sent it home. His brothers bashed it to uselessness.

The media crunch asked Mantle what the pitch was. Berra, walking by, interjected, "Screwball. That's what it was. A screwball," then nudged Mickey in the ribs. Mantle laughed and said the pitch was a chest-high fastball.

Stobbs said he couldn't remember if the pitch was a fastball or a slider, then added, "No matter what it was, he really hit the heck out of it, didn't he?" By the way, the game was Stobbs's first in a Washington uniform.

For the record, Mantle's last two at bats came from the left side in the eighth and ninth innings off Julio Marino. In the eighth he walked. In the ninth, he dragged

---

"How High the Moon?"

Mickey Mantle's home run off Chuck Stobbs was unquestionably one of the longest in baseball history, but was it *the* longest? The question may never be definitively answered, simply because of the controversies surrounding the measurements of certain of the long blasts.

The longest home run ever? That generally goes to a blast Babe Ruth hit in Tampa, Florida, in 1919, while a member of the Boston Red Sox. It reportedly measured 587 feet. Other murkier accounts had Ruth hitting a 612-foot home run in Plant City, also that spring.

Jimmie Foxx is rumored to have hit a 600-foot-plus home run that cleared the left-center roof at Comiskey Park. Legend also has Ruth hitting a 600-foot home run at Briggs Stadium in Detroit in 1926.

The five other acknowledged long home runs before Mantle's were:

Length	Player	Team	Place	Year
560 feet	Ralph Kiner	Pirates	Pittsburgh	1950
538 feet	Ken Silvestri	Yankees	Tampa, Florida	1948
527 feet	Ted Williams	Red Sox	Detroit	1937
500 feet	Hank Greenberg	Tigers	Boston	1937
500 feet	Ralph Kiner	Pirates	Boston	1940

◆

---

a bunt which went all the way into the outfield for a base hit. There were jokes in the press box about its being the longest bunt hit of all time.

The day after, the newspapers screamed their headlines, like a broadsheet advertising the latest screen sensation (the Astounding!-Fantastic!-You'll-Gasp-in-Shock! treatment). It was pure fifties schlock: "Mantle Makes Home Run History at 21" and "Power Kings of the Past, Move Over for Oklahoma Kid" and "Mickey's 565-Foot Drive Recalls Ruth, Foxx Feats"—heavy stuff for a twenty-one-year-old.

On the team train to Kansas City the day after, all the talk was about Mantle's home run. In the hotel lobby, on the streets of New York, across America via wire services, it was Mantle! Mantle! Mantle! Yankee coach Bill Dickey said he played with Ruth, Gehrig, and Foxx, but Mantle had a chance to be the top power hitter of all time. Stengel said point blank Mantle would lead the league in hitting, "this year or next," then made the now-obligatory comparisons to Ruth, Foxx, et al., concluding with an unqualified declaration: "He's the most powerful hitter who ever lived."

Which, of course, meant that no matter what Mantle did from now on, he would be measured against this great, but freaky, home run. For example, when he hit his second home run of the year six days later at Yankee Stadium off Ellis Kinder of the Red Sox—a three-run blast in the bottom of the ninth that broke a 3–3 tie and won the game—the press and the fans noted that the ball "only" traveled 420 feet, ten rows up in the right-field bleachers.

The home run became his curse. He was expected to blast them every time up. The reality is that Mantle, though a great hitter with a high average and mighty power, struck out frequently. Each time, he was booed unhesitatingly by the home fans. Even in 1956, when he put it all together to win the Triple Crown at .356, 52, 130, the fans rode him.

Eventually, this wore him down, and Mantle became moody with the press and the fans. That, along with a seemingly endless procession of injuries, eventually put Mantle's career—as good as it was—into the what-might-have-been category, leaving to the imagination what this shy man from Oklahoma might have accomplished had he been left in peace and in good health.

Stretched to burning by the rack of fame and constant expectation, Mantle would not even find peace within his own self, where the tendrils of his dreams wavered in the tides of this home run.

On the Record: Bill Jenkinson

Baseball historian Bill Jenkinson specializes in long home runs. He is generally considered to be the world's top authority on long-distance blasts.

Valenti: There have been a lot of long home runs hit, but why has Mantle's stood up and out for so long?

Jenkinson: Because Mantle's home run was truly one of a kind. There are very few home runs in major league history as far as distance is concerned that are literally one of a kind. I think the bleachers at Griffith Stadium were built in the mid-1920s. Mantle's was the only game ball that was ever hit over those bleachers. That makes it very special. There have been extremely few plateaus that were reached only one time [in baseball history]. That was one of them. Especially in a ballpark like Griffith Stadium, which was in use for so long. So I think that is critical.

Valenti: What are the unresolved aspects of Mantle's home run, if any?

Jenkinson: One thing which I don't think has been successfully resolved from an investigative standpoint concerns the wind conditions at the time of the home run. Mantle backers tend to quite clearly overstate Mickey's achievements. I'm a Mantle fan, like I'm a fan of all the great tape-measure hitters, and I certainly get as big a kick as anyone out of finding prodigious home runs. But I think [the people who have looked into this home run] have been too much Mickey Mantle fans and not enough of tape-measure home run fans. I make that point now because they [the Mantle camp] make the case that the wind was not blowing out that day, and they do that through what I call "selective information." I see it all the time in their accounts of the Mantle home runs. Mantle himself will tell you, if you ask him, that the wind was really blowing out, and it helped him a lot. He says he remembers looking out at the flag, right after he hit it, and noticing that the wind was blowing out. I have reason to believe that the wind *was* blowing out. But here's the point which I tried to suggest to those guys [Mantle researchers]: whether it was blowing out or not was not the critical factor, because it was surely blowing out many, many other times in the decades the park was in use, and nobody else hit it over the bleachers, with the wind or not. So to me, wanting to preserve my journalistic

Attendance: 4206
Time of Game: 2:27

NEW YORK YANKEES

Name	AB	R	H	RBI
Martin, 2B	4	1	2	2
Rizzuto, SS	5	0	1	0
Berra, C	4	1	1	0
Mantle, CF	3	1	2	2
Bauer, RF	4	2	1	0
Woodling, LF	5	1	2	1
Collins, 1B	4	0	1	1
Carey, 3B	4	1	1	1
Lopat, P	4	0	1	0
Gorman, P	0	0	0	0
Totals	37	7	12	7

WASHINGTON SENATORS

Name	AB	R	H	RBI
Yost, 3B	5	0	2	1
Busby, CF	4	0	1	0
Vernon, 1B	3	0	0	0
Jensen, RF	4	0	0	0
Runnels, SS	3	1	1	0
Wood, LF	4	0	1	0
Terwilliger, 2B	4	2	3	1
Peden, C	4	0	1	0
Stobbs, P	1	0	0	0
Hoderlein, PH	1	0	1	1
Moreno, P	0	0	0	0
Verble, PH	1	0	0	0
Totals	34	3	10	3

Team	1	2	3	4	5	6	7	8	9		
New York	0	0	1	1	2	0	0	3	0		7
Washington	0	0	1	0	0	0	1	1	0		3

Name	1P	H	R	ER	BB	SO
Lopat (W)	8	10	3	3	3	2
Gorman	1	0	0	0	0	0

Name	1P	H	R	ER	BB	SO
Stobbs (L)	7	7	4	4	4	0
Moreno	2	5	3	3	2	0

integrity, if I were a Mickey Mantle fan, and I wanted to make him look as good as I could, I wouldn't go out on a limb and try to say the wind wasn't blowing out when it looked like it probably was.

Valenti: The ball might have gone farther had it not hit the beer sign.

Jenkinson: The ball was impeded by the beer sign. It used to be a scoreboard, but it wasn't in use as a scoreboard at the time. I think it was a beer sign. It deflected off. Then you get into the question of did it really fly. . .565 feet in the air. Of course, Red Patterson is traditionally credited with having measured it exactly, based on an account of a ten-year-old boy outside the ballpark. [Those accounts] are basically baloney. The key here is that Red went outside the ballpark, and he found the boy who had the ball, and [not the ball itself]. And as is oftentimes the case, as I've found out many times in evaluating long home runs—especially people from the Mantle camp—they describe [nonsense]. For example, they've described a 1960 home run he hit in Detroit as 643 feet, claiming that's the longest home run in history. And it's total, total nonsense. To me, anyone who wants to debate the point of that home run being 643 feet would make himself into an absolute fool. I personally investigated that home run, and I spoke to the same sources that they relied upon, and it's a fantasy. I don't know how many times it bounced before the one so-called witness saw it land, but assuredly it bounced several times.

Valenti: And that makes a difference in evaluating long home runs? Is it where the ball stops?

Jenkinson: No. To me, it's where it lands [from the air]. In tape-measure home run history, there are very few occasions where the tremendous home runs have clearly been identified for their specific landing points. The point is, it's awfully difficult to prove where a ball actually lands. Mantle's home run off Chuck Stobbs in Washington is a genuinely historic home run, because it was one of a kind and because of its length. But attributing a specific linear distance to it—I think that's a little tough.

Valenti: You seem to have some reservations about the home run.

Jenkinson: I don't think that home run was necessarily longer than a few others, certainly not many, but maybe a few others he hit up to that point in a Yankee uniform. Mickey was incredibly strong at an early age. But so much of what has happened as a result of that home run was due to the coincidence of Red Patterson being the PR man for the Yankees at the time. A less enterprising PR guy would not have done what he had done [sic]. Especially when you consider the fact that it happened to a New York player. The subsequent attention focused on it was out of proportion to the drive. Not taking anything away from it, because, in my opinion, if I had to put the blue ribbon on the ultimate tape-measure home run, that would probably be it. Because it certainly was one of the longest in the history of the game, and certainly the most famous.

I knew it was going in—or he'd catch it.

DUSTY RHODES
September 29, 1954

12

If there's one subtheme running through this book, it's that circumstance is all. That is, the truth of an event can be realized only if you take into account the other events around which it takes place.

This comes to mind when looking at the box score from Game One of the 1954 World Series. The box score reveals many facts. We see the final score, 5–2 Giants. We see Vic Wertz with an enviable 4–for–5, 2-RBI day. We see Willie Mays 0-for-3 and only two putouts. We see Dusty Rhodes with a pinch-hit, game-winning, three-run home run. We see facts. But we do not see the truth.

Factually, we would expect Wertz ended his day satisfied with his personal effort in defeat. We would expect that Mays was not a factor with his 0-fer and his quiet day in center. And we would expect to hear of Rhodes's monumental blast to win it. For in that beautiful line of the box score, the home run looks titanic:

	AB	R	H	RBI
Rhodes, PH	1	1	1	3

These "facts," however, tell us little. Throw away the numbers of the box score. You with ears, hear what happened.

The 1954 Indians went into the Fall Classic as 8–5 favorites. An Associated Press poll of fifty-four baseball writers found thirty-seven picking the Tribe. United Press polled 154 writers: 110 favored Cleveland. It's easy to see why. This was a team that won 111 games, still the all-time record. How good were they? Casey Stengel would win over 100 games (103) for the first and only time in his managing career, and would finish eight games out.

General Manager Hank Greenberg built his ball club with a rare balance of hitting and pitching. At the plate, Cleveland had Larry Doby (.272, 32 HRs, 126 RBIs), Al Rosen (.300, 24, 102), and Vic Wertz (.275, 14, 48 in just 295 at bats after the trade with Baltimore on June 1 for pitcher Bob Chakales) in the middle. For good measure, second baseman Bobby Avila led the league in hitting with a .341 average. On the mound, the Big Three of Bob Lemon, Early Wynn, and Mike Garcia combined for

65 wins. They were backed up by Art Houtteman at 15-7, and aging Bob Feller at 13-3, and Hal Newhouser at 7-2. Rookie relievers Don Mossi and Ray Narleski pitched in 82 games, winning 9 and saving 20.

This was a team whose depth clearly put the Giants in over their heads. Leo Durocher's team had a maturing Willie Mays, back from two years in the service to hit .345, with 41 homers, and 110 RBIs; they had 21-game winner Johnny Antonelli, an off-season pickup from the Boston Braves; but they had little else. Don Mueller, Al Dark, and pitcher Ruben Gomez had had decent years, but the team was held together more with ace bandages, spit, mud, a few paper clips, rubber bands, and Durocher's indomitable spirit.

The fans lined up early for Game One. George Schnider, a thirty-five-year-old delivery-man from Brooklyn, got the first bleacher ticket and was allowed to sit in the stands at 4 A.M., nine hours before the first pitch. He sat alone for two hours in the haunted, piano-dark expanse of the Polo Grounds, and was then joined by Roy Paul, a disabled World War II vet from Des Moines, Iowa. All the early arrivals received free copies of the special "Home Run Edition" of the *Phoenix Gazette*. A banner headline exclaimed, "Phoenix Cheers Giants in Series." Both the Giants and Indians trained in Arizona, and for the previous nineteen years, had broken camp with a barnstorming tour east. They were well familiar with each other.

A bizarre but humorous incident occurred in the Cleveland dugout before the game. Gordon Cobbledick, sports editor of the *Cleveland Plain Dealer*, introduced Tribe outfielder Al Smith to five writers named Smith: Ken of the *New York Mirror*, Red of the *New York Herald Tribune*, Lou of the *Cincinnati Enquirer*, Chet of the *Pittsburgh Press*, and Lyall of the *Detroit Free Press*. Some anonymous joker near the batting cage saw the group, and yelled with a threatening voice, "Hey, Smith." Six heads shot around fast. Then they all all broke out laughing.

Durocher and Indian manager Al Lopez met at home plate on the sunny early-fall afternoon. No one knew it at the time, but this day would host the second-to-the-last World Series game ever to be played in the crazy-quilt Polo Grounds. Outside the park, hedges breathed fall's early colors. Inside, the park would huddle around 52,751 fans, just three years away from betrayal, a move-west-young-money sadness that would leave hundreds of thousands of New Yorkers feeling as if they'd just seen their birthplace torn down.

But some things are better off not remembered. For this day, the crowd would be content. Their numbers put such a drain on the stadium concessions that workers had to be flown in from Fenway Park in Boston. A Marine color guard raised the flag. Perry Como sang the national anthem. Jimmy Barbieri, captain of the Little League World Champs from Schenectady, New York, threw out the first ball to Giants catcher Wes Westrum. Home-plate ump Al Barlick yelled, "Play ball!"

The Indians came out smoking in the top of the first, making the odds makers look like geniuses. Sal Maglie got off to a shaky start. He went 3-0 to Smith, the leadoff batter, then hit him. Avila singled to right. Mueller juggled the ball, and Smith took third on the error. Maglie seemed over his case of nerves, getting Doby on a routine grounder to Hank Thompson at third and Rosen to pop to Whitey Lockman at first. But Wertz, who would be "on" all day, lofted a booming drive to deep right center. By the time Mays recovered the ball, two runs were in, and Wertz was on third with a triple.

Right fielder Dave Philley then tagged a liner to right. Mueller had trouble judging it, then finally managed to make the grab. It would turn out to be one of the game's several hidden plays, important but long forgotten. If the play is not made, Wertz scores and the whole game turns out differently.

In the Giant first off Lemon, Dark drew a one-out walk and went to third on Mueller's single to right. But Lemon soured the threat, getting Mays on a pop out and Thompson on a 6-3 grounder. The score stayed 2-0 until the third, when the Giants tied it. Lockman led off with a base hit. Dark followed with a single, putting runners at the corners. Mueller's fielder's choice (Avila to shortstop George Strickland) scored Lockman. After Mays walked, Thompson singled home Mueller to make it 2-2. With runners on the corners again, Lemon bore down. He fanned Monte Irvin and got Davey Williams on a harmless bouncer.

The remaining six innings are easy to summarize factually. The game remained scoreless through nine, ending in a 2-2 tie. Again, those are facts. Now let's get to the truth.

The Indians kept putting the pressure on and runners aboard. But they couldn't score. Wertz led off the fourth with a single and died. In the fifth, a couple of singles put runners on the corners. In the sixth, Wertz singled and went to second on Mueller's second error with no outs. He went to third with one out. All these chances were to no avail. Then came the Tribe eighth, and their big chance. It was a half inning that would produce one of the most famous plays of all time.

The tiring Maglie walked leadoff batter Doby. Rosen then ripped a single off Dark's glove. With runners on first and second and no outs, the red-hot Wertz, already 3-for-3, came to the plate. Durocher had seen enough of Maglie and called for lefty Don Liddle to face the left-handed hitting Wertz.

On this day, percentages would matter little to the big first baseman. Wertz clubbed a frightening drive to the deepest part of right center, a ball he would later call the hardest he'd ever hit in his career. As the ball kept carrying, the whole ballpark tallied at least two runs for the Indians. There was only one man who thought the ball could be caught. Fortunately for New York, he was playing center.

Somehow, and no one—not even Willie—can explain it, Mays instantly turned his back to the plate and sprinted with all his might ("like a scared deer," as one newspaper account put it) to an area of the right-center stands where a five-foot green boarding jutted out in front of the high bleacher wall. At the last instant before crashing into the wall and about eight feet to the right of where the wall shoots back to the clubhouse opening 475 feet from the plate, Mays stuck up both hands over his left shoulder. Without looking, he caught the ball over his left shoulder as it was sailing *beyond* him, 460 feet from home.

One writer called the catch "preposterous." It didn't look humanly possible. Who knows, maybe for that instant, Mays wasn't human.

After the catch, Willie slammed on the brakes, wheeled around, pegged the ball back to the infield, and fell to the ground looking. At that precise moment, the Indians lost two runs, the game, the momentum, and the World Series.

The crowd gasped, held its breath, then let out a tumultuous cheer. The catch seemed to leave an imprint of itself somewhere above the sweet-smelling outfield lawn, a kind of hologram of the collective mind that the fans kept going back to like a person slow-sipping nectar throughout an afternoon. Anytime they needed hope, they thought of the cinnamon-voiced outfielder stretching out his searchlight hands one more time. These "replays" were graced in psychic slow motion, actually much the match of the famous black-and-white film footage of the catch itself.

Now the "facts" say that even with this catch, the Indians were still in good shape. On the play, Doby tagged and went to third with one out. Truth knew better.

Hank Majeski was announced to bat for Philley, so Durocher went with the right-hander, Marv Grissom. Lopez countered by sending up Dale Mitchell, who two years later would fan for the last out of Don Larsen's perfect game. Grissom walked Mitchell to load the bases with one out, but the nervous crowd relaxed a bit when Dave Pope was called out on strikes. Jim Hegan put one final scare into them by hitting a ball 400 feet to left. It looked like it had a chance off the bat, but the wind held it up enough for Irvin to make the play. There it was: a single, two walks, two fly-ball outs that totaled 860 feet, and no runs.

In the ninth, the Indians put two more on without result. In the tenth, the tireless Wertz led off with a double deep to left center. Mays tracked the ball down against the center-field bleachers, and only his tremendous throw held Wertz at second on what seemed a sure triple. It would be another of those long-since-forgotten but highly influential plays. Once more, the run would not score.

In the bottom of the tenth, fate would intervene.

Mueller struck out against Lemon, who was still throwing hard. But Mays walked and stole second. The theft would have enormous consequences, since it forced Lopez to give Hank Thompson an intentional pass to get to Irvin, whom Lemon had saddled with an 0-for-3.

Irvin was a surprise starter in left. Before the Series, Durocher said Dusty Rhodes would be in left. But for some reason, he scratched Rhodes at the last minute. Durocher later said he "wrestled with that problem" of who should play left all night before deciding, on a pure hunch, to keep Rhodes on the bench ready to pinch-hit. Rhodes had come through all year as a pinch hitter, racking up a .341 average with several pinch home runs. The Giants, in fact, set a major league record with 10 pinch-hit home runs in 1954.

Here was the perfect spot for Rhodes. The Longines clock above the center-field clubhouse read 4:12. The Chesterfield sign with the enlarged, mutant cigarette prophetically claimed, "It's a Hit!" Lopez left Lemon in against the left-hander. On the first pitch, Rhodes hit a lazy pop fly down the right-field line. Lemon thought it would be a routine out.

Right fielder Pope ran over to the wall several feet off the line and made a desperate leap against the wall, his body contorted, looking like someone doing a flamenco dance while leaping in the air and clicking his heels. Pope strained so hard for the ball that at the height of his jump, his body was crescent shaped.

The runners, of course, had to wait. Mays stood watching about a foot beyond second base. Thompson paused midway between first and second, with Rhodes running full speed around first and getting perilously close to Thompson, who yelled to Rhodes, "Slow down, man!" Then the ball went in. Mays led the trio of runners around the sacks with an incredulous smile.

The ball came down barely in the front row, about 258 feet from the plate, for a 5–2 Giants win. The sphere hit some fan in the chest, then bounced back onto the

Leo Branches Out

◆

Dusty Rhodes gave Leo Durocher enough of a thrill with his game-winning run, but as Leo sat in the clubhouse savoring the moment, he got another one.

A telegram came from Branch Rickey, his old general manager when The Lip piloted the Brooklyn Dodgers. Rickey was kept from attending Game One because of illness. But he wired his one-time field boss: "You did a great job, just as you have done all year. In my book, you rank among the great managers of all time. I just wanted you to know I am thinking about you."

Leo, obviously moved, told writers, "It's one of the nicest things that ever happened to me, especially coming from my old boss." ◆

field where Pope just stared at it. It was, in the parlance of the odd geometry of the Polo Grounds, a cheapie.

When the ball went in, a disgusted Lemon raged and hurled his glove in the air with all his might. A writer cracked that the glove went farther than Rhodes's home run.

Arthur Daley in the *New York Times* had a great description of the home run: "It was a harmless pop-up that peeked timidly above the roof of the grandstand" before gently falling in the stands.

In the locker room, some writers suggested the home run was tainted, a fluke, more the fault of the architect of the Polo Grounds than Bob Lemon. A testy Durocher shot back, "Look, he [Rhodes] had been doing that for me all year. I don't care where they go when he hits 'em. All I know is that you had to have a ticket to catch it."

Lemon's post mortem was succinctly ironic: "They tell me everything hit in this park is 500 feet on paper."

Rhodes gave a cryptic but totally satisfactory account of his "blast": "The minute I hit it, I knew it was going in—or he'd catch it."

Western Union reported that seventy operators moved 200,000 words of copy after the game. Another 250,000 words were sent as overnight copy. The words most frequently used? "Willie Mays" and "Dusty Rhodes."

...midnight words straining to break through the membrane of "fact" and into a morning communion with the truth.

On the Record: Dusty Rhodes

Valenti: How did Leo Durocher use you in 1954?

Rhodes: I was used almost exclusively against hard-throwing pitchers. When somebody was throwing the ball about 100 miles an hour, I played (*laughs*). That's when they stuck me in there. I also had some luck as a pinch hitter.

Valenti: The Indians were heavily favored in the Series. Did that bother the club?

Rhodes: Durocher came in the clubhouse before the Series began, and said, "Look at this. Cleveland's celebrating their victory party already." He got us all riled up. The Indians were favored all four games of that Series. Even when we beat 'em three straight, they were still favored. I'm serious. You know how those odds makers are. But people forget we had a pretty good team ourselves. Mueller and Mays went down to the last game of the season in the batting race. They were both hitting .342, I think. Robin Roberts was pitching (for the Phillies). And don't you know, Mays got three hits. Robin Roberts never walked nobody, but I think he walked Mueller twice. So that's how Mays won the batting championship. All Willie wanted to do was play ball; he played like a kid. He still *is* a kid. He loved the game. We had a pitching staff that won a bunch of games, too.

Valenti: What's the story about Durocher starting Monte Irvin instead of you in left for Game One?

Rhodes: Leo had told us that the guy who started the last game of the season down in Philadelphia was going to start the first game of the World Series. That was me. So it's pregame, the day before Game One of the Series. I was in the Polo Grounds working out, with sportswriters from all over the world there. I was in the cage, hitting. One of the guys yelled, "Could we have the starting lineup over here? I would like to have a picture." So I said, "I'll be with you in a minute." And he yelled back, "*You're* not playing." So I got mad, took my bat, and walked in the clubhouse. I was still mad the next day before we started the game. To add insult to injury, in the ninth inning of Game One, Leo told me to grab a bat and hit for Grissom. So I grabbed a bat. Then Leo said, "Ahhh, never mind. Sit down." So he made me mad again!

Valenti: What about Durocher? How would you rate him as a manager?

Rhodes: He was the greatest manager who ever lived, during that era. Today, I don't know, because these young kids don't listen to nobody no more.

Valenti: Was he tough?

Rhodes: Well, if you made mistakes—stupid mistakes—he'd get mad. If it was just an error, he'd tell you to forget about it. But if you pulled a blunder that lost the game, you didn't even take your hat off in the clubhouse until he got through chewing everybody out. And everybody *listened.* Believe me, they listened. People back then loved the game. Today, they don't give a damn about the game. All they want to worry about is money.

Valenti: Now, to the game. It was tied when Mays made his famous catch off Vic Wertz. What do you remember about that?

Rhodes: Don Liddle was brought in to pitch to Wertz. He hit the ball about 460 feet. Willie made the catch, came back to the dugout, and said, "Ahhh, ain't nothin' to it." That was the turning point in that Series. That killed 'em. That was the longest out I've ever seen. Our reaction to the catch was, "No sweat." He'd made better plays all year. In fact, he put it over just a little bit. He could have got in front of that ball. But he was so good...he had good hands. You know how it is. That play was nothing. You oughta have seen some of the others. The bigger the crowd, the better Willie played. Always, yeah. He was a showman.

Valenti: Tell me about your game-winning home run.

Rhodes: I was on the bench, still mad over not playing. It seemed like any other game to me. So the next thing I know, Willie gets on first, steals second, and they walked

BOX SCORE: The Polo Grounds, 9•29•54

Attendance: 52,751
Time of Game: 3:11

CLEVELAND INDIANS

Name	AB	R	H	RBI
Smith, LF	4	1	1	0
Avila, 2B	5	1	1	0
Doby, CF	3	0	1	0
Rosen, 3B	5	0	1	0
Wertz, 1B	5	0	4	2
Regalado, PR	0	0	0	0
Grasso, C	0	0	0	0
Philley, RF	3	0	0	0
Majeski, PH	0	0	0	0
Mitchell, PH	0	0	0	0
Dente, SS	0	0	0	0
Strickland, SS	3	0	0	0
Pope, RF	1	0	0	0
Hegan, C	4	0	0	0
Glynn, 1B	1	0	0	0
Lemon, P	4	0	0	0
Totals	38	2	8	2

NEW YORK GIANTS

Name	AB	R	H	RBI
Lockman, 1B	5	1	1	0
Dark, SS	4	0	2	0
Mueller, RF	5	1	2	1
Mays, CF	3	1	0	0
Thompson, 3B	3	1	1	1
Irvin, LF	3	0	0	0
Rhodes, PH	1	1	1	3
Williams, 2B	4	0	0	0
Westrum, C	4	0	2	0
Maglie, P	3	0	0	0
Liddle, P	0	0	0	0
Grissom, P	1	0	0	0
Totals	36	5	9	5

Team	1	2	3	4	5	6	7	8	9	10	
Indians	2	0	0	0	0	0	0	0	0	0	2
Giants	0	0	2	0	0	0	0	0	0	3	5

Name	1P	H	R	ER	BB	SO
Lemon (L)	9⅓	9	5	5	5	6

Name	1P	H	R	ER	BB	SO
Maglie	7	7	2	2	2	2
Liddle	⅓	0	0	0	0	0
Grissom (W)	2⅔	1	0	0	3	2

Hank Thompson to pitch to Monte Irvin. And then I went up to hit for Monte. I had hit against Lemon before in spring training for about five years, and I never touched him. He had a fastball that sunk, and he was tough to hit. So I went up with the intention of taking the first pitch. He threw me a curve ball. I held up to the last second, and I swung at it. It hung above the middle of the plate, just about belt high. I couldn't believe it when I seen it. My eyes lit up, and I got on it. The wind then blew it in the seats. I didn't hit it good, but I hit it up in the air. And the next thing I know, the right fielder, Dave Pope, started drifting back, and when I rounded first, the ball was in the seats. Lemon threw his glove in the stands. They say his glove went farther than the ball I hit (*laughs*). I had won about

18 games with base hits during the regular season [.341, with 15 homers in just 164 at bats], so it seemed just like an ordinary game to me. It still didn't dawn on me until fifteen years later about what went on in that World Series. I was in so many tight games that year, one game didn't mean nothing.

Valenti: Did the pressure of clutch situations bother you?

Rhodes: Hell, no. In fact, I loved it. I'd go 0-for-10 with nobody on base. But put me up with the bases loaded, and I'd get a base hit. When I had an idea that a situation was developing, I'd walk over to the bat rack. Leo would look around, but not at me. Then I'd yell, "I'm over here, Leo." He'd then say, "Jim,"—he always called me "Jim," never called me "Dusty"—he'd say, "Jim, grab a bat." I had a bat in my hands, waiting. I loved the game. I loved to win. I hated to lose. I'd try about 300 percent when the game was on the line. But when we were behind by 10 runs, it was different. In fact, the first time I came to bat in the big leagues was in 1952. Leo brought me in to pinch-hit against a left-hander from Philadelphia. I forgot his name. Anyway, we were behind about 16 runs. I went up, looked at three pitches, and struck out. So Leo got on me. And I said, "Well, hell. If I had hit a home run, we'd only got beat by 15." But when it was on the line, that's when I really liked to play.

13

MARK McGWIRE
August 14, 1987

Time is the first point of departure when examining the hitting feats of Mark McGwire. Quite simply, does he belong in this book?

For in a book like this, replete with such legends as Thomson, Mazeroski, Ruth, Williams, Aaron, etc., one must consider the comparative infancy of McGwire's "big" home run. Because McGwire is so relatively new, can he be compared in the same breath with the indisputably legendary? Can he walk the same revered ground as Myth? The answer is "yes"—because he did what no rookie had ever done in the game's 118-year history.

McGwire took the American League by storm in 1987, setting a new rookie home run record. Along the way, he flirted with Maris and Ruth, guaranteeing him an unyielding amount of media attention. That, combined with his long-ball capacities, made him baseball's hottest young star. He was a quantity, an item, a novelty, a walking sideshow—a product exactly fit for baseball in the late eighties.

McGwire was the second oldest of five brothers, a six-foot-five-inch 220-pounder, born October 1, 1963, in Claremont, California. If he had had his way early on, he might never have played baseball. His first sporting love was golf, which he started playing at the age of ten. His first career ambition had nothing to do with sports: he wanted to be a cop, something that fascinates him to this day. But in his sophomore year in high school, the baseball coach took a look at his physique and urged Mark to try out. He did, and made the team, as a pitcher. He was drafted by the Montreal Expos out of high school, but he elected to attend the University of Southern California when the Expos didn't offer enough money.

At USC, he met two people who changed his life. The first was his future wife Kathy, the team's batgirl. The second was Ron Vaughan, USC batting instructor, the man McGwire credits for turning him into a hitter. Vaughan and head coach Rod Dedeaux worked with him on his swing. He made such progress as a hitter that he dropped pitching entirely. The switch to hitting resulted in several USC home run records, and a spot on the 1984 U.S. Olympic baseball team, an awesome collection of young talent that eventually produced more than a dozen major leaguers.

Oakland 7,

California 6

In June 1984, McGwire was the A's first draft pick. He played 16 games that year and all of 1985 in Modesto of the California League, dividing his time between first and third. He led the league in home runs (24) and RBIs (106) in '85, and in '86 hit a combined .300 plus, with 23 homers and 112 RBIs at Tacoma (Pacific Coast) and Huntsville (Southern). That performance earned him the proverbial cup of coffee with the big club, getting in 18 games at third base for Oakland, and hitting 3 home runs in 53 trips.

The A's viewed McGwire almost exclusively as a third baseman, more because of the presence of Rob Nelson than any resemblance to Brooks Robinson. Nelson was himself a highly touted rookie, regarded as can't-miss material by the A's. But because he could only play first base, the club moved McGwire to third, where, in the spring of 1987, he found himself behind former AL batting champ Carney Lansford.

Manager Tony LaRussa handed Nelson the first base job. The A's rated him so highly that they nominated him for the All-Star ballot. The plan had McGwire going down to Triple A. But he impressed the team with a .322 average and a club-high 23 RBIs in Cactus League play. He was the hardest worker in camp, and so he stuck as the last man on the twenty-four-man roster, a projected pinch hitter and backup infielder.

But it didn't work out that way. Nelson, who started at first for a couple of weeks, fell on his face. In the third week of the season, Nelson was the one sent down. McGwire got the call at first. And almost immediately, he started hitting. In May, he hit 15 home runs, and the baseball world took notice. Soon, the old Roger Maris-Henry Aaron treatment took effect.

With each home run, the press horde increased. Soon, this heretofore unknown couldn't go to his locker without people waiting for him, with more questions, wanting more pictures. Gone were the days when he could get to the park early and be alone, just thinking about the game. In June, he hit five home runs in two days at Cleveland. At Chicago, the next stop on the road trip, more than twenty-five media types were waiting for him.

The crush, and the subsequent pressure, increased. Each movement, each swing, came under more intense scrutiny. And so for a time, this unassuming young man stopped having fun. Once, he brushed off a couple of writers because he was tired. The following day came a coast-to-coast story that McGwire was wilting under the pressure, that he was trying to become a recluse.

"I just didn't feel like talking that day," he recalls. "Nothing personal. I just didn't feel like talking. . .I'm not a robot! I can't hit a home run anytime I want, and there are times when I just really don't feel like talking."

Every time he stood on deck, he'd hear people telling him to hit a home run. It started to get to him. But he didn't crack. In fact, McGwire showed remarkable cool for someone so young. He was a twenty-three-year-old rookie. Maris had been in baseball for six years in 1961. Aaron had been in the game almost two decades when he went after Ruth. McGwire was a quiet, almost shy, and simple rookie. How did he handle it so well? There were four reasons.

1. The presence of teammates Reggie Jackson and Jose Canseco. Reggie, a star of the highest order, had been through every kind of media trap conceivable. Canseco, on the other hand, had himself gone through the "Wunderkind-Rookie" syndrome the year before. In '86, he was rookie of the year, hit lots of prodigious home runs,

drove in 117 runs, and had to deal with the Crush. Both men were able to give McGwire a virtual seminar in press relations.

2. Press conference limits. The A's devised a special media policy for McGwire. As the club entered each new road city, McGwire would hold a press conference the first day in. After that, he would be off limits. That didn't completely stop the distractions, but it made the situation more manageable.

3. His teammates in general. The club made a concerted effort to protect McGwire and to keep him loose. They joked with him, gave him nicknames (e.g., "Big Mac" and "Agent Orange"), included him in clubhouse horseplay and practical jokes (during a TV interview, someone squashed a cream pie in Mark's face).

4. His own personality. McGwire came from a stable, loving family, and retained a subdued, good-natured outlook that served him well in maintaining his balance and perspective. An off day wouldn't throw him. When someone or something was bugging him, he kept quiet rather than blurt it out to the press.

He even got pretty good at ducking interviews, retreating to the trainer's room (off limits to the press), or just plain saying, "No."

Most of the early pressure came from his chase of Ruth and Maris. Newspapers started running daily comparison charts. The questions, always the same questions, poured over him in waves. For a while, he was way ahead of the pace (with Ruth, it's deceptive, because the Bambino hit 18 home runs in September of 1927). But a case of the flu (during which he lost ten pounds), plus an 11-game span in which he was homerless in 41 at bats, put an end to that.

The pressure then shifted to the rookie home run record. Wally Berger of the 1930 Boston Braves and Frank Robinson of the 1956 Cincinnati Reds each had 38 for the old mark. On August 10, McGwire tied that with a leadoff homer in the seventh inning off Seattle's Mike Moore in an 8–2 loss. The Kingdome blast cleared the center-field wall.

Four days later, with the A's in Anaheim to take on the Angels, McGwire would become the most prolific home-run-hitting rookie in baseball's 118-year history. His family and friends from nearby Claremont were on hand to make it extra special.

Don Sutton, a 317-game winner, was on the mound for the Angels. In the sixth inning of the 3–3 game, Tony Bernazard opened up with a single to center. Gary Pettis came in slowly on the ball, which then took a strange hop and got past him. Bernazard moved into second on the error. Sutton got Mike Davis on a fly to George Hendrick in left, and Canseco on a bouncer to Doug DeCinces at third.

McGwire dug in on the right side of the plate. On the first pitch, Sutton threw a fastball over the middle. McGwire turned well on the ball and got full arm extension. The ball carried on a line 380 feet into the left-field seats, giving the A's a 5–3 lead and giving McGwire his place in history.

As he rounded first, McGwire saw coach Rene Lachemann give it his home run kick, a special foot movement reserved for whenever someone on the A's hit a home run. That's when he knew it was gone. As he trotted around the bases, the 36,616 fans in Anaheim Stadium gave him a standing ovation that continued until he came out of the dugout for a curtain call. It was an unusual sight: a visiting player called

The Children's Hour

You might say that Mark McGwire's historic night on August 14, 1987 in Anaheim began and ended with kids.

Some ninety minutes before the start of the game, McGwire came out to hit baseballs off a hitting tee. In a front-row seat, a young boy, maybe about ten, screamed endlessly for his autograph. McGwire went about his work, ignoring the boy. During batting practice, the kid continued trying to get McGwire's attention. Finally, he yelled out, "If you won't sign my program, at least look at me."

McGwire laughed, turned around, and smiled at the kid, who went away the happiest boy in the ballpark.

And at the very end, it was another kid. This was Jason De La Garza, twelve, of Rancho Cucamonga. He caught the historic home run ball. He said he'd give it to McGwire, on the condition that he be allowed to enter the Oakland clubhouse to present it to him in person. The A's agreed, and the happy exchange took place. ◆

out for a bow. The home run was only his second of the month and sixth since the All-Star break.

The A's would eventually win the game, 7–6 in 12 innings on Davis's single. That would make the postgame celebration sweeter. In the clubhouse, the team presented McGwire with a bottle of champagne. But there was little time to enjoy it—the media waited for him in the interview room.

"I'm glad it's over," he said, "because now I don't have to think about any records. Nobody has to bring any records up."

It was wishful thinking on his part, since the next questioner asked about the 61 of Roger Maris.

"If somebody brings up the Maris record," he answered with fatigue, "it's still premature."

When he finally got out of the clubhouse, he spent the rest of the night in typical McGwire fashion. He went back to his hotel, ordered room service, then went to bed. The impact of his home run really hit him the next day, when he appeared at an autograph session at a local department store. The endless lines kept bringing him copies of the *Los Angeles Times* for him to sign. The paper had a big picture of the historic home run.

"When I was a kid, I read the *L.A. Times* sports page. Seeing my name and a picture of me on the front page, that really did it."

For the rest of the year, Ruth and Maris would lie quiet. McGwire didn't seriously threaten either of them. But he did end the season with a league-leading 49 home runs. He also established a new club record, beating Jackson's 47, set in 1969. To go along with his 49 round trippers, McGwire batted a healthy .289 and drove in 118 runs.

With one game left in the season, he had a chance to become only the eleventh player in baseball history to reach 50 home runs. But instead of playing, he got LaRussa's permission to go home. He wanted to be with his wife for the birth of Matthew, their first child. Typical McGwire.

In the off-season, he had to contend with his fame. He couldn't go anywhere without being bothered by autograph seekers or people wanting to talk. He confessed that he never wanted any public attention, and that he even wished at times that he had not had the glittery experiences of 1987. "Why me?" he asked.

"Why not?" an unblinking eye answered.

On the Record: Bob Watson

Former slugger Bob Watson was Mark McGwire's batting instructor on the Oakland A's in 1987.

Valenti: When did the pressure on McGwire start to build?

Watson: The hype started building up in that stretch in June when he hit those 14 home runs in about a month's span. The amazing thing about Mark's story is that in spring training, he wasn't playing. In fact, he barely made the ball club. We had a good friend of his, Rob Nelson, playing first base and we also had Ron Cey at first. And so he made the A's as an extra guy on the bench, a right-handed hitter with power. So we go into the first 11 or 12 games of the season, and we played awful. Rob Nelson got off to a terrible start. We sent Nelson back to Triple A and gave Mark a chance to play. He went out, did the best he could, and things started happening for him.

Valenti: Mark's a quiet guy. How difficult was the pressure for him?

Watson: One thing about Mark: he hides his emotions very well. He tries to stay on an even keel. He doesn't get too high, and he doesn't get too low. I think that was the biggest thing that helped him through his rookie year. All of the hype and all of the good things—he never let it get out of proportion. And when he struck out three or four times in a ball game, he didn't let that bother him. He took that as it came. For a youngster to do that, it's unbelievable. I would say Mark is quiet, but I wouldn't say he's a shy person. He's like most big guys. He's six-foot-five and 230 pounds, an imposing figure. And he just tries to be reserved. He comes from a good background. He's married. I think all of that was a big factor in his dealing with the pressures of his rookie year.

Valenti: What do you remember about his record-setting home run?

Watson: He hit it off Don Sutton of the Angels. He had kind of slowed down on his home runs before that, but he was swinging the bat well. It was a time where he didn't hit maybe two or three home runs for about three weeks. He had just tied the record in Seattle. And we went down to Anaheim. His family was there. I mean the whole McGwire clan. I remember him saying, "I'm going to hit this home run the first night in to get the pressure off." Lo and behold, he did. I was in the dugout when he hit it. The team had a two-fold reaction to the home run. One, we were happy for him, elated that he got the home run. That was a big amount of pressure on him and we knew it would relieve him, letting him go about the rest of the season putting together a good month of September, in case we were in the race. We were also happy for his family.

BOX SCORE: Anaheim Stadium, 8•14•87

Attendance: 36,616
Time of Game: 4:06

OAKLAND A's

Name	AB	R	H	RBI
Bernazard, 2B	6	1	2	0
Gallego, PR, 2B	0	1	0	0
Davis, RF	4	0	1	1
Canseco, LF	6	0	1	0
McGwire, 1B	6	3	3	2
Murphy, CF	4	1	2	0
Lansford, 3B	4	0	1	2
Steinbach, C	5	1	2	2
Griffin, SS	4	0	0	0
Polonia, DH	2	0	0	0
Henderson, PH	0	0	0	0
Jackson, DH	3	0	0	0
Totals	44	7	12	7

CALIFORNIA ANGELS

Name	AB	R	H	RBI
Pettis, CF	4	0	0	0
Miller, PH, RF	2	0	2	1
White, RF, CF	4	0	0	0
Downing, DH	5	1	1	1
DeCinces, 3B	5	1	2	0
Hendrick, LF	4	1	2	0
Jones, LF	1	0	0	0
Boone, C	5	1	1	2
Jack Howell, PH	1	0	0	0
Joyner, 1B	5	1	2	0
Schofield, 2B	3	1	2	1
Buckner, PH	1	0	0	0
McLemore, 2B	1	0	0	0
Polidor, SS	5	0	2	1
Totals	46	6	14	6

Team	1	2	3	4	5	6	7	8	9	10	11	12	
Oakland	0	0	0	0	3	2	0	0	1	0	0	1	7
California	0	3	0	0	0	1	1	0	1	0	0	0	6

Name	1P	H	R	ER	BB	SO
Young	7	9	5	5	1	1
Jay Howell	1+	2	1	1	0	0
Cadaret	⅔	1	0	0	0	0
Lamp	1⅓	0	0	0	2	1
Leiper	⅔	2	0	0	1	0
Rodriguez (W)	⅓	0	0	0	0	0
Eckersley (S)	1	0	0	0	0	0

Name	1P	H	R	ER	BB	SO
Sutton	5⅔	5	5	5	1	1
Finley	1⅓	0	0	0	0	2
Minton	1⅓	3	1	1	1	1
Lucas	1	0	0	0	1	0
Buice (L)	2⅔	4	1	1	0	3

Valenti: As a hitter, what did Mark have to learn once he arrived in the majors?
Watson: I had him in the minor leagues also. That was one more reason why I felt so good about it, to see him come from A Ball to the major leagues. Mark had something to show everybody, because he was our number one draft choice. So it's not like a fifteenth round draft choice, such as Jose Canseco, who came in without that pressure. So here's Mark, a guy you knew had talent. He's big and strong. If he got it together, he would hit 30 to 40 home runs in the big leagues. But he had a few things to learn. Like most kids today, he had what I call the

"Aluminum Bat Syndrome." We had to work with him on that. The syndrome is where the aluminum bat does all the work. With a wood bat, you have to have proper mechanics, and you have to stay up through the ball. You can't do anything incorrectly and count on the bat to make up the difference for you. So we had him go to the instructional league, which wasn't easy for him. Here's a guy who was Mr. Everything in school, made the Olympic team. Playing winter ball was a big hurdle for him to get over. But he's a hard worker, and the hard work paid off.

Valenti: Mark handled the hype well, but how did the ball club respond to it?

Watson: They were prepared for it, because the year before, they had the same amount of publicity, or even more, for Jose Canseco. So the ball club benefited, and Mark benefited, from Canseco's experience the year before. We came up with the idea of press conferences for Mark in each city. He ended up being hounded throughout the day, throughout his working period. That is something that we didn't correct with Canseco, and so we said this is the way we could correct it: have a press conference the first day into a city, and then the rest of the time, you talk to him after the ball game. He answered everybody's questions. He's a very cordial, polite young man.

14

REGGIE JACKSON
October 18, 1977

Once upon a time, there was a man who *owned* the World Series. He bought it at a heavy cost.

In the eighth inning of Game Six, 1977, the man uncoiled from a majestic swing. He watched while the white ball moved unmistakably bold into the black of the center-field seats.

And so it was that 51-degree October night as Reginald Martinez Jackson surveyed his kingdom. The home run was his third of the game, his third in as many swings. Wave after wave of rifted cheer descended like a friendly armada upon this Mr. October: REG-gie! REG-gie! REG-gie!

A chant. A mantra. A hypnotic invocation to a near god. A stream of words shooting into the pristine air from a fountain of life center-square in the heart: REG-gie! REG-gie! REG-gie!

As the tumultuous cheering filled the House That Ruth Built (and Jackson remodeled), Reggie soaked it in, a great showman bringing the house down. It was delivery on glory-goods dearly paid for earlier in the year.

The 1977 Yankees were in the toughest division in baseball, and their march to the world title was not an easy one. The Boston Red Sox, led by the hitting of Carlton Fisk and the pitching of Bill Campbell, kept the pressure on all year. The Sox weren't mathematically eliminated until the last day of the season, and they finished just two games off the pace.

But beyond the routine struggles of a chronic pennant race, the Yankees had to deal with some exotic trials as well, trials mainly of their own making. The team was a textbook study in abnormal psychology, or maybe a script from a Hitchcock movie. At its heart was a classic triangle.

George Steinbrenner to Billy Martin to Reggie Jackson. Dynamite to nitroglycerine to smoldering fuse. An around-the-horn lineup with devious variations too numerous to compute.

Steinbrenner rode helm as the grabbiest of hands-on owners. He was paying his team millions and assumed from that a license to set policy—on the field as well

Yankees 8, Dodgers 4

as off. Martin as field manager had to deal with Steinbrenner's interference from the top, player discontent from the bottom. A brilliant strategist but unstable personality, Martin was his own man, a man who hated interference, a street-wise brawler who could not be pushed. Jackson was the self-described swizzle stick that stirred things up, a man whose Christian ethics prevented hatred, but who nonetheless had little respect for his two bosses. His relationship with Martin bordered on the pathologic; he came as close as a player could to not being able to play for his manager.

Thrown into the explosive formula was the makeup of the rest of the Yankee team. There were a few calm and temperate oases, such as second baseman Willie Randolph and reserve catcher Fran Healy. Beyond that you found a neo-Freudian snake-tangle of egos, temperaments, pouters, crybabies, whiners, and mutterers—most all of whom could play the hell out of the game of baseball.

"I'm still the straw that stirs the drink. Not Munson, not nobody else on this club. . . [but] I got to make myself go to the ballpark. I don't want to go."

That was Jackson when things were caving in during July of '77, embroiled in controversy, crushed under the weight of his own oversized and damaged ego, like a beached whale unable to escape from its own bulk. How did he reach this point?

Who knows how he suffered as a child? The family was poor. His father ran a dry cleaning business and also made moonshine on the side to pick up a little extra money. Reggie's mother split from the family with his brothers and sisters, leaving him behind with his father. When his dad did time for moonshining, Reggie had to run the cleaning store. He learned the art of survival.

In high school, Reggie starred on the football team and was heavily recruited as a running back. He selected Arizona State University. His main interest was football. He only made the baseball team on a bet.

The story goes that he needed money for a date, so he bet a friend five bucks he could make the Sun Devils baseball squad—one of the country's best. Coach Frank Kush told him to bat, and Reggie hit some monstrous shots out of the park. He won the bet as well as a spot on the team, was eventually named college player of the year, and in 1966, signed with the Kansas City Athletics for an $85,000 bonus. Football was thrown for a loss.

The following year, he got his first taste of big-league action, appearing in 35 games in K.C. and hitting just .178 with one home run in 118 at bats. But beginning the next year, when the franchise moved to Oakland, Jackson came alive. Over the next eight years, he averaged 25 home runs and 98 RBIs, helping transform the team from losers to champions, with three consecutive World Titles from 1972-74. It would be baseball's last dynasty.

In 1976, Charlie Finley started dismantling the club and its well-paid stars. He traded Jackson to the Baltimore Orioles on April 2 in a blockbuster six-man trade (included in the deal were Ken Holtzman, Don Baylor, and Mike Torrez). Reggie put in his obligatory year with Baltimore, and following a 27-91-.277 season, opted for free agency. After cursory interest from a few clubs, Jackson smelled the Big, Big Money of Steinbrenner. After all the syllables were spoken, all the ink dried, and all the manufactured smiles were affixed for the cameras, Reggie had three million of George's dollars.

Steinbrenner took a lot of heat for paying that kind of money. Even Jackson himself admitted he was overpriced. But when the man stands before you and asks you to fill in the blanks on that bank note, what else can you do?

Jackson and Martin had their troubles from the start: dripping insinuations, spoken and unspoken dark words, a relationship weatherbeaten and wrinkled before it had a chance to begin. Martin would move him around in the batting order, anywhere from third to sixth. He wasn't satisfied with Jackson's hustle. Jackson popped off about it. Then one midsummer's day in Boston, things erupted.

Playing right field in Fenway Park, Jackson played a ball—in Martin's opinion, anyway—nonchalantly. Martin yanked Jackson in mid-inning on national TV. The camera followed Reggie into the dugout, where the two men started yelling at each other. Martin then lost it. Out of control, he charged Jackson. The manager of baseball's proudest franchise was a total wild man, in need of restraints.

The following day, general manager Gabe Paul called a meeting with Martin and Jackson, and according to Jackson, the manager taunted him, saying, "I'll make you fight me, boy."

The affair made headlines across the country, and from then on, the Yankee soap opera became a running entertainment, a running joke, and an embarrassment to baseball.

The immature display would also have another effect, felt later down the line. It would ensure that when the Yankees finally did win the whole thing, the smiles and hugs in that winning locker room—Billy embracing Reggie, Reggie embracing Billy, Steinbrenner praising both of them—would mean about as much as a million three-dollar bills.

So for the rest of the year, the Good Ship New York steered its way through the dangerous icebergs of its own paranoiac creation. Martin ragged Jackson. Jackson put down Thurman Munson. Lou Piniella questioned Martin's ability. Steinbrenner castigated his team for lack of heart.

But they won.

Say anything else about these Yankees, but you must also say that they won. And those three words can excuse almost—almost—any sin, can relieve almost any dose of pain.

They won.

They won because of the unyielding will of Jackson. They won because of the managing of Martin. We must never forget that about Martin. Whatever else he is personally, within the white lines he is an astute and at times ingenious field boss.

So the Yankees won.

They won the playoffs against Kansas City, earning a spot in the World Series for the second year in a row. With it came the chance to make up for the shameful four-game sweep suffered at the hands of the Cincinnati Reds in 1976. This year, they would be ready. Hardened by the millstone hours of a stomach-churning year, they would be ready. For true to form, even in the World Series, even with the chance for baseball's greatest honor, the Yankees feuded.

The Yanks took three of the first four games, with the Dodgers staying alive at home in Game Five with a 10–4 victory. Jackson would homer off the right-field foul pole in his last at bat in the eighth inning.

But as usual, the big news was off the field. That week's issue of *Time* magazine contained a revealing story on the Yankees. The story alleged that Munson and Piniella had gone to Steinbrenner, saying the club was racked with dissension and urging that Martin be fired. The article also claimed that Jackson had recently presented Steinbrenner with an ultimatum: either dump Martin or he [Jackson] would leave.

For the record, Munson denied recommending that Martin be fired, asking angrily, "How long does this crap go on?" Jackson also called the story a lie. Piniella, approached after Game Five for comment, told reporters to stay away, screaming, "No more controversial questions!" Jackson and Martin reportedly had a blowout over the article, and Gabe Paul had to call a press conference to "clear the air." Paul essentially stood behind Martin, after which Martin boasted, "I think we found out who's running this club. I'll stand on my record."

Martin—a believer in absolutes, in blacks or whites, a man who believed that enemies were waiting at every turn to trip him up—claimed that Steinbrenner had planted the *Time* story to pave the way for his eventual firing. He was, in the words of writer Frank Deford, ". . .a kind of Walter Scott knight-errant cast loose into the strange modern world of compromise and convention, where duels are frowned upon, and damsels in distress can be put on waivers."

Before the team headed back to New York for Game Six, there was one more controversy. Ed Figueroa, pouting over his removal from the starting rotation during the Series, demanded to be put back in or he would jump the club. The Yankees called his bluff and gave him permission to go home to Puerto Rico. Figueroa tucked tail and stayed in uniform for the last game but promised he would demand a trade after the season was over.

Game Six, a night game, began before 56,407 in cool but comfortable weather. Joe DiMaggio threw out the first ball. Through three innings, the Dodgers led 3–2. In his first at bat, Jackson walked on four pitches. In the fourth, after a leadoff single by Munson, he lined the first pitch from Burt Hooton—a down-and-in fastball—into the right-field stands, giving the Yankees a lead they would never surrender. In the fifth, with Randolph on first and two outs, Jackson hit his second home run off reliever Elias Sosa, again on the first pitch. The ball, another low, inside fastball, came off his bat like a tee shot before landing in the lower right-field stands. That made it 7–3 Yankees.

Reggie came up for his last time in the eighth, leading off the inning against knuckleballer Charlie Hough. Hough came in with a knuckler that, as they say, didn't knuckle. Jackson timed it perfectly, and hit a gigantic home run 450 feet away into the center-field bleachers. It was another first-pitch home run. Counting his home run in Game Five, his walk on four pitches in the second inning, and the three first-pitch home runs, Jackson had hit four home runs in four swings. Undoubtedly, it was the greatest display of slugging in the seventy-four-year history of the Fall Classic.

The three-in-one game tied Babe Ruth, who did it twice against the Cardinals, in 1926 and in 1928. The home run also set the record of five in a single World Series.

The fans went crazy. As Jackson rounded first, Dodger first baseman Steve Garvey applauded—into his glove so no one would see. As Jackson took his place in right field for the top of the ninth, the crowd began its now famous cheer: "REG-gie! REG-gie! REG-gie!"

Just Like the Babe

When Reggie Jackson hit three home runs in Game Six of the 1977 World Series, he wasn't the first. He was the first to do it on three consecutive at bats, but Babe Ruth had already accomplished the feat itself twice: in the fourth game of the 1926 Series against the St. Louis Cardinals, and in the fourth game of the 1928 Classic, also against the Cards.

The *Sporting News* researched the two games and found some interesting similarities between Jackson's big night and the Bambino's 1926 extravaganza.

Both men were thirty-one years old. Both played right field. Both threw and batted left. Both were members of the Yankees. Each man had four official plate appearances. Each scored four runs. The third homer of each went to center field. The games left each with seven World Series round trippers.

Probably the biggest difference is the fact that Jackson's night helped win the Series. When Ruth hit his three-in-one in 1926, the Yankees lost in seven games. ◆

The Dodgers pushed across a run in the top of the ninth. Then with two outs, Lee Lacy, pinch-hitting for Hough, tried to bunt. He popped it up into the hands of starting and winning pitcher Mike Torrez. The Yankees had their first World Championship since beating the Giants in 1962.

After the out, thousands of fans displayed their idiocy by racing onto the field, tearing up home plate and the turf. Players had to run for their lives to reach the dugouts. For the top of the ninth, Jackson put on a helmet for protection. He needed it. After the final out, he sprinted across center with his old running-back moves toward the visiting third-base dugout. He thought this would allow him to slip off the field easier. It didn't. A mob stopped him. He then started bowling over people. He went back toward right, swinging his fists at the people trying to grab him. He floored several more people before making it back into the locker room.

Torrez said now he understood why they called him Mr. October. It's interesting how that name came about. Late during the regular season, Munson—during another one of his feuds with Jackson—called him Mr. October in derision and with a total lack of respect. Now, people were using it as a title, a badge of honor.

Garvey probably offered the best explanation of Reggie's spectacular night. "I think he was able to release all his emotional tension of the entire season in one game."

Steinbrenner walked through the clubhouse with champagne, praising his players, his manager, and himself. Asked about how a team that had won the World Series could be so disgruntled, Steinbrenner replied, "After this, they got to *want* to remain a Yankee."

Martin, Steinbrenner, and Jackson posed for the photographers. In a joint TV interview, Jackson said, "Anybody fights you, skip, he's got to fight both of us."

Martin replied, "And anybody who fights you got to fight the both of us."

Some thought this was touching. Others almost lost their lunches. Amidst all this, G.M. Paul crumpled into a chair.

"Right now, I feel like I'm a hundred and three."

On the Record: Reggie Jackson

The following is an excerpt from Reggie Jackson's autobiography Reggie *written with Mike Lupica. Copyright © 1984 by Reggie Jackson and Mike Lupica. Reprinted by permission of Villard Books, a Division of Random House, Inc.*

There were really two World Series that year against the Dodgers. First there was the one played over the first five games. We led, 3–2 after that one. It was the Series, but there was nothing memorable or dramatic or startling about those games...

Who could have known that the "second" World Series of 1977, the one played in Game Six, was going to be mine?

People still want to know what I remember best about the sixth game; people will probably always want to know. Was it the chant after that last one? Was it the unbelievable "REG-gie!" chant after the last one? Was it getting showered with confetti out in right field when I took my position in the ninth?

I remember *everything*.

I remember batting practice. The three dingers, off Burt Hooton, Elias Sosa and Charlie Hough. Running the bases after that last one, off Hough. The winning. The champagne. Finding out that only Babe Ruth had ever hit three home runs in a World Series game. Finding out that no one had ever hit five in a Series. Having the writers remind me that I had hit four homers on four consecutive swings, going back to Game Five.

Everything. Don Larsen had his perfect game in 1956. I had mine in '77. Three swings. Three dingers...

By the time the game started, I hadn't spilled any of my adrenaline. Still had a full tank. Still felt pumped up. Even when Hooton walked me on four straight pitches. I wasn't deflated. I still felt *good*. I was going to be ready when he threw me a strike.

He threw me a strike in the fourth. First pitch to me. Nobody out. Thurman on first. I figured Hooton would try to pitch me up and in. That's always been the book on me. Get it up and in. Don't let me extend my arms. Well, Hooton got it up but not in far enough. I got it. I got it a little on the end of the bat, but I got it. It was a line drive to right, and the only thing I worried about was that it might not stay up long enough. It did. We were ahead 4–3.

One.

I was still in batting practice; that is exactly the way I felt. When I came up in the fifth, after we'd scored a couple more times, Hooton was out of the game and Elias Sosa, another right-hander, came in to pitch to me. I stood there next to the plate and watched him warm up and I was thinking, "Please, God, let him hurry up. Let him hurry up and finish warming up so I don't lose this feeling I have." When he was done, I purposely got into the batter's box late so he didn't see where I was standing and start thinking; I just wanted him to throw a strike on the first pitch, try to get ahead.

Attendance: 56,407
Time of Game: 2:18

LOS ANGELES DODGERS

Name	AB	R	H	RBI
Lopes, 2B	4	0	1	0
Russell, SS	3	0	0	0
Smith, RF	4	2	1	1
Cey, 3B	3	1	1	0
Garvey, 1B	4	1	2	2
Baker, LF	4	0	1	0
Monday, CF	4	0	1	0
Yeager, C	3	0	1	0
Davalillo, PH	1	0	1	1
Hooton, P	2	0	0	0
Sosa, P	0	0	0	0
Rau, P	0	0	0	0
Goodson, PH	1	0	0	0
Hough, P	0	0	0	0
Lacy, PH	1	0	0	0
Totals	34	4	9	4

NEW YORK YANKEES

Name	AB	R	H	RBI
Rivers, CF	4	0	2	0
Randolph, 2B	4	1	0	0
Munson, C	4	1	1	0
Jackson, RF	3	4	3	5
Chambliss, 1B	4	2	2	2
Nettles, 3B	4	0	0	0
Piniella, LF	3	0	0	1
Dent, SS	2	0	0	0
Torrez, P	3	0	0	0
Totals	31	8	8	8

Team	1	2	3	4	5	6	7	8	9		
Dodgers	2	0	1	0	0	0	0	0	1		4
Yankees	0	2	0	3	2	0	0	1	X		8

Name	IP	H	R	ER	BB	SO
Hooton (L)	3	3	4	4	1	1
Sosa	1⅔	3	3	3	1	0
Rau	1⅓	0	0	0	0	1
Hough	2	2	1	1	0	3

Name	IP	H	R	ER	BB	SO
Torrez (W)	9	9	4	2	2	6

He threw me a fastball right down Broadway. I call them mattress pitches because if you're feeling right you can lay all over 'em. This was the hardest ball I hit that night, a screaming line drive into right. The one off Hooton worried me because I'd hit it on the end of the bat. The one off Sosa worried me because it was hit so hard I was afraid it might dip short of the stands.

It didn't.

Two.

The crowd really started to come alive then. "REG-gie! REG-gie!" they chanted. We were winning the game that could give us the first Yankee World Championship since 1962. It was only the fifth inning. I had swung the bat just twice, and I already had two dingers. The people in the stadium knew there was a chance for some history.

"REG-gie! REG-gie!"

Finally, it was the bottom of the eighth. We were ahead 7–4.

Tommy Lasorda, the Dodger manager, had brought Hough, a knuckleballer, in to pitch. I stood watching him warm up, and I wanted to yell over to Lasorda, who I like, and say, "Tommy, don't you know how I love to hit knucklers?"

On the first pitch if he got anywhere near the plate, I knew I'd have a good pass at it. The crowd was insane with noise as I dug in. They were expecting a home run. They wanted a home run. They were chanting "REG-gie." Sometimes if you focus in on the crowd noise too much it can become distracting. Didn't matter this night. A plane landing in center field wouldn't have mattered this night.

I just wanted Charlie Hough to throw me one damn knuckleball. I had nothing to lose. Even if I struck out, I had nothing to lose.

Hough threw me a knuckler. Didn't knuckle. I crushed it nearly 500 feet into the black, those beautiful empty black seats in dead center. I found out later that I was only the second man ever to do that in Yankee Stadium.

That wouldn't have mattered a whole lot to me if I'd known at the time. As I began to move around the bases, I felt so. . .vindicated. Completely vanquished. When I passed first, I smiled at Steve Garvey and he smiled back; he'd tell me later he was so excited for me he was pounding a fist inside his mitt so no one would see. I felt so light on my feet, floating on the noise. It was the happiest moment of my career. It *is* the happiest moment of my career. I had been on a ball and chain all year, at least in my mind. I had heard so many negatives about Reggie Jacskon. I had been the villain. Couldn't do this. Couldn't do that. And now suddenly I didn't care what my manager or my teammates had said or what the media had written.

I had three. We were going to win it all. I know I ran hard around the bases, took them fast, but when I think back, the trip seems to have taken an hour. God it was a great moment. A hundred million people had seen that Reggie Jackson was okay, no matter what they'd heard.

I feel like God was with me as I ran the bases. I believe *He* was saying: This is a good man. He survived and triumphed. I don't feel silly or embarrassed saying that. I believe it is true.

BUCKY DENT
October 2, 1978

Yankees 5,
Red Sox 4

15

The full understanding of Bucky Dent's home run can only come from pure darkness, that is, Boston darkness—through the eyes of Red Sox fans.

The Red Sox have not won the World Series since 1918. They have won five pennants since then and have lost four World Series, each in seven games. They lost the American League's first playoff 8–3 to the Cleveland Indians at Fenway Park in 1948. They lost the pennant the next year to the Yankees on the final day of the season. In 1950, they were on their way to a title when Ted Williams smashed his elbow in the All-Star game in Chicago. In 1972, they lost a title by a half game because of a season-opening players' strike.

Yet Red Sox fans have remained the most passionate in baseball. They are different from, say, Chicago Cubs fans, who root for a team of Charlie Browns. Theirs is a light, carefree, comic-strip love. Boston's love is heavy. Not Charlie Brown, but Nathaniel Hawthorne brooding in his home in the Berkshires of Massachusetts on such an imponderable as the Ultimate Sin. The Red Sox were baseball's first dynasty, but after the selling of Babe Ruth, Boston baseball has had to see into the heart of darkness of the baseball soul. What has emerged are the nation's most astute and fatalistic fans.

The 1978 New York Yankees were coming off a World Championship, but also the storm of what had by then become baseball's most popular sideshow: Reggie hating Billy hating George hating everybody. The Red Sox, meanwhile, made some moves. They picked up Yankee postseason hero Mike Torrez, traded for speedster Jerry Remy, and in what was called The Trade in Boston, obtained fireballing twenty-three-year-old righty Dennis Eckersley. With a frightening offensive powerhouse and a rotation of Torrez, Eckersley, Luis Tiant, and Bill Lee, they had the best talent in baseball.

And they opened that way.

After an 11-9 April, the Red Sox went 41-14 in May and June, opening up a nine-game lead by the All-Star Game. They had the best winning percentage in all of baseball, and were winning with bunts, home runs, pitching, and defense. They had played nearly .700 ball for half a season and seemed certain to win if only they played .500. They did that, playing at a .524 clip in the second half. But who would have counted on the Yankees to play .700 in the second half?

In the first half, the Bronx Bummers feuded, scratched at each other's eyes, poked their own flesh with red-hot pokers, and scrubbed the wounds with volcanic pumice.

First-half injuries to such key players as Dent, Thurman Munson, Willie Randolph, Mickey Rivers, and Catfish Hunter left New York without a representative team for the early months. The mess culminated on July 24, both collapsing on itself and rising out of its own ashes. That's when George Steinbrenner fired Martin (it was announced as a forced resignation). In his parting shot, a teary-eyed Billy blasted Reggie Jackson and pointed a finger at Steinbrenner's conviction on a felony rap.

Bob Lemon, the soft-spoken antithesis of Martin's exposed raw nerve, was named manager. He looked into a mirror and saw in the second half the reflection—or mirror image—of Boston's first half.

The season flip-flopped. The Yankees healed and played .700 ball. The Sox got injured. They suffered 34 separate injuries, losing over 200 player-games. Carlton Fisk cracked his ribs. Remy smashed his wrist. Dwight Evans was seriously beaned (a Mike Parrott pitch cracked his helmet) and suffered continued dizzy spells. Rick Burleson lost three weeks to ankle ligament damage. Torrez's hand went numb, Carl Yastrzemski's back went out. Bill Campbell, who the year before saved 33 games, tore a shoulder tendon. Butch Hobson had bone chips doing a dead man's float in his elbow—more chips than Billy Martin had excuses for getting fired.

From July 20–28, Boston lost 9 of 10 games. August was better, at 19-10, but in the first two weeks of September, specifically, September 1–16, the bottom dropped out. The Sox went 3-13 in those games, hit .184 as a team, were outscored 86-43, and made a whopping 31 errors. At the black heart of this horrendous stretch was a four-game set at Fenway Park now known as the Boston Massacre. The Yankees came into Boston on September 7, four games out. They left four games later with a tie, and all the momentum. The Sox were pummeled by scores of 15–3, 13–2, 7–0, and 7–4; they made 12 errors, and were outhit 67–21. It would be impossible for a team—any team—to play worse baseball. But it was staggering that a talented team such as this could play this way, at home, where they were a .720 for the year.

The recollection of the stretch of games from the All-Star break to the end of the Boston Massacre is a schizophrenic, word-salad memory. When smoke from the Massacre lifted, the Red Sox found themselves 4½ games behind the Yankees. A win in New York made it 3½, and then just as incredibly, this team that had been so hopeless played once more as they did in the first half. The Red Sox won 12 of their last 14, including 8 in a row. On the season's last day, Tiant shut out the Toronto Blue Jays at Fenway, while Rick Waits beat the Yankees in New York, 9–2. People forget. The Yankees, not the Red Sox, folded in the stretch.

A one-game playoff would be played the next day at Fenway Park. Zimmer named Torrez to start. Lemon countered with his ace, Ron Guidry. The Red Sox and Yankees in a one-game showdown. The culmination of baseball history.

"This is what they pay me for," said Mike Torrez.

October 2 was not a good day in Red Sox history. Some twenty-nine years earlier, they lost the pennant on the last day to the Yankees at the Stadium. Torrez was reminded of this. He replied, "History owes us one."

As the game began, the fans looked for any advantage. Yankee rooters pointed out that their team would have extra incentive in beating ex-mate Torrez. Boston fans pointed out that the only three losses for Guidry in his remarkable 24-3 year had been to pitchers with the first name of Mike.

The Red Sox got an early 1–0 lead on Carl Yastrzemski's home run down the right-field line in the second. They were on Guidry. In the third, George Scott doubled deep off the wall on center, but did not score. In the sixth, Burleson doubled. Remy bunted him to third, and he came home on Jim Rice's single, making it 2–0. Fred Lynn, up with two outs, hit one deep into the right-field corner. Piniella lost it in the sun but made a fortuitous recovery to make the grab and save a run.

Torrez, meanwhile, had a brilliant two-hit shutout going through six innings. But in the seventh, with one out, Chris Chambliss and Roy White singled. Jim Spencer, pinch-hitting for Brian Doyle, flied out. That brought Dent to the plate. Dent had managed just four home runs all year. In the last 20 games, he had hit an anemic .140. Lemon was out of middle infielders. He had just hit for Doyle. Randolph was injured. Dent would have to hit for himself.

Torrez's first pitch came in for a ball. Dent fouled the second pitch off his right foot and collapsed to the ground in pain. The trainer came out to freeze the foot. Dent struggled to his feet, shaking off the pain.

Mickey Rivers then made the biggest play of the game—from the on-deck circle.

The roots of it go back to batting practice. Rivers advised Dent to hit with a Roy White model. Dent agreed. But unknowingly, Dent had slightly cracked the handle in batting practice; the crack, however, was covered by tape and could not easily be seen. When Dent got to his feet, he walked to shake off the pain. Rivers came to him from the on-deck circle. Rivers then noticed the crack in the bat. How did he notice? He had used the bat in the fifth, bouncing to third, and saw the crack then. Dent had flied out and popped out using the faulty stick.

Rivers rushed back to the dugout, pulled out one of his sticks, and gave it to Dent. Why was Rivers so eager to give Dent this particular bat? It was corked. At least that's what Rivers told Torrez at the Yankees' Old-Timers Game in 1987. Rivers asked Torrez, "Did Bucky ever tell you?"

"Tell me what?" Torrez replied.

"You mean to tell me that Bucky didn't tell you I gave him my bat, and my bat was corked?" Rivers revealed.

Dent confirms that exchange took place, but, unlike Torrez, he says Rivers was joking.

A game to be decided. A pennant on the line. A possibly illegal bat.

Jackson yelled from the dugout, "Hit the tin, Bucky," referring to the Green Monster in left.

ANNOUNCER: "Here's the pitch. Dent lofts a fly to left. Yaz moves back. Waiting. It's gone! It just made the screen in left!"

Dent's flyball, aided by the wind, just settled in the netting above the Green Monster. Yaz looked like he would have a routine play. Instead, the Yankees took a 3–2 lead. Torrez was shocked. Unglued, he walked Rivers. Zimmer lifted Torrez for Bob Stanley, who gave up an RBI double to Munson, making it 4–2 New York.

The Yanks made it 5–2 in the eighth when Jackson hit his 27th homer deep into the center-field bleachers. But true to their character, the Red Sox would not die.

As they had in the regular season, they came back. Off Goose Gossage in the bottom of the eighth, they pushed across two runs. Remy doubled. Yaz singled him in, then came in himself on singles by Fisk and Lynn. It was 5–4, with the tying run on second and just one out. But Gossage got Hobson to fly to right and fanned George Scott. After Andy Hassler and Dick Drago held the Yankees in the ninth, the Sox would have one more chance.

With one out, Burleson worked Gossage for a walk. Remy then hit a sinking line drive, which Piniella lost in the murderous sun field in right. Now, understand. Piniella had just lost a tricky liner in the sun. Once the ball landed, the reaction time would be close to nonexistent. In the back of his mind was Remy's speed. If the ball got by him, Burleson would score.

The ball landed. Piniella stuck out his glove—thrust it out randomly, on a guess, on a hope,—and the ball bounced into it. He didn't catch the ball. The ball caught him. Burleson, playing it conservatively, held at second in case Lou made the play. Rice flied to deep center, and Burleson tagged and went to third. It came down to Gossage vs. Yastrzemski, one-on-one.

The stands were up. On the first pitch, Yaz lofted a towering pop fly to the left side of the infield. Burleson, head down, trotted home. Nettles squeezed it.

In the five-second arc of a pop fly, the legacy of a baseball team from Boston, Massachusetts, was apotheosized. This pop-up was the summation of an ideal, the ideal of a simple fly—just a bat hitting a ball, really—so accurately summing up a franchise's knowledge of itself. A hit by Yastrzemski could not have had this effect. It was as if this out had been chosen by destiny to punctuate a remarkable game whose seeds had been sown fifty-nine years earlier with the sale of Babe Ruth.

Seen in this way, the outcome of this game was no accident, for accidents are imperfect: it *had* to end the way it did.

After the game, Jackson visited the Boston locker room, shaking hands with everyone.

"Both of us should be champions."

Later, someone asked him if the Yanks could have won with Billy Martin. Without a second's pause, Reggie yelled back, "No."

On the Record: Bucky Dent

Valenti: What was the feeling coming into the game, especially facing ex-mate Mike Torrez, who the year before had done so well for the Yankees in postseason play?

Dent: I think our biggest concern was having to go play in Fenway itself, in a one-game playoff. If you lose, you go home. I think we were more concerned with that than worrying about who was pitching. It was such a pressure game. The two teams had played so well all year, and to come down and have to play each other in Fenway was tough. It's a difficult park for the visitors. The pitcher didn't matter. What mattered was the loser had to go home.

Valenti: What was the mood of the club going into Boston that day?

Dent: I think we were a little shocked. We knew we could have put it away on the last day by beating Cleveland, and we didn't do it. But I felt like the team was loose and very determined. It was a very determined ball club, a team that felt

Thank the *White* Sox, Too

The Yankees, of course, had much to be thankful for regarding the Red Sox in 1978. But a tip of the hat could very well have been in order for the *White* Sox.

The three key performers of the playoff showdown at Fenway Park had recent Chicago ties.

First was superhero Bucky Dent. Dent had been the White Sox shortstop for several years before coming to New York. Second was Dent's roomie in Chicago—none other than Goose Gossage. Gossage was actually used as a starter in the Windy City, before hitting megastardom as the fearsome Goose in Gotham.

Finally, there was Bob Lemon. The White Sox had fired Lemon as their manager on June 30. A mere twenty-five days later, after George Steinbrenner axed Billy Martin, Lemon found himself at the helm in New York.

Under Lemon, the Yankees went 48-20 to stage a startling comeback, topped in baseball history only by the 1914 Miracle Boston Braves and the 1951 Giants. ◆

like it couldn't get beat. I personally was struggling a little bit at the plate. I missed most of the year with a hamstring pull. But I guess I picked a good time to come out of it.

Valenti: The Red Sox went up 2–0. People forget Torrez was working on a two-hitter through six innings. How did he look to you early on?

Dent: He was throwing the ball pretty good. We had some opportunities to score. In the first inning, right off the bat, Rivers got on, stole second base with nobody out. I think a couple times Munson came up with men in scoring position and struck out early in the game. But Mike was throwing the ball well, and so was Guidry. It's just that Yastrzemski hit the home run to put them up. But we just felt like if we stayed close, that we were going to score some runs. There wasn't much talk on the bench at that point. It was more like everybody was concentrating on what they had to do. We knew that we didn't want to give them any more, and if we held them right there, something was going to happen. We just could feel that, that something was going to happen.

Valenti: In the seventh inning, the Yankees put a couple of guys on, then you came to the plate with two outs. Before you got up to the plate, Bucky, did you have any feeling whatsoever that anything unusual was going to happen? Or was it just another at bat for you?

Dent: It really was just another at bat. I knew that we had an opportunity to score some runs, and I was just looking for a pitch that I could drive, something that I could hit hard someplace and hopefully knock in a run or two.

Valenti: On the pitch before, you fouled it off your ankle. You went down in pain. And I guess the trainer had to come out and actually freeze it, is that right?

Dent: Yes. I had had some problems with my ankle all year. You know, I fouled a ball off it in spring training and developed a blood clot. I had worn a shin guard most of the time after that. And I had taken it off, because I hadn't fouled a ball off my foot in quite some time. And it just so happened that I hit one off my ankle. I looked around a little bit. The trainer came out, started putting some freeze on it. That's when Rivers came over to me and he said, "Hey, Homey, you're using the wrong bat. You're using the one that's cracked." We had only had two of that model, because our bat orders hadn't come in, and we were using the same bat. I don't know for sure which model it was. I think it was a Mac 44. We had broken one in batting practice, and it had a hairline crack just under the tape, and he came over to me and he says, "Here. You're using the wrong bat." He says, "That's the one that's cracked."

Valenti: How did he notice that?

Dent: Well, we only had two, like I said. One was newer than the one we had in batting practice. He gave me a bat and said, "Here, take this one. This is the one that's not cracked." I didn't think nothing of it. He just gave it to me, and I said, "Okay." I got back up there, and that was it.

Valenti: Mike Torrez said Rivers told him at the Yankees' Old-Timers Game in 1987 that he gave you one of his bats, and it was corked.

Dent: Nooo! That's crap! (*laughs*) That's not true! (*still laughing*) Me and Mickey were joking around. At the Old-Timers Game last year, we started joking, and I said, "Mickey, it's a wonder somebody hasn't said we used a corked bat that day." And we started laughing.

Valenti: Torrez was telling the story as if he believed it.

Dent: Ah, no. That bat wasn't corked.

Valenti: Was it a Mickey Rivers model?

Dent: To tell you the truth, I don't know which model it was. I think it was Rivers' model. But the bat—it wasn't corked. If it was, I didn't know it.

Valenti: What about the pitch you hit out?

Dent: It was a fastball down and in. That's the pitch I could hit well. He made a mistake. When I hit the ball, I couldn't tell how far it would carry. There's kind of a shadow on the wall at that time, and when I hit it, I thought it was going to hit the top of the wall. I really didn't know it had gone out until I had rounded first base and saw the second-base umpire signal that the ball had gone out. I knew I had hit it pretty good, at least good enough to get up on the top of the wall. I never did see it go out. My feeling was that it put us ahead. I didn't realize at the time what kind of impact it was going to have, because you don't think of things like that when they happen. We were only up 3–2, and anything can happen in Fenway. It didn't sink in until after we had won, and we were on our way to Kansas City.

Valenti: Anything can happen in Fenway, and almost did. The Red Sox came back with a couple of runs after they got down, 5–2.

Dent: Yes, they did come back. The thing I'll never forget is Yastrzemski coming up with two outs in the bottom of the ninth and Rick Burleson on third base and Gossage standing there on the mound. And we're going, "Well, this is it." I kept saying to myself, "This is the whole game, right here." Goose threw a fastball. Yastrzemski swung and popped it up. He just missed it. He had a pretty good

BOX SCORE: Fenway Park, 10·2·78

Attendance: 32,925
Time of Game: 2:52

NEW YORK YANKEES

Name	AB	R	H	RBI
Rivers, CF	2	1	1	0
Blair, PH, CF	1	0	1	0
Munson, C	5	0	1	1
Piniella, RF	4	0	1	0
Jackson, DH	4	1	1	1
Nettles, 3B	4	0	0	0
Chambliss, 1B	4	1	1	0
White, LF	3	1	1	0
Thomasson, LF	0	0	0	0
Doyle, 2B	2	0	0	0
Spencer, PH	1	0	0	0
Stanley, 2B	1	0	0	0
Dent, SS	4	1	1	3
Guidry, P	0	0	0	0
Gossage, P	0	0	0	0
Totals	35	5	8	5

BOSTON RED SOX

Name	AB	R	H	RBI
Burleson, SS	4	1	1	0
Remy, 2B	4	1	2	0
Rice, LF	5	0	1	1
Yastrzemski, LF	5	2	2	2
Fisk, C	3	0	1	0
Lynn, CF	4	0	1	1
Hobson, DH	4	0	1	0
Scott, 1B	4	0	2	0
Brohamer, 3B	1	0	0	0
Bailey, PH	1	0	0	0
Duffy, 3B	0	0	0	0
Evans, PH	1	0	0	0
Torrez, P	0	0	0	0
Stanley, P	0	0	0	0
Hassler, P	0	0	0	0
Drago, P	0	0	0	0
Totals	36	4	11	4

Team	1	2	3	4	5	6	7	8	9	
Yankees	0	0	0	0	0	0	4	1	0	5
Red Sox	0	1	0	0	0	1	0	2	0	4

Name	1P	H	R	ER	BB	SO
Guidry (W)	6⅓	6	2	2	1	5
Gossage	2⅔	5	2	2	1	2

Name	1P	H	R	ER	BB	SO
Torrez (L)	6⅔	5	4	4	3	4
Stanley	⅓	2	1	1	0	0
Hassler	1⅔	1	0	0	0	2
Drago	⅓	0	0	0	0	0

swing at that ball. Nettles caught the ball. Afterward, the locker room was total chaos. There must have been a thousand people in there. It was almost like, "We did it. We finally did it." It was just a tremendous feeling.

Valenti: Someone asked Reggie Jackson if the team could have won if Billy Martin had stayed on as manager, and he answered a very emphatic "No." What's your feeling on that?

Dent: I don't know. There was so much going on. What happened to me when Martin got fired, I was hurt. I had a hamstring pull. They had sent me to Florida [for reha-bilitation]. So I wasn't around when he got fired. When Lemon came in, he kind of like just soothed everybody down. He told us to just go out and play. He came in and he said to us "You guys were World Champions last year. You're capable of doing it again. Just go play." It was a soothing type thing.

Valenti: What do you say to Mike Torrez when you see him now?

Dent: I see Mike. I've talked to him at the Old-Timers Game. We joke about it a little bit. I saw George Scott a couple of years ago at a card show, and we started laughing over it, joking around.

Valenti: How has the home run made a difference for you?

Dent: Naturally, it's made me a household name in Boston. Everybody remembers it. Everybody that reminds me of it knew where they were at the time. They say, "Geez, you know, I was driving down the street when you hit that home run." Which is something you don't realize when it happens, but only later when you start talking to people. I find it to be kind of interesting.

If I had any guts, I'd retire right now.

16

GEORGE BRETT
July 24, 1983

Royals 5, Yankees 4

If men play baseball long enough, everything that is possible on a diamond will some-day occur. Everything. Even as bizarre a play as George Brett's famous "Pine Tar" home run.

Little did Brett realize that when he hit his ninth-inning home run off Goose Gossage to—seemingly—beat the Yankees, he would set off one of the most bizarre sequences ever to end a game (or not end a game). It involved the measuring of a bat, unleashed screams, a total loss of perspective, wrestling matches, and the chasing of a ball player by security guards up the runway into the locker room. It was something worthy of a Fellini movie, or maybe stylized Kubrick—the closeup stare where the madman knows more than we do.

For Brett, it would be just another eventful day shared with the New York Yankees, a team that elicited the best, and most unusual, in him. For three straight years from 1976 to 1978, the Royals won the American League West crown, only to lose to the Yankees in the playoffs. In the '76 playoffs, Brett hit .444 in the five games. His dramatic three-run homer in the eighth inning in the final game tied the score. But Chris Chambliss was even more dramatic with his ninth-inning home run to win the pennant.

In 1977, the Royals lost again in five games. Brett batted .300, but he's remembered mostly for his fight with Graig Nettles at the third-base bag after a Brett triple and Nettles's hard tag. In '78, Brett slugged .389 and slammed three home runs in the third game—only to see his team lose the game, 6–5, and the series, 3–1. The three years of defeat went down hard.

Even when the Royals swept the Yankees in the 1980 playoffs, there was still a resi-due of emptiness from past failures against New York. In the '80 playoffs, Brett clinched the series winner with a mammoth three-run homer off Gossage at Yankee Stadium in the seventh inning of Game Three, keying a 4–2 K.C. victory and a World Series berth.

So, well before that July afternoon in 1983, Brett already had a colorful history involv-ing New York. Just as he had an interesting journey from unknown rookie to superstar.

Brett's development as a hitter was just that—a development, the result of deliberate action and hard work. He was made a hitter, not born one. He came from a baseball family, but growing up as a kid in Hermosa Beach in southern California, he was more interested in surfing than in baseball. When George was twelve, his seventeen-year-old brother Ken signed as a pitcher with the Red Sox for $85,000. Two years later, Ken made history for Boston as the youngest man ever to pitch in the World Series.

When Ken went off to the Instructional League in Florida in 1965, young George looked to brother John for guidance. John was seven years older and was himself signed by the Red Sox, though he didn't get far. John, recognizing his kid brother's talent, urged young George to drop his surfboard and begin practicing. Goodbye, Endless Wave.

"John was a bigger influence on me than anyone. He was not the best ball player in the family, but he wanted to play more than any of us," Brett said. "He forced me to practice for hours. John had great desire. Ken was different. If he hadn't received a big bonus for signing, I think he would have stayed home and just become a beach bum."

John's work ethic rubbed off on George, and in 1971 the Royals drafted him on the second round. Ken had urged Boston to sign George, but the Sox weren't interested, not believing Ken that his brother was that good.

George was only a slightly better-than-average minor league hitter. At Billings in the Pioneer League in 1971, he hit .291. The next year at San Jose of the California League, he fell to .274. In '73 at Omaha in AA ball, he hit .284 with little power. But in '74, he got his big break. Sixteen games into his season at Omaha, the Royals called him up. That's when he met the next big influence on his baseball career—Kansas City's batting coach, Charlie Lau.

Lau got Brett to change his swing, lowering the bat from a Carl Yastrzemski-type stance and putting it almost on his shoulders. Lau said that would give him bat speed, and he advised his pupil to try to hit everything over second base. He and Lau conferred before and after every at bat. The advice worked. Brett went from .199 to finish the year at a respectable .282. For the next nine years, he would not hit under .300. Superstardom followed with two batting crowns, and the MVP Award in 1980, when he hit .390, the highest average in baseball since Ted Williams hit .406 for the Red Sox in 1941.

But all this would mean little to Brett in the shocking conclusion of Sunday afternoon's game on July 24, 1983, at Yankee Stadium. Through eight innings, things proceeded normally, with the Yanks holding a 4–3 edge. New York got the lead with three runs in the sixth on Don Baylor's two-run triple followed by Dave Winfield's single. It stayed that way until the ninth; Dale Murray, pitching well in relief of Yankee starter Shane Rawley, got the first two outs. But when U.L. Washington singled, Yankee manager Billy Martin summoned Gossage.

The scene was reminiscent of the final game of the 1980 playoffs, when Brett scalded the Goose with his huge, series-winning home run. But this was another time, and the fate of the action about to unfold would rest on a sharp observation, a dirty piece of wood, the baseball rule book, and a little more than one inch.

The observation was made by Nettles, Brett's long-time third-base rival and former playoff sparring partner. During New York's visit to Kansas City after the All-Star Game about ten days earlier, Nettles watched Brett closely. The bat looked awfully dirty to Nettles, and he was convinced that Brett had the pine tar too far up on the bat. Nettles mentioned this to Martin. Martin did nothing with the tip, cleverly waiting for a more important moment to bring the matter to light.

The question arises as to why Nettles would notice Brett's bat. The answer is that he had had previous doings with illegal bats. Nettles himself had once had bat trouble. He lost a hit in a 1975 game when his bat broke in two, and several small "super balls" that he had illegally placed inside rolled out. He also remembered when Yankee catcher Thurman Munson was called out after a base hit against the Minnesota Twins for having the pine tar too far up on the handle. Nettles was sure that's what Brett was doing. If it was an out for Munson, then why not for Brett?

As Gossage came in from the bull pen, Nettles told the reliever that if Brett got a hit, the bat should be checked for too much pine tar. As Gossage warmed up, Nettles also reminded Martin in the Yankee dugout.

Brett fouled off Gossage's first pitch. The next one was a high, inside fastball, which Brett crushed 400 feet deep into the lower deck in right. The home run put the Royals ahead 5–4. As he went around the bases, all seemed normal. But by the time he got to home plate, he saw Martin there talking with home-plate umpire Tim McClelland. It couldn't have been a more perfect time for Martin to resort to his legalism.

From the dugout, Brett didn't know what Martin was saying. All he knew was his clutch home run gave his team the lead. But as the session with Martin, Nettles, and the umpires became more animated, he became aware that something was wrong. McClelland and crew chief Joe Brinkman were examining his bat. McClelland then laid it down across the 17-inch width of home plate. McClelland, bat in hand, then walked toward the K.C. dugout, came up with his right hand, and called Brett out for using an illegal bat. The game was over. The Yankees, instead of trailing 5–4, walked away with a 4–3 win.

McClelland ruled Brett out under two regulations of the official baseball rules.

The first was rule 1.10(b). This states that any foreign substance, including pine tar, may not go up the bat farther than 18 inches from the handle. "Any such material," the rule states, "including pine tar, which extends past the 18-inch limitation, in the umpire's judgment, shall cause the bat to be removed from the game." Brett's bat had pine tar about 19 inches up on the handle.

The second rule was 6.06(d). This says a batter using such an illegal bat shall be called out. Furthermore, ". . .the player shall be ejected from the game and may be subject to additional penalties as determined by the league president."

With the decision made, Brett tore out of the dugout. It's hard to adequately describe the depth of his rage. He was totally consumed, with the wild eyes of a madman and the countenance of one hatched prematurely from the Rubber Room. He was screaming at McClelland so loudly that the veins in his head were popping out in an odd, cartoonish manner. Brinkman, Royals manager Dick Howser, and several others restrained Brett—barely—as Nettles and Martin looked on. Several of the Royal ball players came out of the dugout as well, arguing. The scene was total chaos. Yankee Stadium security guards poured onto the field to lend the umps a hand, should a riot break out.

In the midst of all this, Kansas City pitcher Gaylord Perry, a collector of sports memorabilia, snatched the bat from McClelland's hands. When the umps and security guards got to him, he tossed the bat to Steve Renko. Renko dashed for the dugout, with Yankee players and umpires pointing to him. The security guards, with walkie-talkies in hand, tore off after him like Secret Service agents after a would-be assassin. They finally caught Renko in the runway leading from the dugout to the Royals' clubhouse. They wrestled, and managed to get the bat. The fans were yelling. Few people had ever seen, or even heard of, such a strange series of events on a baseball field. It was freaky. It was a black-and-white Universal horror feature. But it was surely not baseball.

Well, yes, baseball. The umpires confiscated the bat. The teams walked off the field, everyone talking about the play, everyone in disbelief, even the Yankees. Howser closed the Royals' dressing room for twenty minutes so he could address his club and try to calm Brett down. When the press got in, Brett was still in a tizzy, and launched into a tirade.

"I'm furious. Pine tar? That was the farthest thing from my mind when they were checking the bat...Christ, I've seen it all now in my career. If I had any guts, I'd retire right now," Brett raged.

Crew chief Brinkman said after the game that the bat definitely was illegal. He added that, because the bat wasn't tampered with, there wouldn't be a suspension. "But we measured it across the plate," he said, "and it went past the 18 inches allowed."

Directly after the game, Howser phoned in a strong protest to Bob Fishel, assistant to American League president Lee McPhail. Howser followed this up with a written protest. His appeal would be based on an assertion that the rules were interpreted too strictly, that Brett wasn't warned, that there were precedents for allowing the home run, and that, in any case, use of the pine tar could not add distance to a batted ball. Such a bat, therefore, could not be considered doctored.

Howser was controlled but firm in his postgame comments. "For a game to be decided on some technicality like that, it's tough for me to swallow," the upset manager said.

Martin, looking like the Cheshire cat, like a man who had something on the rest of the world, defended his action. He said the rule was there, and it should be enforced.

"We've known about [Brett's bat] for awhile, but why bother saying anything after he makes an out? Look, the guy was using an illegal bat," Martin explained. Perry Mason would have been proud.

The following morning at about 10 A.M., the American League office on Park Avenue in New York received the bat in a carefully wrapped, yellow package from a Yankee employee paid by Brinkman to deliver the bat safely. About an hour later, Murray Cook, Yankee general manager, showed up in Fishel's office with a videotape of the incident. He spouted the official party line, of course, when asked about the appeal, saying the rules were on the books and had to be enforced.

All day, reporters and curious fans dropped in to try to look at the bat, but the league had it in a safe pending McPhail's decision on Kansas City's protest. The league announced that after McPhail ruled, the bat would be sent back to Brett.

Joe Brinkman defended his crew's ruling on Brett, but he quickly added that the rules on pine tar and bats were "terrible" and the penalties "too severe." A similar incident had occurred earlier in the year in Boston. With Jim Rice of the Red Sox at the plate, Cleveland manager Mike Ferraro told Brinkman that Rice's bat had too much pine tar on it—before Rice batted. Brinkman refused to measure Rice's stick, though, saying it wasn't necessary because a visual inspection showed it was clean.

Going Against the Grain

The bat that George Brett used to hit his famous disallowed-then-reinstated home run was a T-85 Marv Throneberry model. It weighed 32 ounces, and was 34½ inches long. But more than that, it was a "seven grainer."

That's what Brett told Rex Bradley, vice-president of Hillerich & Bradsby, the bat makers out of Louisville. Bradley went on to explain that most bats have five grains, with each grain indicating a year's growth of the tree. He said Brett had been using the bat for weeks, and that it became his favorite.

Would the extra two years of growth make a difference in a bat? Bradley didn't think so. He said the main thing is weight distribution and not the age of the wood. He said if the weight is evenly distributed in a bat, and the rings have grown evenly, the bat will be a good one, no matter how many grains.

Bradley also pointed out that the bat's superior performance indirectly helped set up the furor. Brett had used it for some time. Each time he touched the pine tar, the substance would creep up the bat just a little bit more. It eventually ended up in the illegal zone. ◆

Phones in Kansas City, New York, and at the league office rang incessantly. Surprisingly, the calls in New York were almost universally against the ruling. Dave Glazier of McPhail's office said not one call came in supporting the umps. Even Yankee fans felt they'd rather lose than take the home run away, Glazier said.

Apparently, most everyone felt that way. Including Lee McPhail. Four days after the circus eruption at the stadium, McPhail overruled the umpires, reinstating Brett's home run and the Royals' 5–4 lead. It was a gutsy decision, since it dropped the Yankees out of a first-place tie in the American League's Eastern Division.

McPhail essentially stated that the pine tar was irrelevant to the home run, that it didn't give Brett an undue advantage against Gossage. He said that while McClelland's decision was "technically defensible," it wasn't in keeping with the intent, or spirit, of the baseball rules.

"The important thing is something should be done before the bat is used. The pine tar was excessive," McPhail said, "but the fact that it was beyond the 18-inch limit is not sufficient reason to call him out."

Yankee owner George Steinbrenner reacted vehemently to the ruling, claiming that it was incorrect because it cost the Yankees a share of first place.

"If the Yankees should lose the Eastern Division race on the ruling...I would not want to be Lee McPhail living in New York City," the Boss said ominously. "He better start house hunting in Missouri, close to Kansas City." Steinbrenner added that the ruling didn't surprise him and that he had expected the worst. Asked to sum up McPhail's decree in one word, he called it "ridiculous."

McPhail's ruling meant the game wasn't over but suspended. It would be picked up at a later date with the Royals up in the top of the ninth with two outs and a 5–4 lead.

The two teams finished the game later in the year on an off day. The Royals stopped at Yankee Stadium on their way to Baltimore. Brett was barred from taking part, since he had been thrown out of the game by the umpires. Hal McRae made the last out in the top of the ninth. In the bottom of the ninth, Dan Quisenberry came on in relief and got the side in order. The final score stood at 5–4, Royals. As it turned out, the game had no influence on the pennant races. Both teams failed to make the playoffs. But they did give baseball one of its more bizarre moments.

The league office returned the bat to Brett, who loaned it to memorabilia collector (and part owner of the Yankees) Barry Halper. Halper put it on display in a case.

And baseball rested. Another possibility realized.

On the Record: George Brett

Valenti: Was the bat questioned before that play?

Brett: No. It was never brought up. No one on the team ever said anything to me. No team ever questioned the pine tar on the bat. I used the bat for about six weeks. It just came up that one time in Yankee Stadium.

Valenti: There was a story that Graig Nettles had noticed something unusual about your bat sometime before. He said something to Billy Martin, and Martin filed it away for future use, at a good time.

Brett: I read about that the next day in the paper. We had played the Yankees about ten days or two weeks before that. Graig had noticed my bat was pretty dirty, full of pine tar. He said something to Billy Martin about it. Billy said, "Well, let's just wait, and maybe some day he'll be using that same bat, get a base hit that could have an impact on the ball game, and then we'll bring it to the umpire's attention. There's no use bringing it up now, after he makes an out." About ten days go by, and I'm facing Gossage in the ninth inning with two outs, and hit a home run off him. The next thing you know, there was a big discussion. I think everybody knows what happened after that.

Valenti: At what point in that discussion did you realize something was wrong?

Brett: When I got to the dugout. By the time I touched home plate, Billy was already talking to the umpires. I got back to the dugout. Somebody said, "They're going to check your bat for cork." I started laughing, because I don't use cork in my bats. Finally, someone said, "They're going to check your bat for pine tar." And I didn't even know there was a rule on pine tar. I looked at the bat when it was in [home-plate umpire] Tim McClelland's hands, and I said, "That bat does look pretty dirty," but the bats I use are unfinished, and the pine tar was up to here (*he picks up a bat and indicates an area approaching the barrel end*). But it wasn't just pine tar. It was a lot of dirt.

Valenti: What kind of bat was it?

Brett: A Marv Throneberry model, T-85. That was the bat I used that day and still use quite a bit. I've been using that model for fourteen years. The style just feels comfortable in my hands. I don't use the bat because Marvelous Marv used it. I use the bat because it feels comfortable in my hands. My bats are unfinished. Raw wood. A lot of guys get them flame-tempered, they get them burnt, they get them stained black, they get them varnished. I just get raw wood. It's comfortable for me.

Valenti: When McClelland made the call and nullified your home run, what was going through your mind?

Brett: I can remember that like it was yesterday. I was talking to a couple of guys on the team. I think it was Leon Roberts and Joe Simpson. And I was standing in the dugout thinking I had just hit a home run that was going to give us the lead in the game, 5–4, in the ninth. They're measuring my bat. I just got through saying, "If they call me out, I'll go out there and kill that son of a bitch [meaning McClelland]." As soon as I said that, he walked over and called me out. I ran out of the dugout, started going crazy. Everybody on our team was going crazy. We walked back in the locker room. Howser had a few choice words to say. He was mad. I think he was a little mad at me for using an illegal bat, which was something I didn't even know about. He was understanding to the fact that I didn't know it was a rule. I had no idea that the bat was illegal. We had a closed meeting for about fifteen minutes to keep the media out of the locker room. I went and showered, and just had to deal with the media, answering questions.

Valenti: The bat was sent to the commissioner's office, and the Royals appealed the ruling. What was it like in the intervening period waiting to hear from the league office?

Brett: I didn't know how it would turn out. I tried to forget about it as much as was possible. The next day, we had a game in Kansas City. The applause I got was unbelievable. The support we got from the Kansas City people was great. I went up to the plate, and I felt so good. I tried to hit one even further. I think I was still upset at what had happened in New York. I struck out my first three times up that day. I didn't make any changes in my bat. I just tried to keep an eye on the pine tar a little bit, measure it off 18 inches up the bat, find out where the 18 inches was on the bat. I just tried to keep an eye on it to make sure that I would not be called out again.

Valenti: American League President Lee McPhail upheld the Royals' appeal, reinstating the home run. When was the game resumed?

Brett: The game was replayed on our last trip of the year into New York. We had to stop in the city for one day to finish the game. We had to stop off there on a day off on our way to Baltimore so we could finish the game. I was kicked out of the game for my actions. So I didn't even go to the ballpark. I went out and had dinner in New Jersey. I stayed at the airport for a while, then I said, "Screw this, let's get something to eat." In the game, Hal McRae made the last out in the top of the ninth. The Yankees went out 1-2-3. Dan Quisenberry got them out 1-2-3, and the game was over. There were about 1000 people in the stands, and we ended up winning the ballgame, 5–4.

Valenti: Do people still ask you about the bat?

Brett: Yeah. My family and I have a restaurant in southern California, in Hermosa Beach. And the bat's there on display. It's a sports bar and restaurant. We have a lot of sports memorabilia there. The bat's in a nice case with a lot of clippings around it, and photographs. The case is probably the most looked-at case in the restaurant.

Valenti: What happened to the bat immediately after you got it back?

Brett: I gave it to Barry Halper, a good friend of mine. Everybody wanted the bat. All these collectors wanted it. I gave it to Barry, who had the best individual collection

Attendance: 33,944
Time of Game: 2:40

KANSAS CITY ROYALS

Name	AB	R	H	RBI
Wilson, CF	3	0	0	0
Sheridan, PH, CF	2	0	0	0
Washington, SS	5	1	1	0
Brett, 3B	5	1	3	2
McRae, DH	3	0	0	0
Otis, RF	4	0	1	0
Wathan, 1B, LF	3	2	1	0
Roberts, LF	3	0	2	0
Aikens, PH, 1B	1	0	0	0
White, 2B	4	1	2	2
Slaught, C	4	0	3	1
Totals	37	5	13	5

NEW YORK YANKEES

Name	AB	R	H	RBI
Campaneris, 2B	4	1	2	0
Nettles, 3B	3	0	0	0
Piniella, RF	4	1	1	0
Mumphrey, CF	0	0	0	0
Baylor, DH	4	1	1	2
Winfield, CF, LF	4	1	3	2
Kemp, LF, RF	4	0	0	0
Balboni, 1B	2	0	0	0
Mattingly, 1B	1	0	0	0
Smalley, S	3	0	1	0
Cerone, C	2	0	0	0
Totals	31	4	8	4

Team	1	2	3	4	5	6	7	8	9*		
Royals	0	1	0	1	0	1	0	0	2		5
Yankees	0	1	0	0	0	3	0	0	X		4

*Game suspended with two outs in top of ninth

Name	IP	H	R	ER	BB	SO
Black	6	7	4	4	0	2
Armstrong	2	1	0	0	2	0

Name	IP	H	R	ER	BB	SO
Rawley	5⅓	10	3	3	2	2
Murray	3⅓	2	1	1	0	2
Gossage	—	1	1	1	0	0

of anybody, I think. He's part owner of the Yankees, and he's been a very good friend of mine over the years. He put it in a nice case in his basement. After a while, when we got our restaurant going, we decided the place to put the bat would be in the restaurant. In the summertime, the Hall of Fame will call up and say, "Can we have the bat, and in turn, we'll give you Babe Ruth's uniform or Ty Cobb's uniform?" So we just kind of trade back and forth. So it's always either in our restaurant or at the Hall of Fame.

Valenti: Would it be fair to call the play the strangest thing to happen to you in your career?

Brett: So far, yeah. But the way things are going, something stranger may happen.

Valenti: Are there any other aspects of the play we haven't covered or that you want to mention?

Brett: Gaylord Perry was on our team then. He was always known for his "mysterious" sinker ball and for not getting along too well with umpires. Gaylord's a pretty good collector of sports memorabilia himself. When the umpire called me out, Gaylord went over to Tim McClelland, who still had the bat in his hand, and wrestled it away from him. When the umpires and the policeman...saw that, they started chasing Gaylord and the bat. Gaylord threw it over to Steve Renko, who in turn started running to the locker room with it, running up the runway to the locker room. And the policemen are chasing him with walkie-talkies, saying, "The bat's going up to the locker room!" They ended up wrestling it away from him. They in turn gave the bat to whomever. I don't know who they gave the bat to. And the bat was sent back to me through Emery Air Freight. I ended up doing a commercial for Emery Air Freight and made about eighty grand on the deal. So it ended up pretty good.

155

17

KIRK GIBSON
October 15, 1988

In the theater of the improbable, faith is a backstage doorman, the anonymous, behind-the-scenes character who controls events by deciding which people, and what possibilities, to admit inside. When hope comes knocking, faith—when it is strong enough—will say yes...as it did to Kirk Gibson and the Los Angeles Dodgers in the 1988 World Series.

Dodgers 5, A's 4

Few will argue: the World Series is controlled by TV, and may yet become just another billboard for corporate America. But the nation still takes it seriously. The Series is not a manufactured event, as is the Super Bowl. It isn't played at the wrong time of year, as are the NBA and Stanley Cup finals. It retains its capacity to transform baseball into something larger than itself, into a rejuvenating experience for millions of people. That is its beauty.

The incredible postseason of the Dodgers bears this out. For it was a case of the little guy triumphing. Against all odds, a group of men proved that to win in the face of adversity was not only possible, but also the sweetest of victories. Underdogs and the downtrodden everywhere could profit from this lesson: if you don't give up on yourself, you can make something happen.

Winning the Western Division of the National League but stumbling slightly down the stretch, the Dodgers went up against the mighty New York Mets, a team apparently without a weakness. The national press touted the Amazins as unbeatable playoff foes. The experts had spoken. Mets in five.

The few who thought the Dodgers had a chance jumped ship after Game One of the playoffs, when they blew a three-run, ninth-inning lead at home. But undaunted, they won in seven behind the astounding pitching of Orel Hershiser and the bat of Gibson, who beat the Mets twice with home runs in consecutive games.

As the playoffs climaxed, Gibson painfully planted the seeds of what would become one of the greatest moments in sports history.

In the ninth inning of the final game at Shea Stadium, Gibson stole second. But in doing so, he severely pulled his left hamstring. As Gibson limped off the field, the Mets fans—on the verge of falling behind three games to two—cheered the injury, a classic case of soreheads eating sour grapes.

Gibson added to his leg woes, and to the ultimate melodrama, in the seventh game at Dodger Stadium. Running stiffly because of his pulled hamstring, he broke up a double play at second. But, favoring his bad left leg, he slid awkwardly and strained the ligaments in his right knee. Gibson didn't know at the moment how seriously he was hurt. But in the next inning, the pain flared up—enough pain to make the hamstring pull seem insignificant. It was like the guy who cures his headache by smashing his foot with a sledge hammer: the greater pain erased the lesser.

Afterward, the skeptical press and fans alike viewed the Dodger triumph as a fluke, a result that wouldn't come up one time in a hundred. The better team lost, while the inferior club advanced against another, more imposing, obstacle: the Oakland A's.

The A's had Jose Canseco and Mark McGwire. They had defense, speed, starting pitching. They had Dennis Eckersley, who had shaken off a career of unfulfilled potential as a starting pitcher with the Indians, Red Sox, and Cubs to be reborn as the American League's top closer. The A's were, in short, even more unbeatable than the Mets. With 103 wins and coming off a methodical four-game playoff sweep of Boston, they could have just mailed in the World Series results.

By beating the Mets, the Dodgers didn't earn respect. According to observers, they simply signed their own death warrant. Almost no one could envision the A's losing . . . not just the Series, but a single game. The consensus: Oakland in four, five if the Dodger luck continued.

Who, even among the Dodgers, believed? Really believed? It may have been the entire team. Or it may have been just one man. It didn't matter, as long as that one man was Kirk Gibson, whose season-long hustle would earn him the National League's 1988 Most Valuable Player award. All year, he had sparked the Dodgers, beginning in the hot spring training sun of Vero Beach, Florida.

To welcome his new teammate to the Dodgers, relief pitcher Jesse Orosco secretly put lamp black under the rim of Gibson's baseball cap. On the first day of workouts, Kirk took the field with his loaded cap. Soon, trickles of black sweat inched down into the eyes of this Man of Sorrows.

Gibson's response stood the team on its head. He stormed off the field, confronted manager Tommy Lasorda, and blew out of the locker room, slamming the door behind him. The next morning at a team meeting, Gibson blasted his laid-back mates, making his feelings known in the sharpest of terms. It was a moment of reckoning for the once-proud Dodger organization. Coming off two years of abject mediocrity, they had fallen into an abyss, a petrification of desire, a mellow, uncaring acceptance of losing that seemed complemented by their mild, Left Coast environs.

All this was not lost on the rugged Gibson, who played baseball like a linebacker in the middle of a crunching hit. He was the cold, harsh Michigan wind, not the sea breezes of the Pacific. Gibson's Rust Belt ethic, learned in Detroit under Sparky Anderson, seemed out of place in the serene apathy of L.A.'s palm-tree mentality. Another ballplayer might have forgiven Orosco's prank. Another might have laughed it off. Still another might have seethed inwardly while outwardly holding his tongue.

But Gibson, the new kid in town, took on the whole team. He told the Dodgers point blank that he was here to win, here to play hard, here to be serious. He expected the same from his teammates. He issued a warning to leave his equipment alone, and not to mess around with his mind while he was preparing to play baseball.

The swift kick was exactly what the Dodgers needed. The avocado green was flushed out of their veins, replaced by pulsing Dodger Blue.

The transfusion worked. They won the division. They beat the Mets for the pennant. But here they were, on the eve of their confrontation with the mighty A's, with Gibson unable to play—unable even to hit, to run, to move comfortably, to walk. Their go-to guy was moving around with all the athletic grace and fluidity of Amos McCoy, resembling Tommy Kirk more than Captain Kirk.

Because the Series opened at Dodger Stadium, Lasorda could not even try to put Gibson in at DH. In the World Series, the DH is used only during games played in American League parks. But it was academic anyway. Gibson had not run since Thursday, when he wrecked the knee. At home on Friday, he tested the leg. He tried to jog lightly across his living room into the next room. He couldn't. The best he could manage was a hop. Disgusted, he threw himself down on the sofa, knowing he would miss Saturday night's opener, and possibly the entire Series.

By the time he drove to the park for Saturday night's game, the pain had increased. When the lineups were introduced and the players took their spotlit bows, Gibson sat scowling and depressed in the trainer's room. He was given two options: take to the field for the introductions and have no chance of playing, or take a long needle in his ice-wrapped right leg and have a remote—a very remote—chance of playing.

Only an immediate shot of xylocaine and cortisone into the knee would give him any hope that night. The long needle was not without risk. The anti-inflammatory shot would temporarily increase the soreness and pain in the knee joint. The ensuing ice treatments would numb the joint, meaning that if Gibson played, he might not be able to feel any further damage to the deadened joint. He ran the risk of completely shredding the knee before he could notice.

What would it be?

"Stick me," a resigned but determined Gibson told team doctor Frank Jobe. "Do it now. I hate this. Get it over with."

The outfielder wrapped the knee with a huge ice pack, and sat alone watching on TV as rookie Tim Belcher threw the first pitch to Oakland leadoff man Carney Lansford.

Belcher got out of the inning with no runs. The Dodgers quickly took the lead in their half of the first, giving the A's a taste of what was to come for the rest of the series. Steve Sax was hit by a Dave Stewart pitch. After Franklin Stubbs flied to center, Stewart balked, sending Sax to second. Mickey Hatcher, a journeyman outfielder playing in place of Gibson, poled a two-run homer to left-center field for a 2–0 lead.

The next major development came in the following half inning, when the A's looked like they would live up to their advance billing. Glenn Hubbard singled. After striking out Walt Weiss, Belcher walked Stewart and Lansford. The pitcher regrouped to fan Dave Henderson, but paid the price for his largesse when Canseco hit a vicious, jet-propelled line drive over the center field fence for a grand slam and a 4–2 Oakland lead. The ferocity of the smash shocked the Dodger fans, and Lasorda as well.

"I still can't believe how fast that ball got out of the park," Lasorda said after the game. "[Canseco's] got an awesome swing. He just hit a line drive, and it was gone!"

The game stayed that way until the sixth, when the Dodgers closed the gap to 4–3 as Mike Scioscia single home Mike Marshall. Meanwhile, Gibson stayed in his ice-bound solitude, showing up in the dugout only in the third inning to see if family members had arrived and found their seats. Finding all well on that front, he painfully limped back to the trainer's room and his TV set. He heard something that got his attention.

Vin Scully, calling the game for NBC, mentioned that Gibson would not be available for the game. That's all Gibson needed to hear.

"Bull!" Gibson bellowed to the set.

Any second thoughts about trying to get himself ready left his mind. The pain, the physical inability to perform, the sapping of strength induced by the shot and the two serious leg problems, were now irrelevant. Gibson slowly peeled off the ice pack from his knee, flexing the traumatized joint. He had resolve.

For the next several innings, he repeated the ritual of icing the leg, then removing the ice pack to test the limb. He found that for a brief period, ten minutes at most, the joint would be numb enough for him to stand and move around a little bit—not exactly like Fred Astaire, but certainly better than Walter Brennan. Then after the few minutes of amnesty, the pain would come back, first in a murmur, then in a screaming stab. Shot up as heavily as it was and iced only into a temporary oblivion, the knee kept its fiery-hot foothold on agony. But the key discovery had been made: for those brief few minutes, Gibson could maneuver his body into something resembling fitness, a kind of counterfeit of true athletic readiness.

The game made its way through the seventh and eighth innings, with Oakland still hanging onto the 4–3 lead. Stewart had settled down nicely, cruising through eight with a neat six hitter. Oakland manager Tony LaRussa's plan was to get eight innings from his starter, maintain a lead, then give the game to Eckersley. Things were going just that way.

But in the eighth inning, Gibson made his big decision. He would try to pinch hit if the situation came up. He told Dodger batting coach Ben Hines that he wanted batting practice. Hines couldn't believe it. He saw a man out of uniform, with a gigantic ice pack strapped to his knee. He saw a man who could barely walk. Still, he summoned the clubhouse batboy, Mitch Poole.

"He wants to hit. You go with him," Hines told Poole. Gibson got into his uniform. Together, the batboy and the wounded star made their way to the batting cage at the end of the runway off the Dodger dugout and underneath the stands. The cage is a ten-foot square enclosed by black netting. Batters hit off a tee, driving the balls into the net. Poole's job would be to put a fresh ball on the tee after each swing. Gibson was in no shape to reach down for a ball and tee it up himself. Hines shot back to the dugout, telling a surprised Lasorda what Gibson was doing. Poole kept setting the balls up; Gibson knocked them off just as quickly, his demeanor intense, savage. The sound of the bat meeting the ball echoed in the Dodger dugout, dull and thunderous, like an amplified heartbeat. Poole and Gibson continued their ritual in silence. About halfway through the sixty swings, Gibson stopped and spoke his only words to Poole.

"Mitch, this could be the script."

Gibson continued hitting, visualizing Eckersley throwing at him from the mound. As the A's batted in the ninth, Gibson stopped hitting and took the basketball-sized ice pack off his leg. The A's went down quickly, and the Dodgers came up for their last chance.

Eckersley looked unhittable in the bottom of the ninth. Scioscia popped up to Weiss at short. Third baseman Jeff Hamilton struck out. Two outs, nobody on. Things could not look bleaker. With Alfredo Griffin due up, Lasorda went to the bench, sending up lefty Mike Davis. In the meantime, Gibson sent Poole to summon a harried Lasorda. At first, the manager chastised the batboy for bothering him at such a time, but Poole persisted, saying it was important. Gibson wanted to talk to him.

Tommy hurried down the runway, where he saw Gibson in uniform.

"If Mike gets on, then I can hit," Gibson yelled.

Armed with this trump card, Lasorda went back to the dugout, where he could only sit and wait, the situation now out of his hands. Gibson's chance would depend solely on what Davis could do against the Oakland ace. Davis, who signed with the Dodgers as a free agent the previous winter, was coming off a terrible 1988 season. He was projected as a starting outfielder. Instead, he hit a paltry .196, with just two home runs and 17 RBIs.

Eckersley then made his first big mistake. Instead of going after Davis, it appeared he was trying to finesse him. He nibbled. All five pitches were close, but four of them were balls.

"He was real close on the plate, but they weren't strikes in my opinion," Davis said.

With his walk, Mike Davis became a midwife to history.

What happened next puts to shame even the most melodramatic, concocted, implausible, Hollywood Grade-B script. Gibson entered the dugout from the runway. Lasorda told him to grab a bat.

In the dugout, Gibson's teammates were surprised to see the slugger.

"I didn't even think the guy could walk," said Brian Holton.

"I'd forgotten all about Kirk," Hatcher added.

"I didn't even see him all night," Sax said.

But here he was, getting his bat, and walking slowly to the plate as Davis trotted to first. The 55,983 fans broke out in a spontaneous ovation that veteran observers said was perhaps the loudest ever heard at Dodger Stadium.

Eckersley had saved 45 games in 1988, plus a record-setting 4 more against the Red Sox in the playoffs. He hadn't given up a home run in two months, and in all his appearances during the season, lost only one lead in the ninth inning.

Eckersley started Gibson off with three fastballs. Gibson came up swinging, fouling off the pitches and falling behind 0-and-2. His swing looked pathetic. He was hitting with just his upper body, and was unable to catch up with Eckersley's smoke. After each swing, Gibson staggered on his aching right leg, doing a sorry dance of pain. A hitter couldn't have looked more overmatched.

On the CBS radio broadcast, Jack Buck rightly questioned Gibson's fitness to hit.

Eckersley wasted a fastball for a 1-2 count. Gibson doggedly fouled off another fastball. Eck missed with his next pitch for ball two. This diet of high fastballs on the outside corner had Gibson overpowered. Then Eckersley made his second blunder, going with catcher Ron Hassey's call to abandon the fastball in favor of the slider.

Eck went into his motion, and Davis broke for second. There was no throw as the ball missed, running the count to 3-2. On the play, Gibson's bat hit Hassey's glove, and Hassey didn't make a throw. If he had gotten off a throw, Gibson could have been ruled out for interference. Such a call would have ended the game. But with no throw, no call could be made, according to baseball rules.

Davis's steal opened first base, and the debate raged in the stands and across the nation: should LaRussa order Gibson to be intentionally passed, setting up a force play at any base and bringing right-handed Sax to the plate? The A's decided to play it both ways. They'd try to get Gibson with a back-door slider, a pitch that comes into the left-handed batter low and outside, looking like a ball, but that curves in quickly at the last moment to pick up the outside corner. The strategy was this: if the "back door" worked, they would freeze Gibson's swing and maybe pick up a called third strike. If it missed, they would have Gibson harmlessly on first with a walk.

With the way Gibson had looked against the fastball, the decision to go again with the slider was baffling. The back-door breaking ball came in. Gibson swung his one-legged swing, lunging with extended arms to the outside corner of the plate. He connected, his body coming out of its all-day snarl. Upon impact, his left leg lifted from the ground, his right leg stayed planted in the dirt. His left hand came off the bat, giving the swing a "one-arm" effect. The result seemed to defy the laws of physics. Somehow, with this reaching, rusted hinge of a swing, he had managed to *pull* the outside pitch.

The ball climbed into the night air, riding the hysterical cheering of the fans. They cheered with a voice that had shed all restraint, finding in their wildest reverie not a hallucination, but a dream that actually comes true. The ball landed in the right-field seats over the head of Canseco, whose second-inning grand slam was instantly reduced from a bold headline to a lost footnote. With one swing, Gibson had turned a 4–3 loss into a 5–4 win.

Vin Scully broke with a wonderful call for the TV audience: "A high fly ball to right field. She is *GONE!*" On the radio, Jack Buck exclaimed: "I don't believe what I just saw!" Eckersley stood shocked on the mound.

Gibson then set out on his way-of-the-cross circuit of the bases, a tortured but joyful trot that was at once agony and ecstasy. He broke out in minced, baby-like steps, watching the ball land. He nearly stumbled going into first, timing his steps so he would hit the bag. Between first and third, adrenaline took over as he waved his arms, yelled, and shook his fists. On his way into the plate, Gibson slowed down, the pain catching up to him. He took the last ninety feet in short, stiff shufflings, so his bad knee wouldn't lock.

It would turn out to be one of the most productive at bats in World Series history, for as it turned out, it would mark Gibson's only appearance in the '88 Fall Classic. The home run made history in another way: it was the first time in Series annals a batter hit a ninth-inning home run to rescue a game from defeat to victory. The closest thing to it was in Game Four of the 1947 Classic, when Brooklyn's Cookie Lavagetto hit a two-run double against the right field wall at Ebbets Field with two outs in the ninth off Bill Bevans of the Yankees. Bevans had held a 2–1 lead, but more importantly, had a no-hitter going until Lavagetto's hit gave the Dodgers a 3–2 win.

At home plate's mob scene, Gibson was met by Lahugga, who wrapped the hero in both arms. Gibson did a quick network TV interview, then headed into the delirious clubhouse. Above his locker, someone had printed a new name sign: "Roy Hobbs"—the hero of Bernard Malamud's novel *The Natural*.

"A Call for the Ages"

Veteran broadcaster Jack Buck called Kirk Gibson's home run for CBS radio. He made it a memorable one, repeating: "I don't believe what I just saw." Here, he describes the moment.

"After Davis stole second, I was thinking there's no way Gibson will hit a home run. I knew he wasn't trying to hit a home run, especially with the tying run at second and first base open. I figured he'd get nothing to hit with Sax, a right-handed batter, due up. Or, if Eckersley did make a mistake, Gibson would go the other way or try to hit the ball up the middle to score the runner. So when Gibson got out in front of the pitch, when he pulled the ball, I was totally surprised. That's why the surprise showed in my voice.

"When he hit it, I didn't think it would go out. Gibson kind of let go of the bat with his left hand. He had a one-handed swing. And I'm used to the Dodger Stadium where the ball never left the park, unless someone really crunched it. But I looked up, and that sucker was still going. It got back in the seats by about five or six rows. And that's what shocked me too. I was shocked he pulled the ball. Then I looked up, and was astounded that the ball was still going, because I didn't think he hit it that well.

"My call of the home run wasn't an act. It was genuine. I didn't preplan it, or tell myself how excited I was going to get, or whether I was going to under-play it. Sometimes you do that on radio. So it was all spontaneous." ◆

Lahugga could not contain his joy.

"I wasn't surprised that he hit a home run," the excited manager said. "The man can hit the ball out of the Grand Canyon. . .I've seen him get big hits all year. What surprised me is that he played. . .When I saw the ball go out, I said 'Thank God.' We were staring defeat right in the eye. He did it before 50,000 fans who were cheering for all they were worth. It was great!"

Gibson called it "a great moment." He said he felt "fortunate to be in there and be a part of it. This was a classic. A good game for the fans and the people around the world to see."

To his credit, Eckersley did not try to duck out of the postgame interviews.

"It was a terrible pitch," the stunned reliever recounted. "But I've got to live with it. And he looked so bad swinging on the previous strike. I gave him something he could hit. If I could throw it again, I would throw a fastball."

The home run turned the tide of the Series. The A's, with their momentum abruptly halted, lost three of the next four games. They didn't see Gibson any more, but were pushed head-on into Orel Hershiser's buzz saw. Hershiser shut them out in Game Two, and threw a complete-game win for the clincher in Game Five.

The mighty A's ended up hitting .177 for the five games. Their two big guns, Canseco and McGwire, were a combined 2-for-33. The ragtag Dodgers outplayed them in every facet of the game. It was, in short, a shocking, historic upset.

For all time, the composite box of the 1988 World Series will show Gibson's one game, one at bat, one run scored, one hit, one home run, two RBIs, and his 1.000 batting average.

1.000. Never will a number seem more fitting.

On the Record: Kirk Gibson

Valenti: What's your view of the misfired spring training practical joke played on you? How important was it in turning the 1988 Dodgers around?

Gibson: It was a key incident, no doubt. But I thought it got blown out of proportion. The day after it happened, I knew something had to be said. The situation needed to be defused. It was obvious that what happened the day before wasn't a good situation. So, at our daily team meeting the next morning, we talked it out. I explained myself and we went on from there. The team didn't dwell on it for very long. Really, the only people who brought it up very much were the media. But we did learn from it, I think, and moved on.

Valenti: What did you learn? And how, after two mediocre years, did the Dodgers get so good, so fast?

Gibson: We became a team. As far as the turnaround, I think the off-season acquisitions played a major role. I'm talking not only of myself, but also of Jay Howell, Rick Dempsey, Alfredo Griffin, and Mike Davis. I think we had good athletes, good professionals, who played with a lot of desire and heart. We built character throughout the year and gained momentum as we moved on. We answered every challenge. And we played our best baseball down the stretch against the Mets and A's. We became the type of team that did what it had to do to win. Some people might have thought we didn't have the talent to do what we did, or that we were winning ugly, or they couldn't figure out why we were winning. But we weren't concerned about that. We were concerned about the end result: being World Champions. As the season went on, we just felt we were good enough, that we had enough composure, that we wouldn't snowball into a losing streak. I don't think we lost more than three games in a row all year. Plus, we had some outstanding pitching and individual performances. But I think the World Series signified what we were all about. We had people hurt, and everybody just did their job. I said in spring training that we were going to be World Champs, and that everybody on the roster was going to contribute. It ended up being that way.

Valenti: What happened during the last playoff game in New York when you hurt your hamstring? What was your reaction to the Met fans, who cheered your injury?

Gibson: I think we were up by a run or two. They weren't paying attention to me over at first base. There were two outs. I felt that if I could get to second base, it might get us a run, which was important against a team like the Mets. You can never really feel secure against them. I stole the base, but before I got to the base, I popped my left hamstring. I knew I had to come out of the game. I called time and started to walk off. The fans cheered the fact that I was hurt. I took it as a compliment. I knew they didn't want me in there. The background is that there were comments from some Met players about the way I was playing during the series, about my hard play. But I didn't listen to any of that. I just played my game.

Whatever anybody else felt about my style didn't affect me. We were the people who went on to become World Champions, so I couldn't have been all wrong.

Valenti: When did you hurt your knee?

Gibson: In game seven against the Mets, going into second base. I was pushing it pretty hard. Because of my hamstring problem, I had a funky slide trying to break up the double play, which I did. My toe caught in the ground, and I twisted my knee. I didn't know it was hurt right away. But the next inning, I knew that something crazy was going on in there.

Valenti: In the ensuing couple of days after you beat the Mets and before the World Series opened, did the knee get worse?

Gibson: It's not that it got worse. It just didn't get any better. I had it examined and X-rayed. Everything looked intact. The morning before the opener, I tried to do a little jogging in my living room, hopping to the next room and back. I knew I was in trouble. On the day of the game, I went in. The doctor decided to inject it, which he did about the time they were doing the introductions. The knee was very sore. I just sat in there [the trainer's room] all game, icing it. You know, I was hurting.

Valenti: Had you not had the shot, could you have played?

Gibson: No. But I thought I couldn't play regardless. The shot acts as an anti-inflammatory [agent] within the area. The purpose is to take some inflammation out and speed up the healing process. After the shot, it was sore. I numbed it with ice. As the game rolled on, I realized that every time I took the ice off, for about five or ten minutes after, I could kind of walk on it. So I'm sitting there watching the game on TV, and see the camera pan the dugout, and Vin Scully says, "No. He's not there. There's no way he's playing." And I wasn't expecting to play. But I saw what was ahead of us. Looking ahead to the bottom of the ninth, I saw who was coming up, who we had available, and who they had on the mound. So I put more ice on the knee, got dressed, and grabbed the batboy [Mitch Poole]. We went into the little batting cage. Mitch put some balls on the tee. I took some swings. I looked at him and said something to the effect of "The script is written." I was hurting, but I told myself to suck it up. I then told Mitch to get Tommy [Lasorda]. Now the cage is right near the dugout, and I could hear Tommy really annoyed at Mitch, saying, "What do you want? I got a game going on here. Don't bother me." Mitch says, "No, Tommy, it's really important. It's Gibby. I think he thinks he can hit." So Tommy ran up there, and I said to him, "Let Davis bat for Griffin, and I'll hit next." He didn't say anything. He just took off. So after there were two outs and Davis came up to the plate, I came down to the dugout and I sat there as it all unfolded in front of me.

Valenti: Did anyone say anything to you when you came into the dugout?

Gibson: No. I don't even think a lot of the guys realized I was there. I just came in and sat down. I had accepted the fact that I wasn't going to be playing regularly, and I was prepared for that type of situation. Mickey Hatcher was basically filling in for my role, and I had prepared myself for his role.

Valenti: Did you have an idea of what Dennis Eckersley might do with you in that situation?

Gibson: Yes. Before the Series began, Mel Didier, one of our scouts, stood up in front of us and read the scouting report. He looked at us and said, "Partners, as sure as I'm standing here breathing, if Eckersley gets you 3-and-2 and you're a left-handed

BOX SCORE: Dodger Stadium, 10•15•88

Game One, 1988 World Series
Attendance: 55,983
Time of Game: 3:04

OAKLAND A's

Name	AB	R	H	RBI
Lansford, 3B	4	1	0	0
Henderson, CF	5	0	2	0
Canseco, RF	4	1	1	4
Parker, LF	2	0	0	0
Javier, LF	1	0	1	0
McGwire, 1B	3	0	0	0
Steinbach, C	4	0	1	0
Hassey, C	0	0	0	0
Hubbard, 2B	4	1	2	0
Weiss, SS	4	0	0	0
Stewart, P	3	1	0	0
Eckersley, P	0	0	0	0
Totals	34	4	7	4

LOS ANGELES DODGERS

Name	AB	R	H	RBI
Sax, 2B	3	1	1	0
Stubbs, 1B	4	0	0	0
Hatcher, LF	3	1	1	2
Marshall, RF	4	1	1	0
Shelby, CF	4	0	1	0
Scioscia, C	4	0	1	1
Hamilton, 3B	4	0	0	0
Griffin, SS	2	0	1	0
Davis, PH	0	1	0	0
Belcher, P	0	0	0	0
Heep, PH	1	0	0	0
Leary, P	0	0	0	0
Woodson, PH	1	0	0	0
Holton, P	0	0	0	0
Gonzalez, PH	1	0	0	0
Pena, P	0	0	0	0
Gibson, PH	1	1	1	2
Totals	32	5	7	5

Team	1	2	3	4	5	6	7	8	9		
A's	0	4	0	0	0	0	0	0	0		4
Dodgers	2	0	0	0	0	1	0	0	2		5

Name	1P	H	R	ER	BB	SO
Stewart	8	6	3	3	2	5
Eckersley (L)	⅔	1	2	2	1	1

Name	1P	H	R	ER	BB	SO
Belcher	2	3	4	4	4	3
Leary	3	3	0	0	1	3
Holton	2	0	0	0	1	0
Pena (W)	2	1	0	0	0	3

batter, you're gonna see a back-door slider." Well, I got behind 0-and-2, fouled off some pitches, and worked the count to 3-and-2. If you watch the tape, you'll see at that point I called time and stepped back out. I said to myself, "Partner, as sure as I'm standing here breathing, you're going to see a 3-and-2 back-door slider." I stepped back in, and that's exactly what I saw. The thing about it is, you've got to understand, it wasn't a bad pitch. It was a good pitch. I was prepared for it.

I was gambling he would throw me that. Dennis got a lot of people out with that same pitch. So we can't take anything away from him. But give credit to the guys who prepared me with the scouting report.

Valenti: Let's go back earlier in the sequence, when you were down 0-and-2. Eckersley was throwing fastballs. With your legs the way they were, it looked like there was no way you could catch up with the fastball. People were almost shocked when he decided to go with the slider, a breaking ball.

Gibson: What happened was this. The more pitches I saw, the better I felt, and the more confident I was he couldn't strike me out. I felt that on all the fastballs, I could foul them off. I thought the worst I'd get out of it was a walk. When I got down 0-and-2, I was thinking about changing my approach. On 0-and-2, you've got to give yourself up a little bit. You've got to dig in a little. You've got to scuffle. You've got to fight him, and hopefully get into a situation where you can hit a ball. And that's exactly what happened.

Valenti: On the 3-2 pitch, it appears as though your bat hit catcher Ron Hassey's glove, raising the possibility of an interference call. What happened there?

Gibson: I checked my swing, and kind of fell across the plate. Hassey ran into me. Let me put it this way. He was trying to make it look [like I hit him]. He's been around a while. So I think it was half me falling over the plate, and half him trying to get a call. But the whole thing is, you have to throw the ball to get an interference call, and he didn't throw it. So you can't call it.

Valenti: When you connected, did you think the ball would carry that far?

Gibson: I knew it was gone as soon as I hit it.

Valenti: What about making it around the bases. It looked painful.

Gibson: It didn't hurt at all, believe me. It was just an outstanding moment. It was the greatest moment of my professional baseball career. It was amazing. When I came out in the on-deck circle, I knew the fans would be excited. I knew that would excite me, and that my adrenaline would take over. When I go into an important series, I affirm that I'm going to have an impact on the series. I did in the playoffs, and fortunately, in the World Series. That's the way I picture myself. As an impact player. I picture myself having great moments like that.

Valenti: As you think back on the home run, is the play distinct in your mind, or is it all a blur?

Gibson: No. It's clear. Very clear. I could close my eyes right now and see it. I can just close my eyes, and see the whole thing, just as clear as it comes. I was fortunate. I was lucky. I don't know why, but fate was on my side.

APPENDIX:
THE "OTHERS"

There you have it—the top home runs in baseball history. Is this the absolute, definitive discussion? The inarguable list? No. And it's no big deal. Such selections are always open to debate. That's as it should be. But what of those other home runs? What of those that could very well have made it into this book, if only I could have doubled its length? They deserve at least a mention. So here's my list of the "other" Top Ten.

1. Dave Henderson, Boston Red Sox, fifth game of the 1986 playoffs. Batting against California's Donnie Moore, Hendu clocked a home run that gave Gene Mauch nightmares, saved the Red Sox from extinction, and ultimately got them into the World Series.

2. Ted Williams, Boston Red Sox, 1941 All-Star Game. The Splinter hit a tape-measure blast off Claude Passeau of the Cubs with two outs and two on in the ninth, giving the American League a dramatic 7–5 win.

3. Babe Ruth, New York Yankees, 1932 World Series. Against the Cubs, the Babe hit his famous "called shot" off Chicago's Charlie Root in the fifth inning. Actually, there's much doubt over whether Ruth called the home run. With two strikes and the Cubs riding him, Babe stepped out of the batter's box, looked at the Cubs' dugout, and made some sort of gesture. That's all we know.

4. Al Weis, New York Mets, 1969 World Series. An otherwise anemic hitter, Weis hit his one and only Shea Stadium home run in the seventh inning of Game Five off Baltimore's Dave McNally. Weis's home run tied the score. The Mets went on to win the game, and with it, the Series.

5. Chris Chambliss, New York Yankees, 1976 playoffs. Chambliss unloaded his ninth-inning missile off Mark Littell to give the Yanks a 7–6 playoff win over the Royals.

6. Hal Smith, Pittsburgh Pirates, 1960 World Series. He hit the home run that set up Bill Mazeroski's famous game-winner (see Chapter 3).

7. Bernie Carbo, Boston Red Sox, 1975 World Series. A latter-day Hal Smith. His setup home run made Carlton Fisk the ultimate hero (see Chapter 7).

8. Babe Ruth, New York Yankees, 1926 and 1928 World Series. Three home runs in Game Four against the St. Louis Cardinals in both series (see sidebar, page 131).

9. Babe Ruth, Boston Braves, 1935. The aging Babe hit the last three home runs of his career in one game (for a related discussion, see Chapter 5).

10. Dale Long, Pittsburgh Pirates, 1956. He hit a home run in eight consecutive games and just missed the ninth.